TREASURES

ALLAHABAD MUSEUM

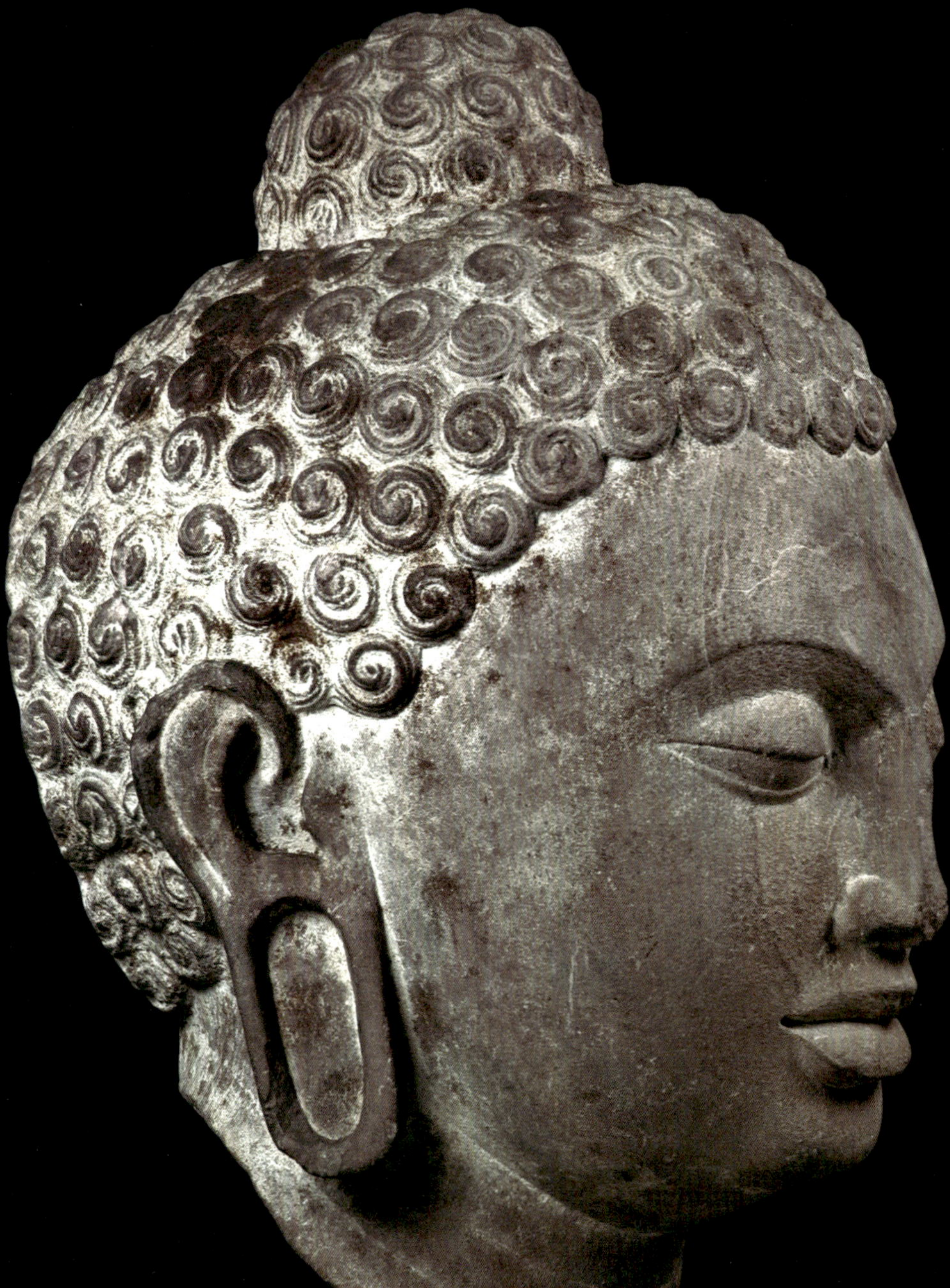

Buddha Head (p. 35)

TREASURES

ALLAHABAD MUSEUM

ALLAHABAD

Allahabad Museum

NATIONAL CULTURE FUND

NIYOGI
BOOKS

Produced in collaboration with National Culture Fund, Ministry of Culture, Govt. of India
Puratatva Bhawan, 5th Floor, D-Block, GPO Complex, INA, New Delhi: 110023

Jointly published and marketed by
NIYOGI BOOKS
Block D, Building No. 77,
Okhla Industrial Area, Phase-I,
New Delhi-110 020, INDIA
Tel: 91-11-26816301, 26818960
Email: niyogibooks@gmail.com
Website: www.niyogibooksindia.com

Series Editor: Malavika Singh
Editor: Rajesh Purohit
Design: Hajra A. Ahmed
NCF Team: Shri Padma Loachon Sahu, Reshmi Ghosh, Dr Monika Chaudhary

ISBN: 978-81-926939-5-8
Publication: 2017

Printed at: Niyogi Offset Pvt. Ltd., New Delhi, India

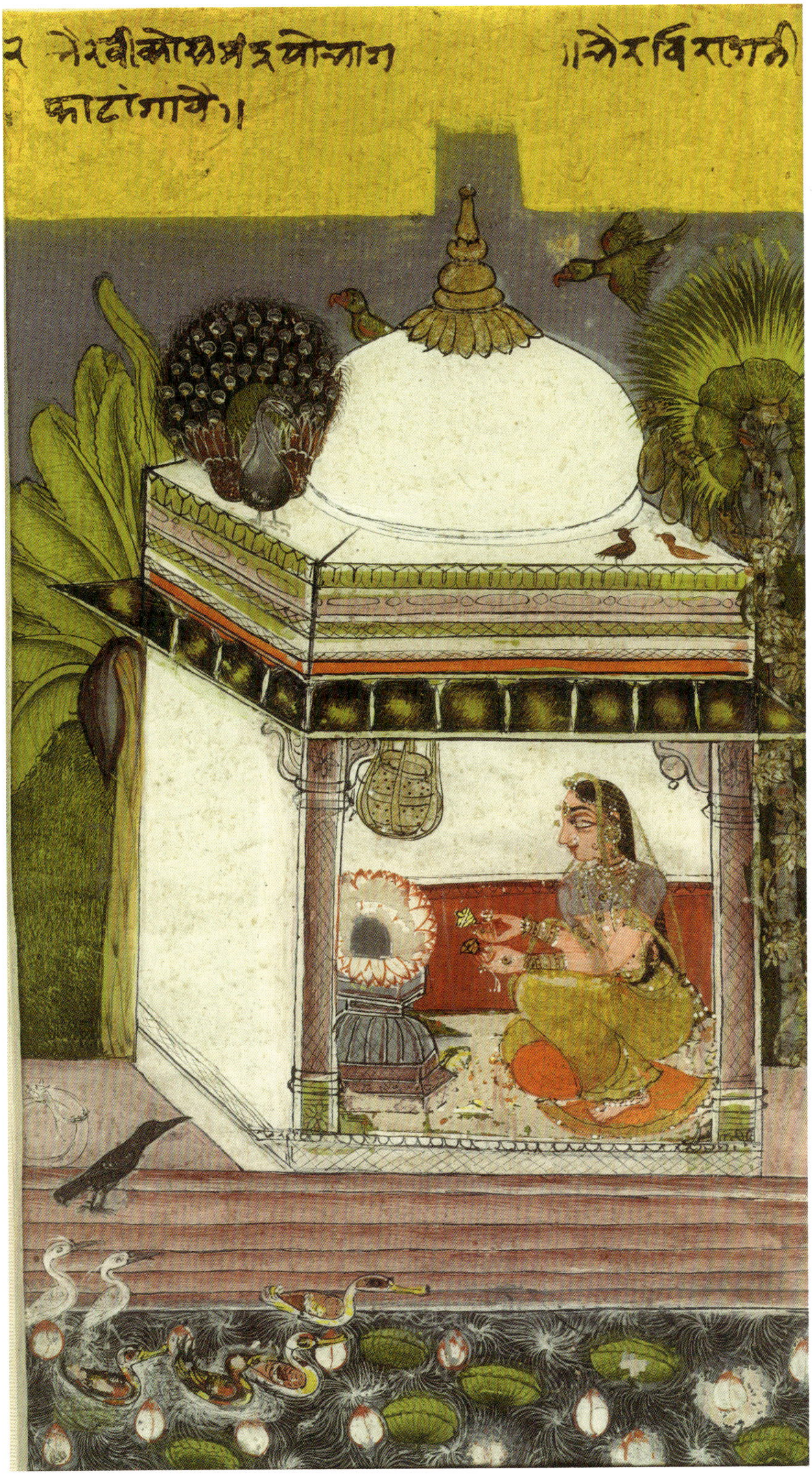

Ragini Bhairavi; Raagmala painting, Bundi, Rajasthan, 17th century

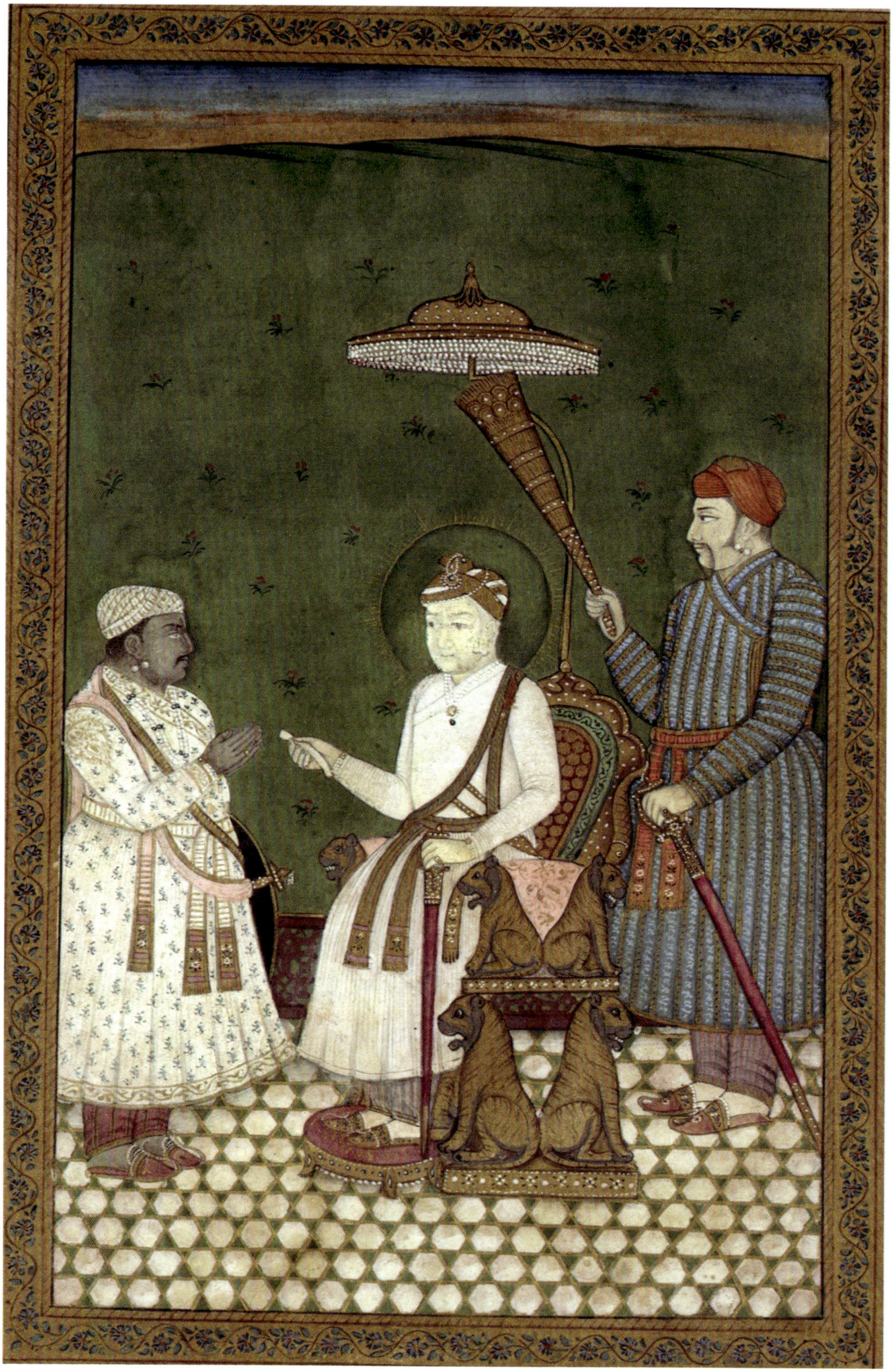

A portrait of the Mughal Emperor Akbar from 19th century CE

संस्कृति मंत्री
भारत सरकार
शास्त्री भवन, नई दिल्ली-110001
Minister of Culture
Government of India
Shastri Bhawan New Delhi-110001

सत्यमेव जयते

MESSAGE

National treasures are unique cultural assets that are symbols of a civilisation, its history and its people. *Treasures,* of Indian Museums, is a series that reflects the aesthetic sensibility of Indian artists and their patrons, through the ages. Indian art is rooted in different philosophies. This series of museum publication aims to share this extraordinary repository with the world.

'Treasures' are objects of great aesthetic quality and historic value. In some instances an object is considered a 'treasure' in a particular museum if it is one-of-its-kind in the collection, offers an insight into Indian history or through association the object is linked to a historic personality. There are also treasures that exemplify craftsmanship in a particular medium or style of a given historic period.

Each book has an introduction to the particular museum. Set in broad thematic sections, several significant treasures have been selected by the Director and staff of the specific museum. The museum staff has provided information on the date, provenance, as well as a brief introduction to each object. The selected 'masterpiece' is represented by a photograph from which an interesting detail has been highlighted, to enable readers to fully appreciate its finer aesthetic details and understand its visual message.

This series was initiated by the Ministry of Culture, Government of India under the Museum Reforms programme. The Ministry of Culture entrusted the responsibility of the production of this series with the National Culture Fund, New Delhi. We hope that this series will initiate a lasting interest in Indian art and inspire more people, especially the younger generation, to come to Indian museums and share in India's great cultural legacy and her rich cultural heritage.

Dr Mahesh Sharma

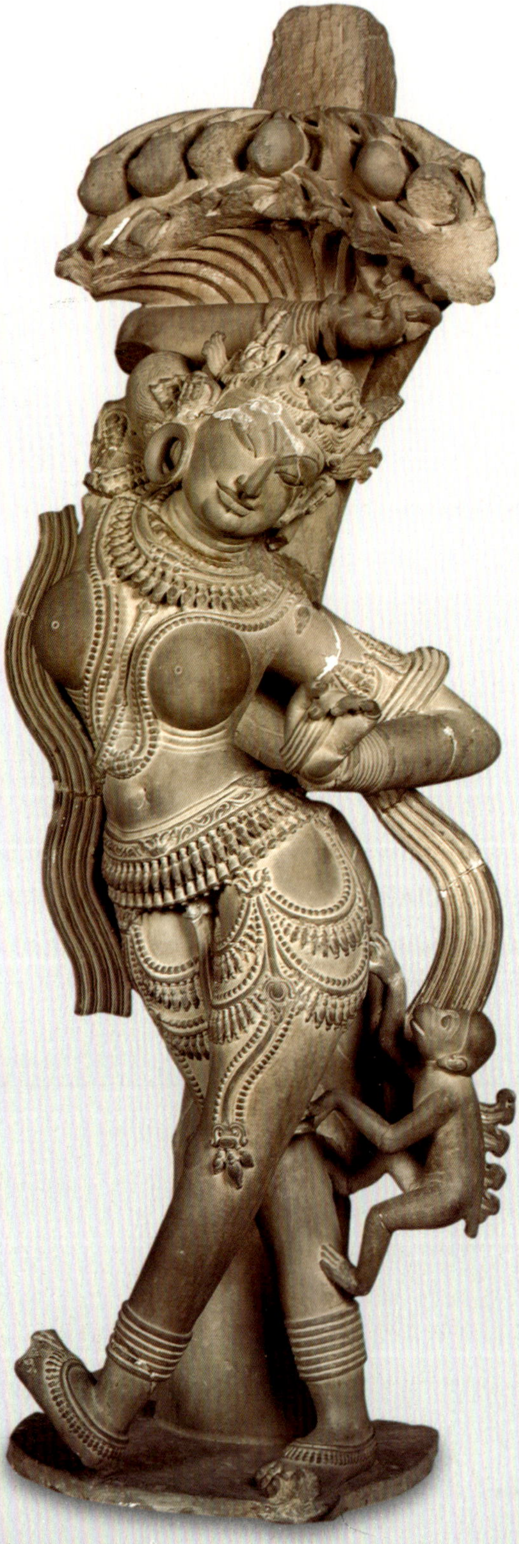

Dancing Damsel in Bracket Figure (p. 39)

INTRODUCTION TO ALLAHABAD MUSEUM

The Allahabad Museum is centrally located in the Civil Lines area of the city, in a lush green thickly forested historic park called Chandrasekhar Azad Park. It is about 3 km from the Allahabad Junction Railway Station, almost equidistant from Prayag and Rambagh railway stations and about 12 km from Bamrauli Airport.

In 1863, the Board of Revenue requested the Government of North-Western Provinces for the establishment of a public library and a museum. With donations from the provincial government, the famous Orientalist, Sir William Muir, and the Maharaja of Vijaynagaram, an ornate building was inaugurated in 1878 to house the collection, and a superintendent of library and museum was appointed for its upkeep.

For unforeseen reasons the Museum closed down in 1881. The initiative to reopen the Museum was taken by Pt Jawaharlal Nehru, who was the president of the Allahabad Municipal Board from 1923–24. Under the operational direction of Pt Brij Mohan Vyas, the then executive officer of the board, the Museum was opened in the Municipal Building in 1931. Under his guidance, the Museum acquired important collections, including ancient sculptures from Bharhut (Satna district of Madhya Pradesh) and Bhumra (Madhya Pradesh).

In 1942, S.C. Kala, the first curator, gave the much needed impetus to enriching the collection of the Museum, especially by adding the Nehru personalia collection and the Bengal School Paintings. As space became a constraint, it was decided that the Museum should be shifted from the Municipal Board building to the present building at the Company Bagh or Chandrasekhar Azad Park. The foundation stone of the present museum building, which was then known as Prayag Sangrahalaya, was laid on 14 December 1947 by Pt Nehru and the Museum was opened to the public in 1954.

The real turning point of the fate of the Museum, however, came in the year 1986. Realising the significance of the diversity of its archaeological artifacts, the Museum was taken over by the Ministry of Culture, Government of India, after constituting an autonomous body called Allahabad Museum Society, and it was declared a museum of national importance. At present, the Museum is under the financial control of the Ministry of Culture, Government of India, and the ex-officio chairman of the Museum is the Governor of Uttar Pradesh.

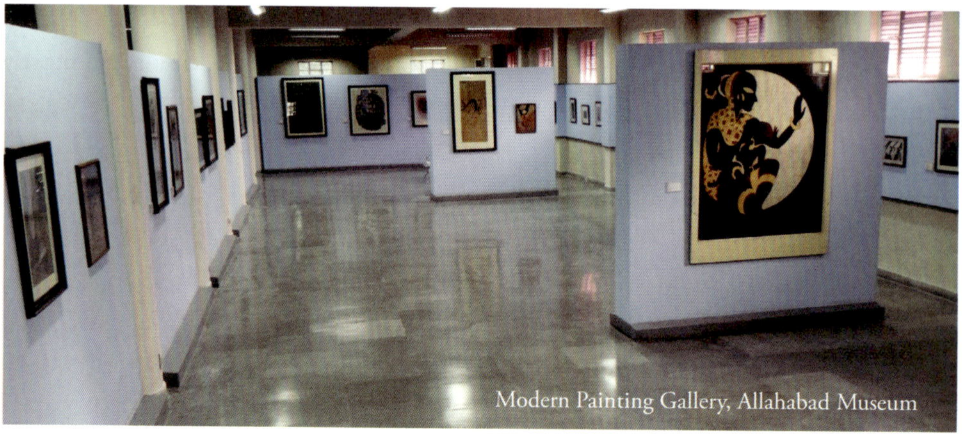
Modern Painting Gallery, Allahabad Museum

THE COLLECTION

The Allahabad Museum has a rich and diversified collection of art, antiquities, paintings, sculptures, coins, ceramics, archaeological objects, illustrated manuscripts, firmans, decorative art objects, arm and armours, textiles, natural history specimen, photographs, prints and personalia collections pertaining to Gandhi, Nehru, and literary personalities of Allahabad like Sumitra Nandan Pant, Suryakant Tripathi 'Nirala', Premchand, and Mahadevi Verma. The artefacts are displayed in sixteen different galleries including an exhibition in the Memorial Hall, in the memory of A.K. Coomaraswamy, and in the Central Hall, where from time to time various temporary exhibitions on different themes are organised for the rotation of art objects and antiquities from the reserve collection of the Museum.

Central Hall Collection

The Central Hall is mainly dedicated to the representative collection of modern paintings of the Bengal School of Art maestro, Asit Kumar Haldar. Besides, a few rare stone sculptures and decorative pillars are also on display here. However, the most coveted piece of the introductory gallery is the pistol of the martyr of the Indian Freedom Struggle, the youth icon of Allahabad, Chandra Shekhar Azad.

Stone Sculpture Collection

Allahabad Museum has an extraordinarily rich collection of exquisite stone sculptures, which also includes stone carvings, fragments of panels, coping stones, and railing stones from the remains of the great stupa of Bharhut discovered by Sir Alexander Cunningham in 1873. The theme of the Bharhut collection are mostly from the Buddhist *Jataka* stories and the life of Buddha. Apart from the Bharut collection, the Museum also houses some interesting Brahmanical (Hindu) images such as Shiva, Krishna, Durga, Kartikeya, Vishnu, Ganga, Gana, Yaksha, from the periods of the Shunga, Kushana, and Gupta dynasties. These have been acquired from Bhumra, Nachna, Khoh (Madhya Pradesh), and Kaushambi (Uttar Pradesh). However, the centre of attraction of this gallery is a tussle head of Shiva emerging out of stone linga, portraying the classical Gupta Art. The collection also includes the images of Bodhisattva Maitreya, resembling the Greek God, Apollo. It also has some beautiful specimens of the Gandhara School of Art, such as stone reliefs depicting the scenes of the birth and death of Buddha and the stories connected with Buddha's life.

Under the early medieval stone sculpture collection, the Museum has a wide variety of images dedicated to Brahmanical cults like Shaivism (Shiva), Vaishnavism (Vishnu), Shakta (Mother Goddesses), Saura (Solar), Ganapatya (Ganesha), which includes the prominent images of Uma-Maheshwara, zoomorphic incarnations of Vishnu such as Nrisimha, Varaha, the Shakta images like Chamunda, and Saptmatrikas. The Museum also has Jain images of Adinath, Ambika, and Saraswati. It also houses four exquisitely carved images of nymphs from Jamsot, Allahabad, and Uttar Pradesh.

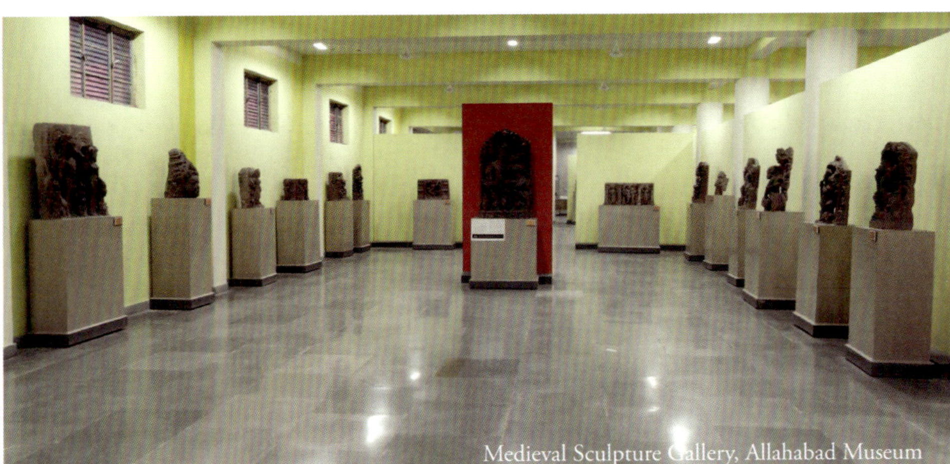
Medieval Sculpture Gallery, Allahabad Museum

Terracotta Collection

The Allahabad Museum has a very rich collection of more than six thousand terracotta images from the major centers of terracotta art in the Ganga valley, like Shrugna in Haryana, Mathura, Kaushambi, Jhusi, and Rajghat in Uttar Pradesh; Ahichhatra and Chandraketugarh in West Bengal; Patna and Buxar in Bihar. The terracotta collection includes narratives from Indian mythology and Puranas, the secular images like toy carts, animal, and human figurines highlighting the folk expressions of Indian art in ancient and medieval times.

Decorative Art Collection

Beautiful wooden furniture, glazed pottery, including Delft pottery of Holland and porcelains from China, and ivory carvings are the most attractive items in the collection housed here. It also contains several exquisite textiles, including baluchari sari and zardozi or zari work.

Arms, Armour, and Bronze Collection

There are about more than 220 weapons in all in the Museum, majority of which belong to 17th to 20th century CE. A large number of them have been acquired

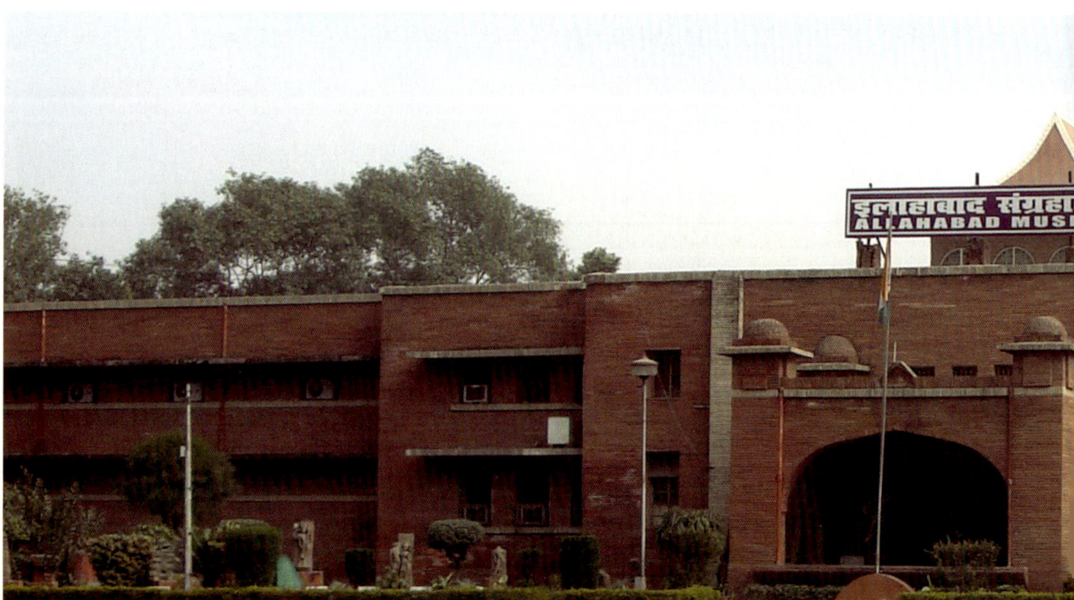

from the old Manda state near Allahabad. They are of both offensive and defensive types. The offensive weapons are the sword, the spear, battle axe, *gurj, khukhri*, dagger, *khanjar*, muskets, guns, rifles, bayonets, field guns, machine guns, pistols and revolvers etc. The defensive weapons are the shields of different sizes, the chain and plate armour, arms guard with or with chain, etc. The pride of the arms collections is a gold scabbard, which was gifted to the Governor of Uttar Pradesh by the Shah of Iran, who later handed it over to Allahabad Museum.

Personalia Collection

It contains photographs of Mahatma Gandhi from his birth to his death and also historic scenes of his struggle from his early days in South Africa to his struggle for Indian Independence, the Non-Cooperation Movement, Civil Disobedience Movement, and the Quit India Movement. As a symbolic gesture of his Civil Disobedience Movement, the original salt he prepared at Dandi is on display. The brass casket in which Mahatma Gandhi's ashes were taken to Sangam at Allahabad is also on display. The Ford vehicle that carried the ashes of Gandhi to Sangam for immersion is parked in a separate enclosure, outside the Museum. The Museum also contains valuable letters of Mahatma Gandhi.

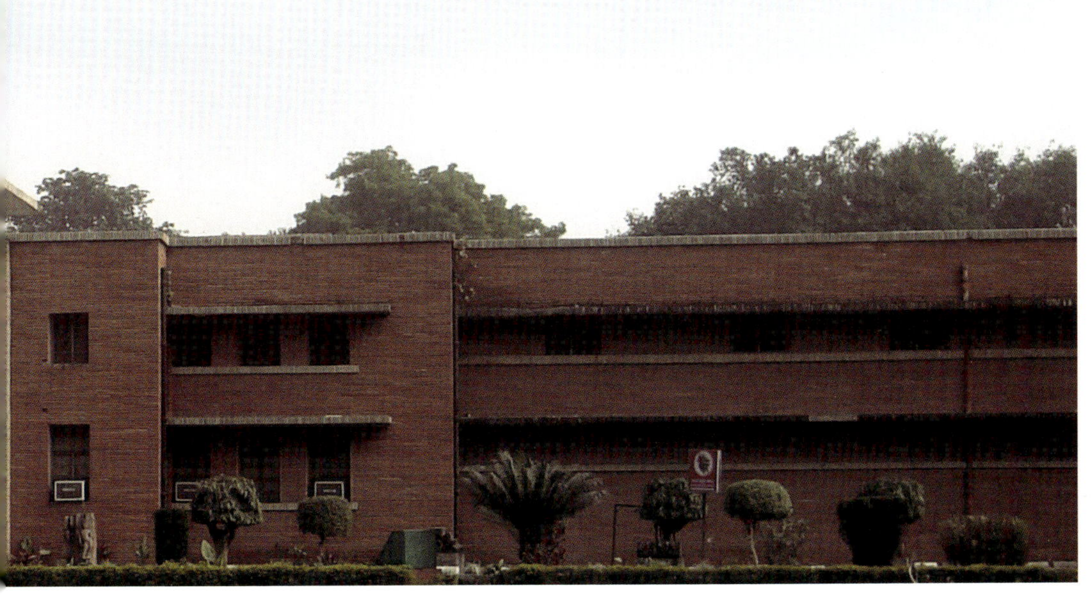

The personalia collection of Pt. Jawaharlal Nehru includes welcome addresses, his autobiography, caskets, and photographs from his childhood to his last days, and a golden stick among other things. There is also a collection on Indian Freedom Struggle containing the photographs from Revolt of 1857 to India's independence. The Museum has in its possession the sword and dress of Liaquat Ali Khan, the hero from Allahabad of 1857, the First War of Independence. There are also some valuable match-box labels printed in Sweden, Japan, and Australia.

Archaeological Collections

Allahabad region is abundantly rich in archaeological sites from the prehistoric times to Mughal period, which have been explored and excavated over a period of time. The Allahabad Museum has a few of the representative collections in the form of microliths, tools, ceramics, fossils, and antiquities and artefacts belonging to the Chalcolithic, Neolithic, and Early Historic periods. These include Neolithic celts, blades and burins, bone points, needles, etc. Besides, the archaeological findings from this historical period include seals, sealing, coins, and inscriptions. They are preserved and displayed along with some photographs of pre-historic rock paintings of the Sonbhadra, Mirzapur, and the other regions of Vindhya range to understand them contextually in relation to different archaeological sites from where these have been unearthed or acquired. The archaeological collection also includes terracotta toy carts, bulls, spoked wheels, and the grave goods from Mohenjodaro of the Indus Valley Civilization.

Miniature Painting Collection

The Allahabad Museum has a fine collection of miniature paintings of c.18th to 19th century CE. The collection of miniature painting includes styles and schools such as Deccani, Rajasthani, Mughal, Pahari, and Company Schools of Paintings. Among these paintings, the Sikh painting of Guru Arjunadeva listening to Gurubani; the Darbar scene of Bahdurshah Zafar; the Raga and Ragini of Deccani and Pahari paintings, the image of classical singer Tansen of Mughal Darbar are conspicuously significant among the paintings.

Modern Indian Painting Collections

Allahabad Museum, though an archaeological museum, is also known for its modern art collection. The modern art collection has a large number of paintings both in oil and tempera. It has a water-colour collection from the Bengal School of Art, which includes paintings of Abanindranath Tagore, Jamini Roy, Nandal Bose, Kshitindra Nath Majumdar, and Asit Kumar Haldar. Besides, the Museum also has the prized collection of the German painter and monk, Anagarika Govinda, the precious collections of two Russian painters Nicholas Roerich and his son Svetoslav Roerich. Apart from these, there are a good number of modern paintings by eminent artists of contemporary times.

Natural History Collection

One of the oldest collections of Allahabad Museum is the Natural History Gallery, which contains the taxidermy collections of animals, birds, reptiles, and mammals, including migratory birds, leopards, tigers, and peacocks. It also has in its possession an Ostrich egg cell.

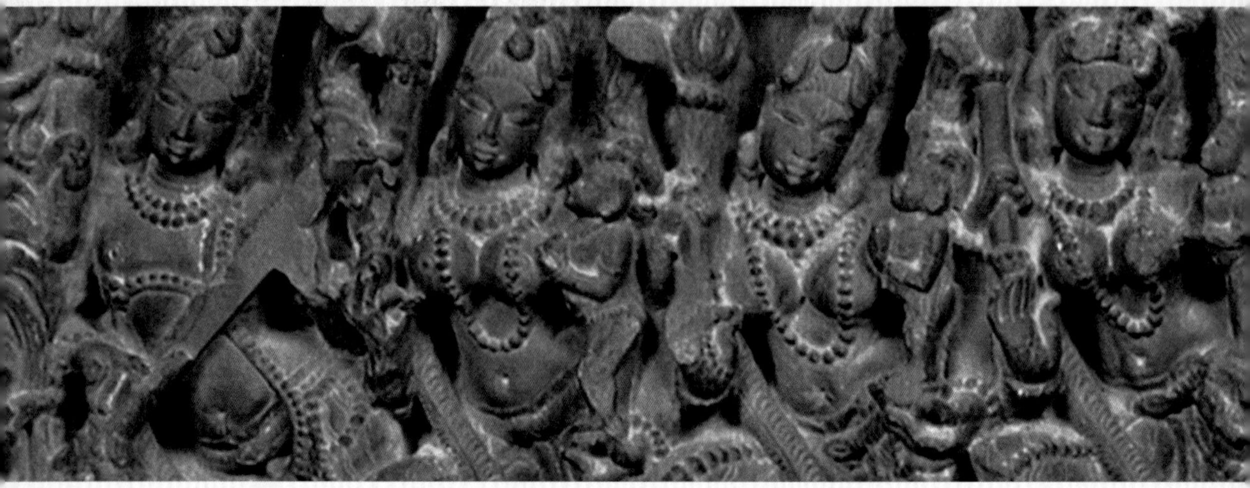

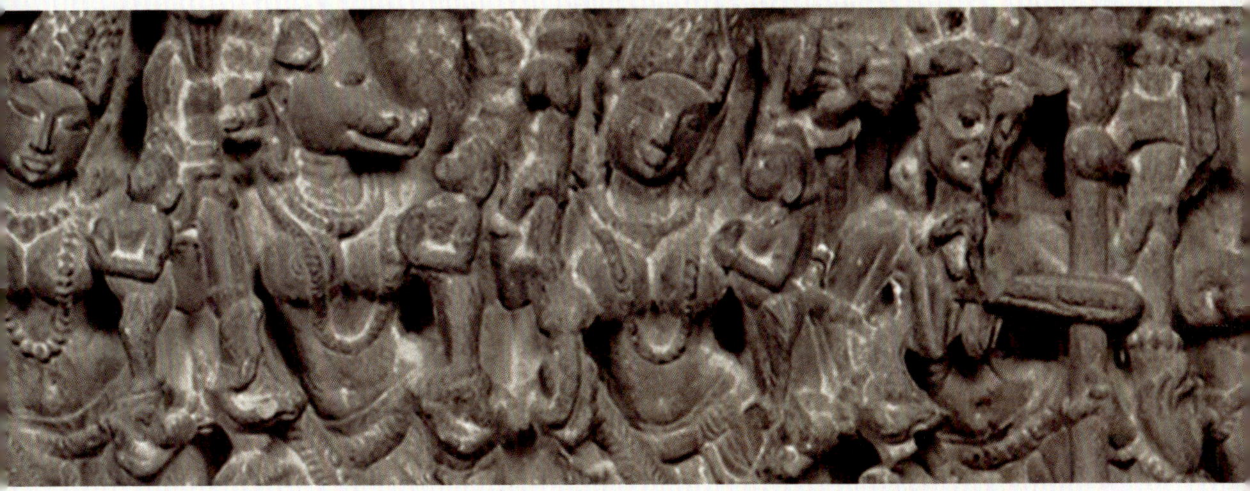

STONE SCULPTURE GALLERY

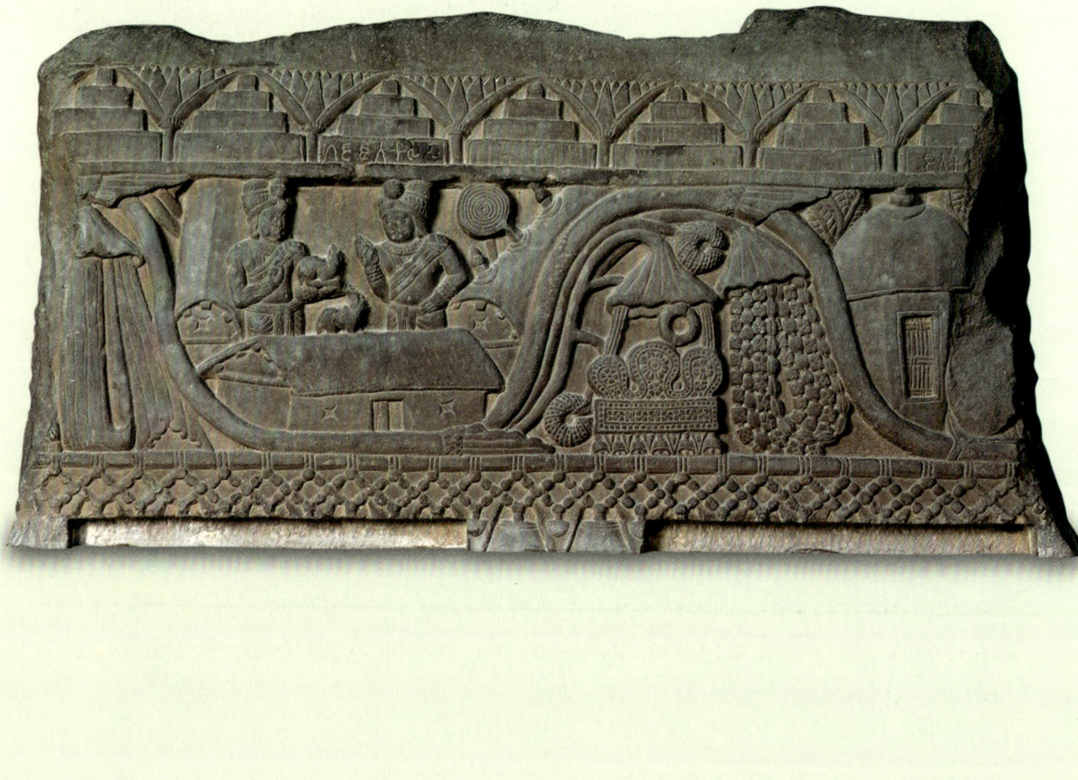

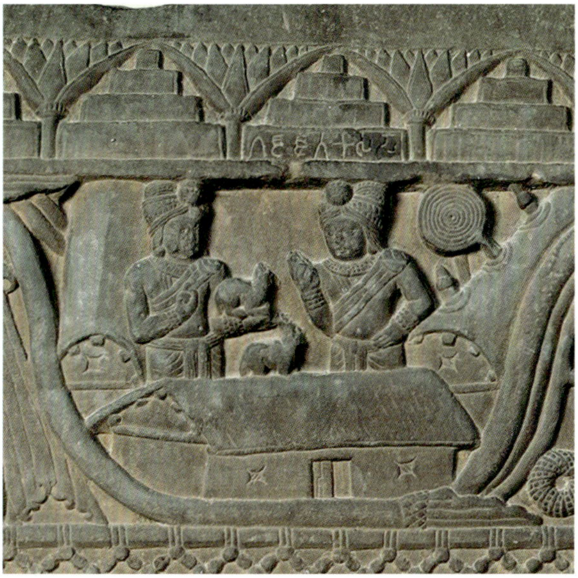

FRAGMENT OF A COPING STONE RAILING

One of the architectural remains of a fragment of the huge stupa of Bharhut, this displays the inner face of a coping stone of a railing. Between the usual upper and lower borders of stepped merlons and pendant bells are reliefs, which fill the four compartments, formed by the undulating creepers (*kalpavalli*). On the left, we first see a calyx, yielding a cloth; two men engaged in conversation in a courtyard formed by three buildings; and finally three finials. The figure on the left has the right hand raised in the attitude of exposition while the left hand holds an animal. Another animal can be seen perched on the roof of the house in the foreground. This roof is gabled, consisting of sloping rafters thatched with grass; the other two roofs are vaulted.

Provenance: Bharhut, Satna, Madhya Pradesh
Material: Sandstone
Date: 2nd century BCE
Dimension: 91.5 x 49.5 x 22 cm
Acc. No.: AM-SCL-45

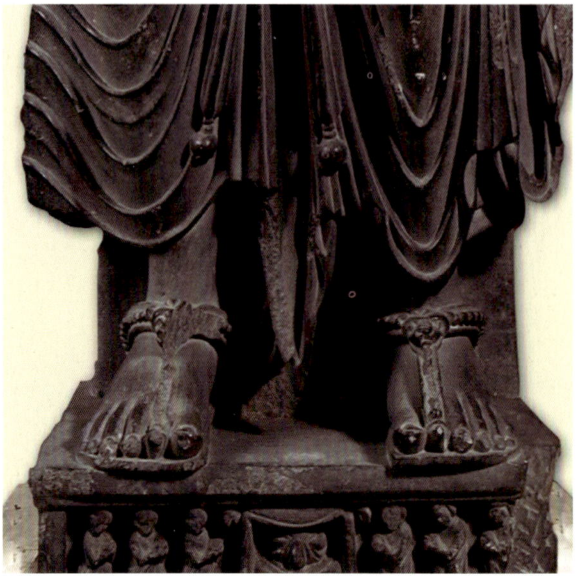

THE BODHISATVA MAITREYA

The Bodhisatva Maitreya is supposed to be the future Buddha, who will appear on this earth to attain complete enlightenment. This compassionate figure of Maitreya is exquisitely carved on blue schist stone. His hands and halo are partly damaged. The image wears a dhoti, a crown, a broad necklace, an amulet with two *gandharva*-like figures holding it, and a *yajnopavita* tagged with bunch of amulets. He is adorned with beautiful ornaments of fine workmanship. A pair of wooden sandals, each held by a leather strap, carved with lion heads establishes his royal associations. His hair is wavy and parted at the centre, and tied in a bun (*ushnish*) on the top. A pearl fillet circles the brow and is looped around the bun. Worshippers are shown on either side of the central image. The Buddha has a moustache, resembling the Greek God, Apollo. The sculpture belongs to the Gandhara School of Art, developed in the north-west frontiers of India.

Provenance: Gandhara
Material: Blue Schist Stone
Date: 2nd century CE
Dimension: 84 x 31.8 cm
Acc. No.: AM-SCL-130

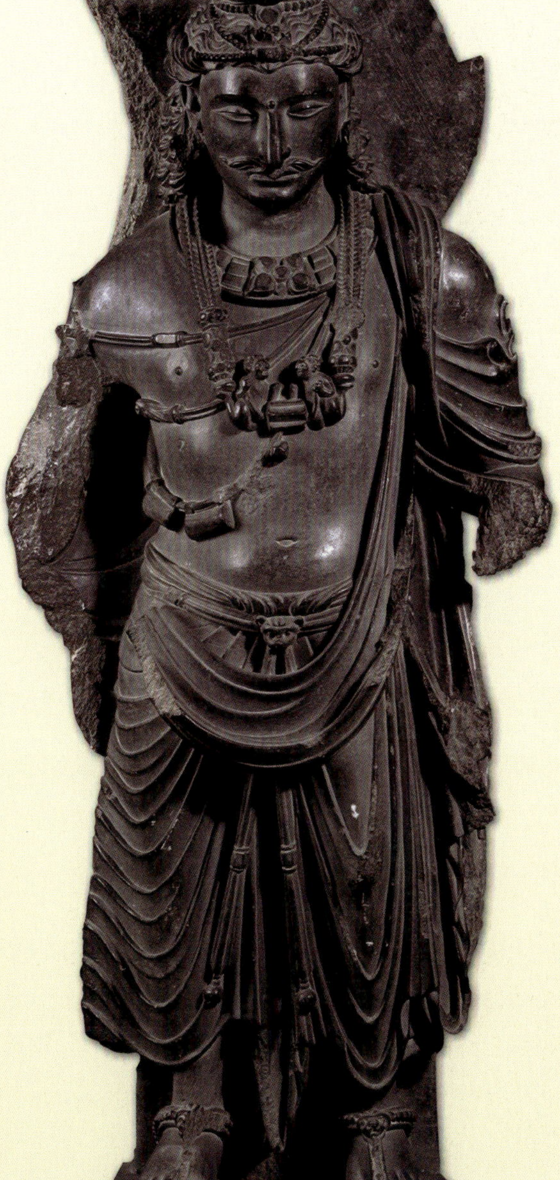

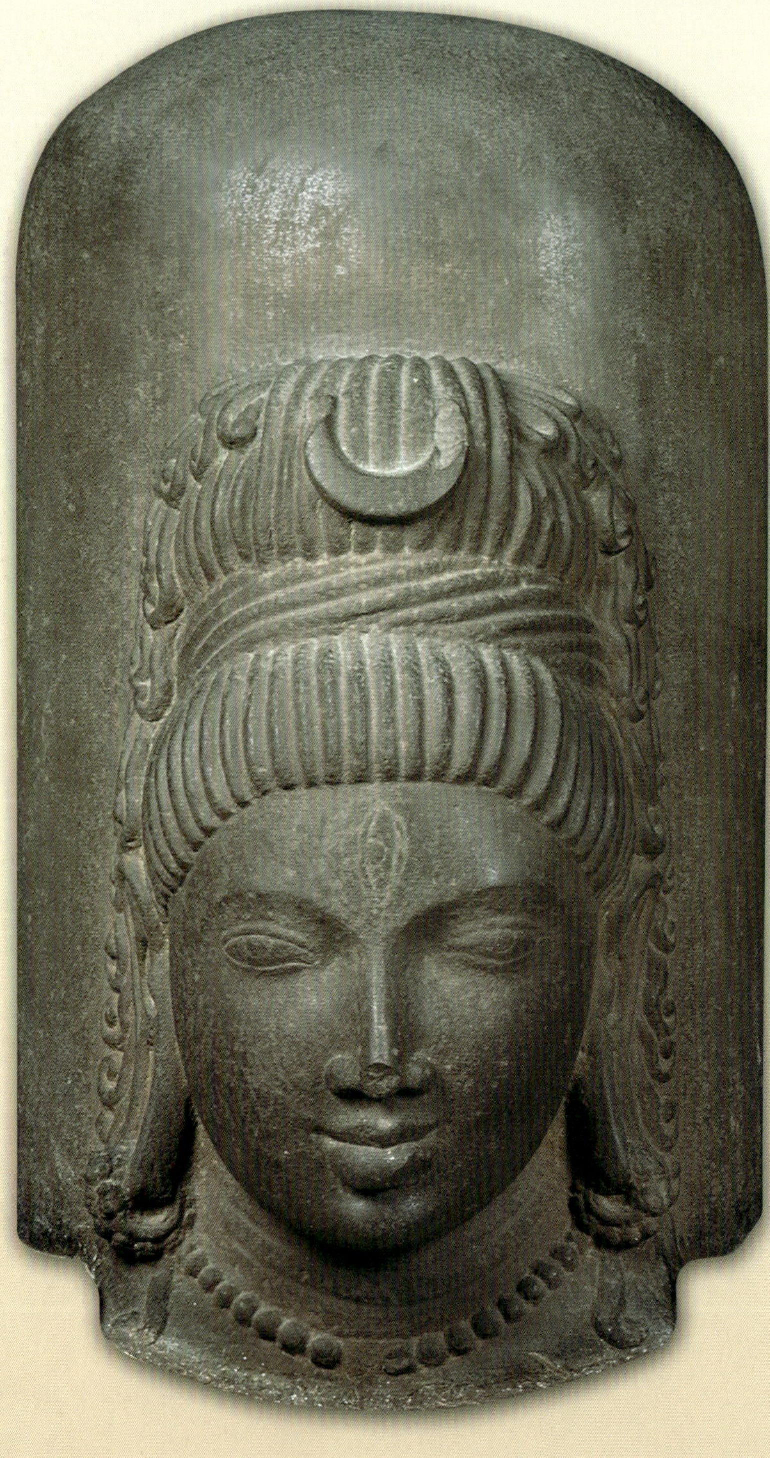

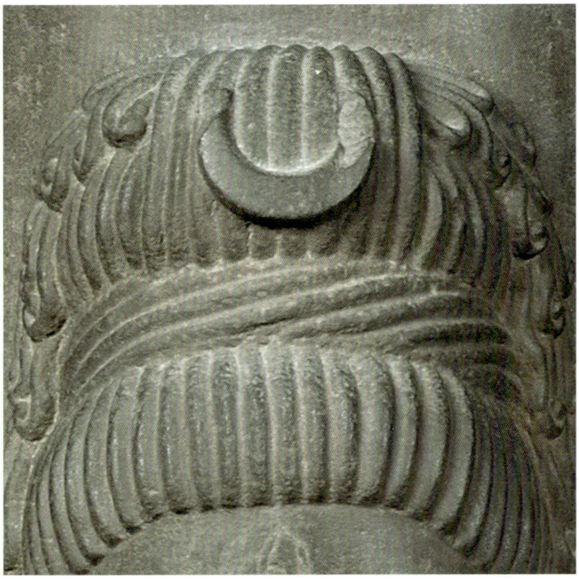

EKMUKHA SHIVA LINGA

This linga, with the relief image of Shiva emerging out of it, was recovered in situ from a site at Nat-ki-talai in village Khoh, Satna, Madhya Pradesh. The base is a square undressed tenon, which was once sunk into a *pitha*. The beautifully carved image of Shiva has a calm and serene look. He is bejewelled with a pair of a small circular pearl earrings and an *ekavali* (beaded necklace), close to his neck and adorned with *jatamukuta,* with a crescent moon on it, which signifies his godhood. Curly hairs are seen falling down over his shoulder from the *jatamukuta,* and his drooping eyelids signify a yogi in a meditative mood.

Provenance: Khoh (village), Satna, Madhya Pradesh
Material: Pink Sandstone
Date: 5th century CE
Dimension: Ht: 66 Dia.: 38 cm. (outside pedestal)
Acc. No.: AM-SCL-153

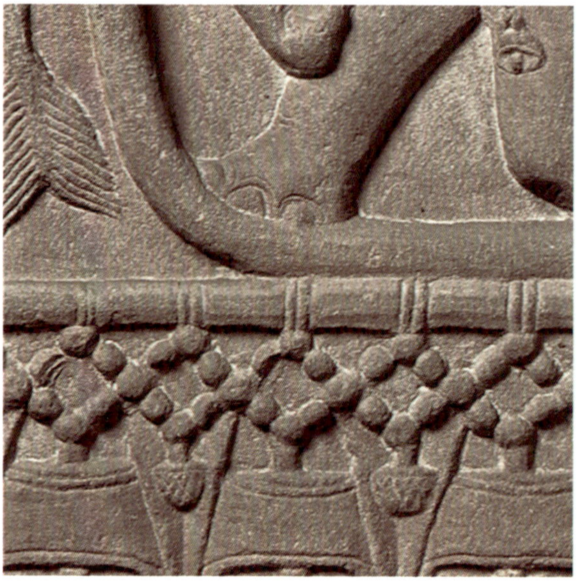

ELEPHANT CARRYING CORPORAL RELICS OF THE BUDDHA

After the *mahaparinirvana* (death) of the Buddha, his corporal remains and associated materials were buried inside a stupa by the kings of eight kingdoms, where these were enshrined and worshipped. This coping stone is part of the stone panel depicting series of scenes of elephants in procession, carrying the relic caskets as can be seen from the tail of the elephant at the end. The scene is depicted within the loop formed by the lotus rhizome. The upper border of the coping stone show a row of stupa, like pyramidal miniature structure on low relief, each stupa is flanked on either side by lotus petals. The border on the bottom shows a row of bells hanging on a chain like design. One of riders is shown holding the relic casket while the other holds a banner.

Provenance: Bharhut, Satna, Madhya Pradesh
Material: Sandstone
Date: 2nd century BCE
Dimension: 44.5 x 40.5 cm
Acc. No.: AM-SCL-47

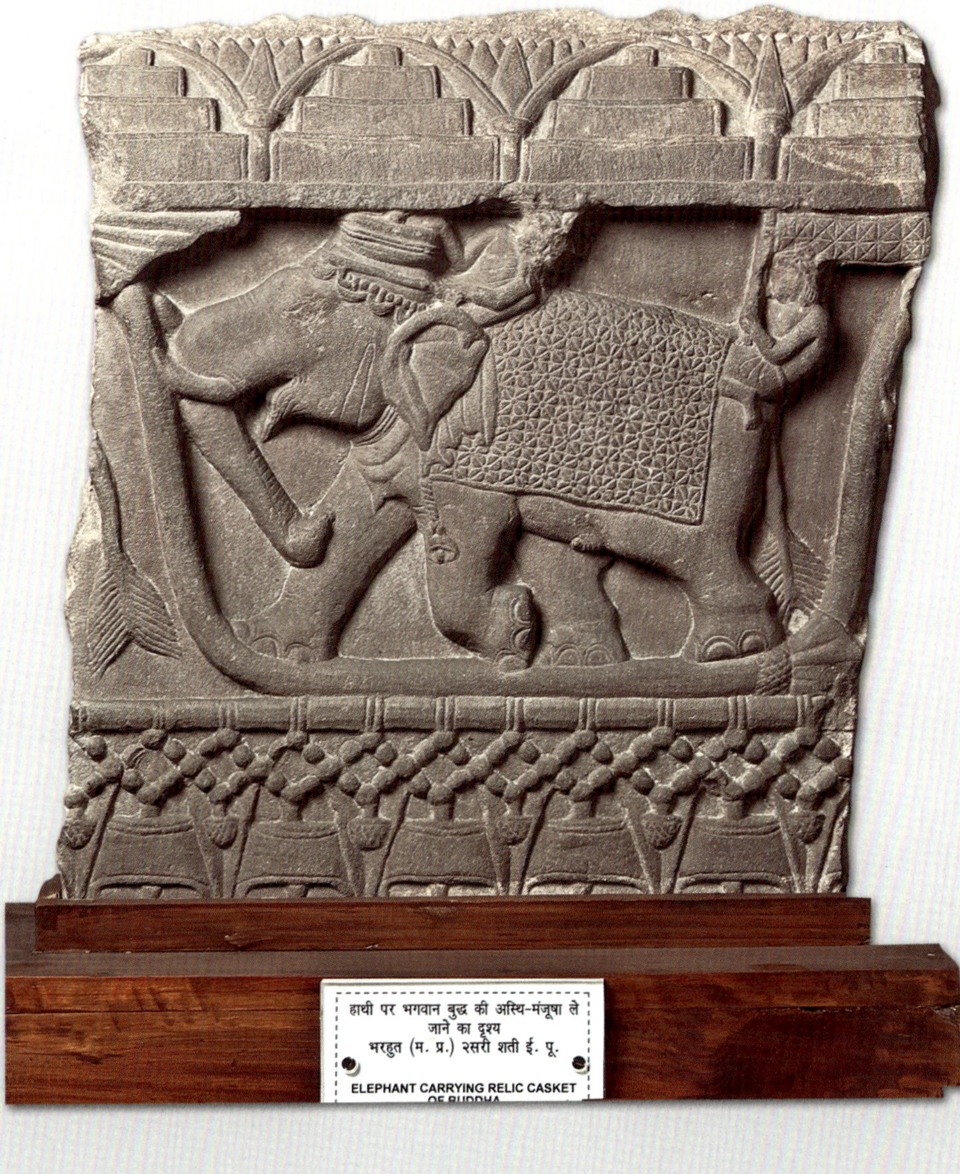
हाथी पर भगवान बुद्ध की अस्थि-मंजूषा ले
जाने का दृश्य
भरहुत (म. प्र.) २सरी शती ई. पू.
ELEPHANT CARRYING RELIC CASKET

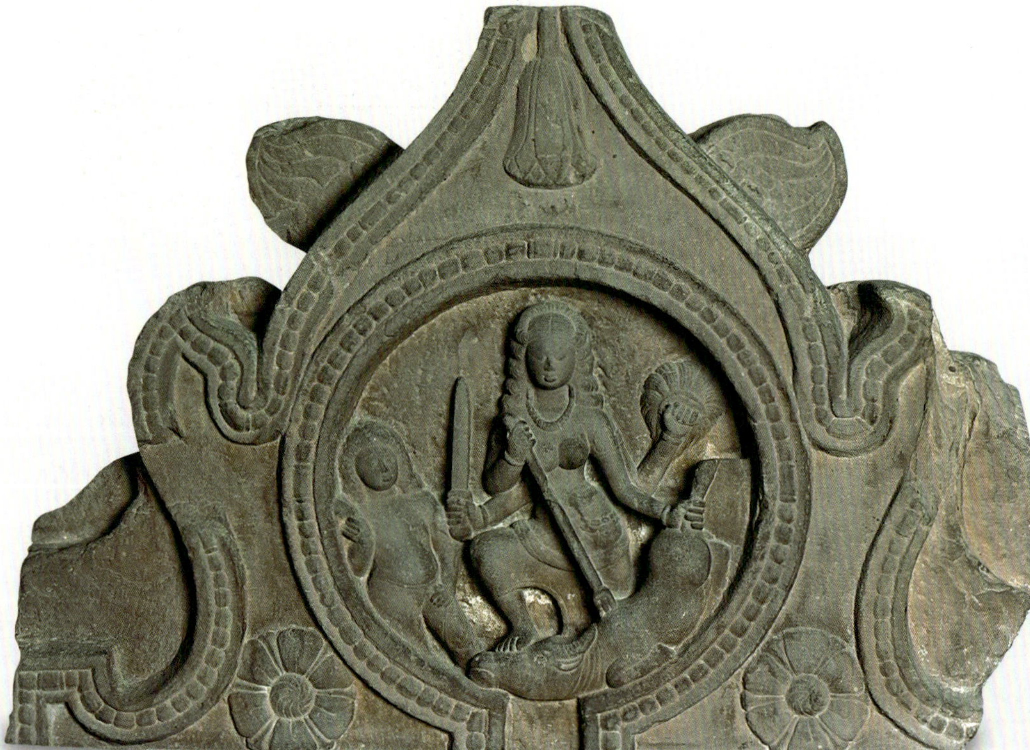

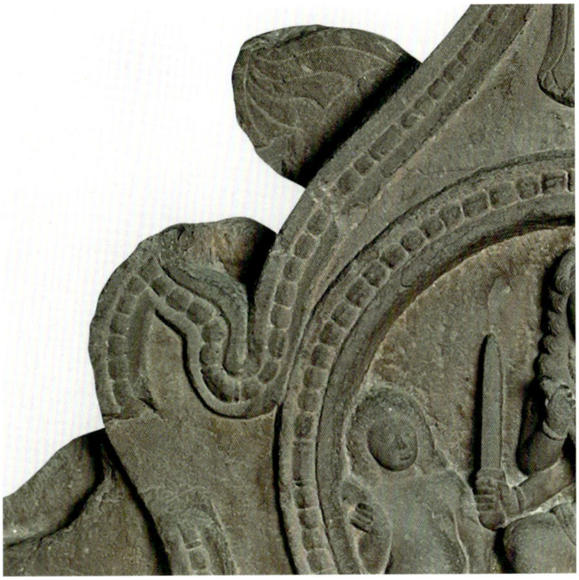

CHANDRASALA WITH MAHISAMARDINI

Chandrasala is an architectural fragment canonically called *chaitya.* It is a window of a Shiva temple of Gupta period, recovered from Bhumra, Madhya Pradesh. As the name suggests, Chandrasala is a moon-shaped circular niche, with the image of four-handed Mahishasurmardini Durga, the Goddess who killed a buffalo-headed demon, Mahishasura, carved on it. It is an anthropomorphic image of the demon emerging out of the buffalo's neck. Durga holds a shield (*dhal*) in her upper left hand. With her lower right hand she holds a sword (*khadga*). Her right leg is raised, resting on the head of the buffalo, and her lower left hand holds the tail of the buffalo. She holds a trident (*trishul*) in her upper right hand, which is piercing into the body of the buffalo. A *gana* is seen holding an unidentified object in his right hand, his left hand resting on his thigh.

Provenance:	Bhumara, Satna, Madhya Pradesh
Material:	Dark Pink Sandstone
Date:	5th century CE
Dimension:	56 x 72.5 cm
Acc. No.:	AM-SCL-151

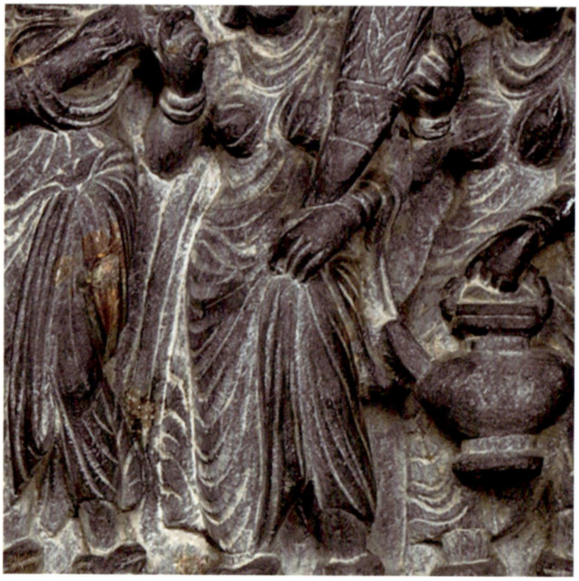

NATIVITY OF THE BUDDHA

Queen Maya, mother of the Buddha, stands in *tribhangamudra* in this panel. She is at the centre, holding a branch of the *shala* tree with her right hand. Her left hand is placed around the shoulder of her sister, Maha Prajapati, on whom she leans for support. Left of Maha Prajapati, a female figure holds a flywhisk. Another one carries a spouted vessel of holy water to bathe the baby. The newly born baby is held by a male figure—Lord Indra as per the Buddhist text. He holds a towel to carry the baby. The male figure immediately beside him stands with folded hands, and the one next to him carries a flywhisk and has an astonished look on his face. The halo behind the head of the baby signifies the divinity of the child. On the top of the panel are floating musical instruments signifying a joyful moment in heaven on the birth of this divine child.

Provenance: Gandhara
Material: Blue Schist
Date: 2nd century CE
Dimension: 30.5 x 45.8 cm
Acc. No.: AM-SCL-125

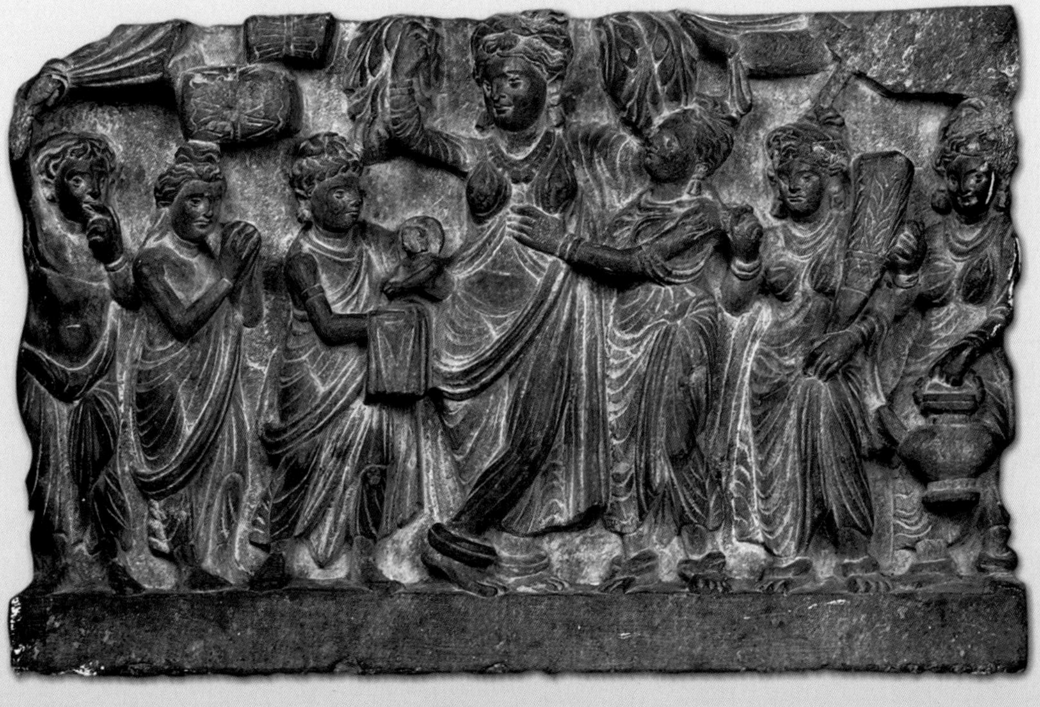

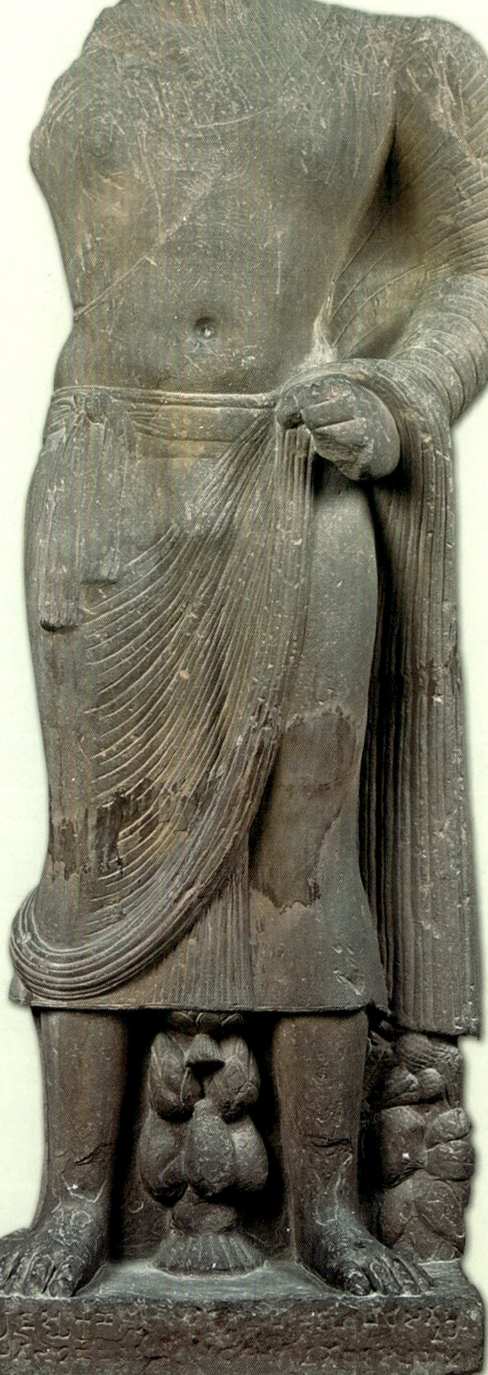

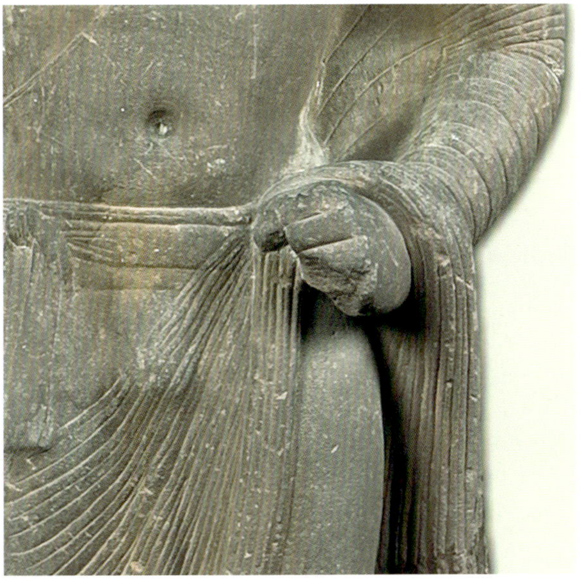

STANDING BODHISATTVA DEDICATED BY BUDDHAMITRA

The figure stands in *samabhanga* posture. The legs are apart, and between it is a bouquet consisting of five lotus buds and one full-bloomed lotus flower. The Buddha wears a diaphanous *antarvastravasaka* reaching below the knees. A *samghati* covers his left shoulder and arm. A ribbon-like girdle is knotted on the right side with the loose ends falling over the thigh. The folds are indicated by light incisions and grooved ridges. The powerful legs and the broad shoulders are features shared with other images of School of Mathura Art, sculptured during the early phase of the Kushana period. On the back of the figure there are traces of a halo with scalloped edge. This figure is a product of the great workshops at Mathura from where it was exported to Kaushambi, where it was found. The monk Buddhamitra, who dedicated this image, is also associated with the image at Sarnath.

Provenance: Kaushambi, Uttar Pradesh
Material: Spotted Red Sandstone
Date: 1st century CE
Dimension: 113 x 40.5 cm
Acc. No.: AM-SCL-68

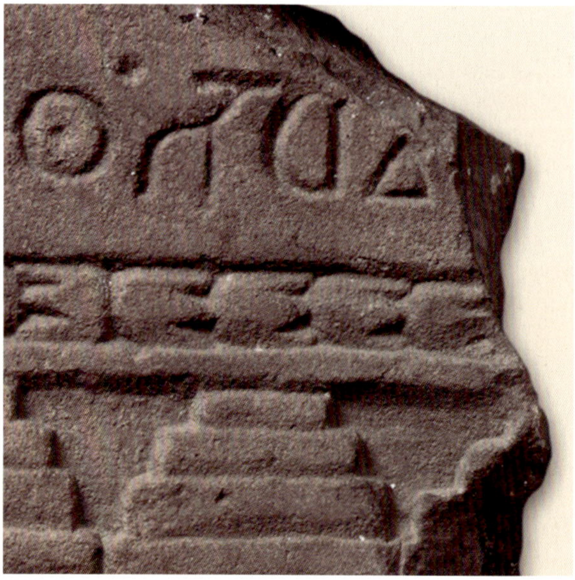

SHALBHANJIKA

The pillar fragment depicts a female figure standing under a *shala* tree, holding its branch with her right hand in front of the Ashokan pillar, decorated with floral designs and stepped merlons. The top portion just below the inscription is decorated with a series of four-stepped pyramids. The border is made of floral designs and stepped merlons (part of a crenelated parapet between two embrasures). An inscription is engraved on the top reads: *pusasa thabhodhama*. The panel may well be a representation of the nativity of the Buddha in the *shala* forest at Lumbini, in which case the female figure is identified as Maya. This identification would be further reinforced if the creature depicted on the *stambha* were indeed a horse, as it has been conjectured that the pillar set up by Ashoka at Lumbini was crowned with a horse capital.

Provenance: Kaushambi, Uttar Pradesh
Material: Pink Sandstone
Date: 2nd century BCE
Dimensions: 21 x 18 cm
Acc. No.: AM-SCL-63

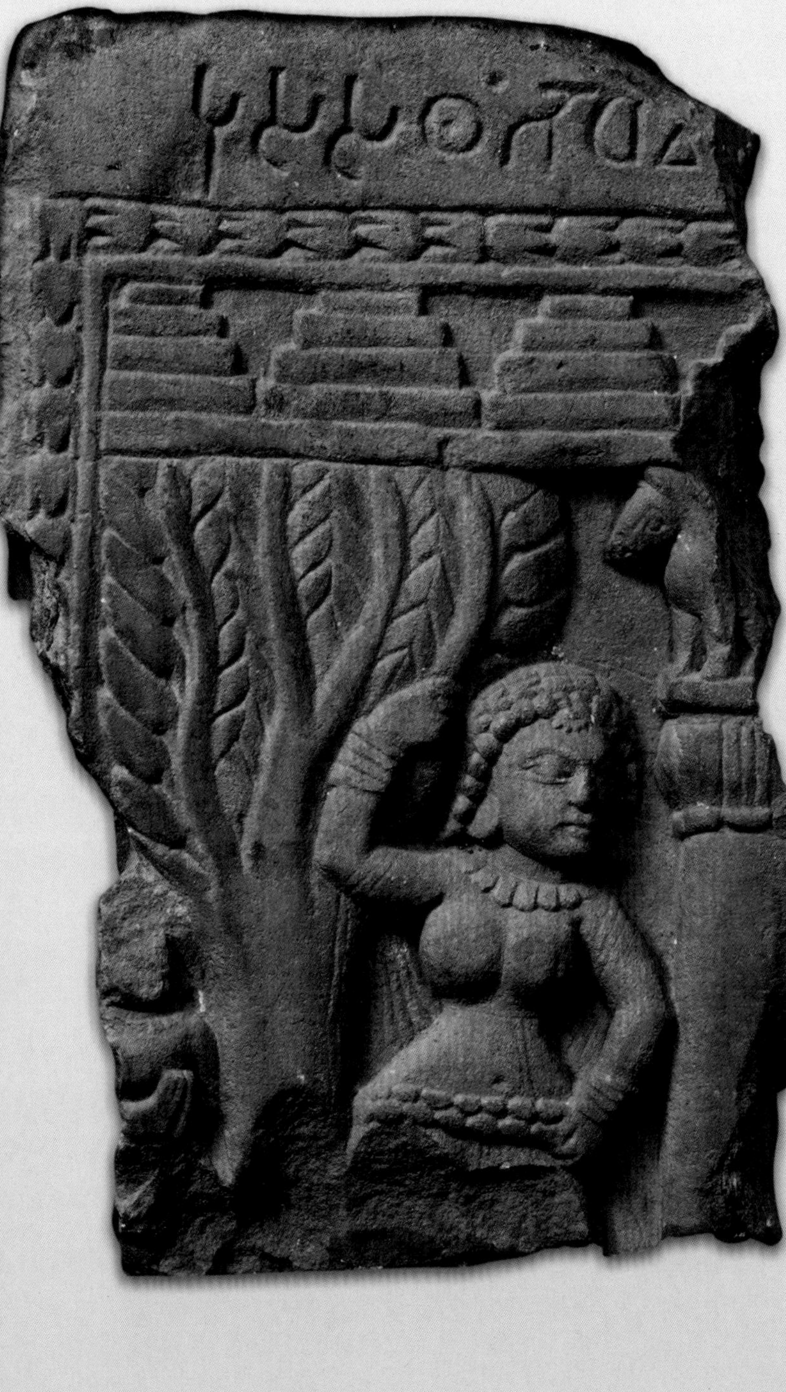

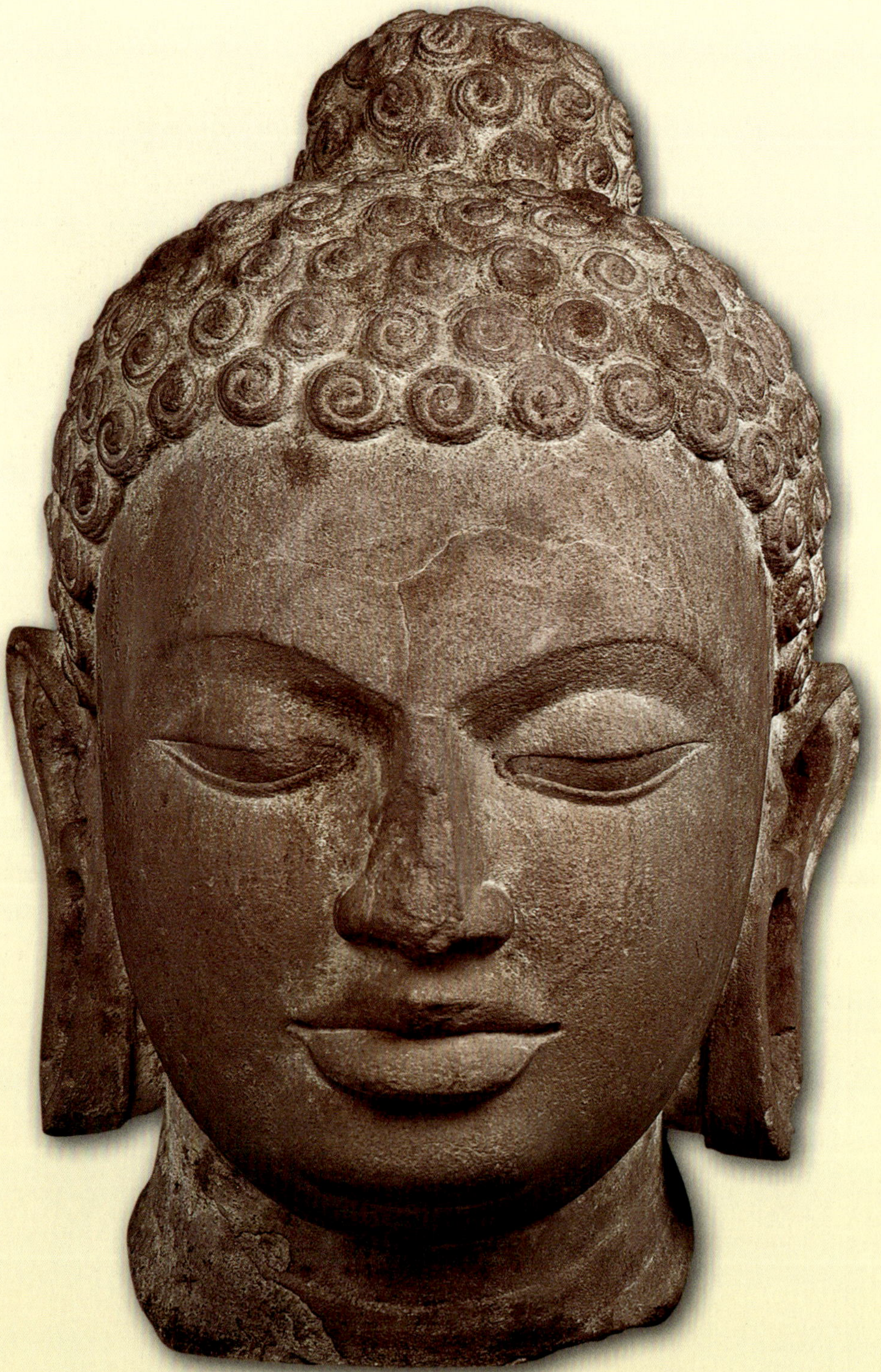

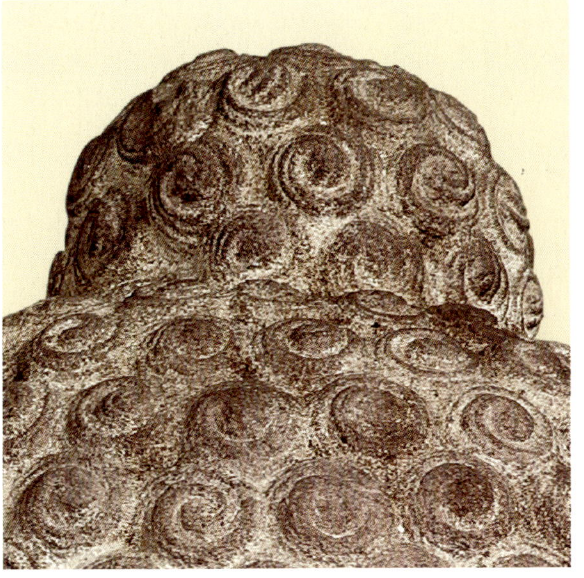

BUDDHA HEAD

This Buddha head has been recovered from Bhita in district Allahabad, Uttar Pradesh. The centre of the attraction of this image is the coiffure of Budhha, his hair arranged in snail-shell curls, culminating in a raised bun-shaped *ushnisha*, representing a typical Gupta-style sculpture. The linear features of the face and delicate handling of the sculpture recall the Sarnath School. The almond-shaped eyes and drooping eyelids imply a meditative *dhyanamudra*. His long ears and the *ushnisha* are some of the *mahapurusha lakshan*s, or signs of a great soul, seen in this image.

Provenance:	Bhita, Allahabad, Uttar Pradesh
Material:	Pink sandstone
Date:	5th century CE
Dimension:	33 x 20.3 cm
Acc. No.:	AM-SCL-229

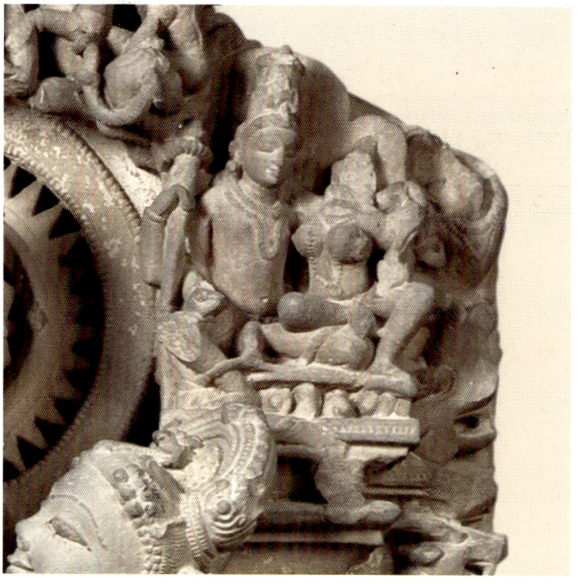

UMA-MAHESVARA

It is an amorous sculpture of Uma-Maheshvara, seated on a lotus platform in *lalitasana* (a seated posture). The lotus seat is borne on a stock with winding shoots and leaves. A bull, the vehicle of the Shiva, and a lion, the vehicle of Uma, are shown on either side of the pedestal. There are other devotees around them. Ganesha and Kartikeya (mutilated) images are shown on the either side of the panel, along with four attendants, two on either side. Seven *ganas* (dwarf images) are shown at the bottom-most register with the one at the centre supporting the slab. Behind the coupe are pilasters with *alingana-murtis* of Brahma and Vishnu with their consorts by their side. The side offsets contain the decorative motifs of *vyalas* on elephant heads and the *makaras* (crocodile) with warriors. Above the two pilasters are the mutilated images of flying Vidyadhara couples.

Provenance: Khajuraho, Chhatarpur, Madhya Pradesh
Material: Sandstone
Date: 11th century CE
Dimensions: 124.5 x 71 cm
Acc. No.: AM-SCL-291

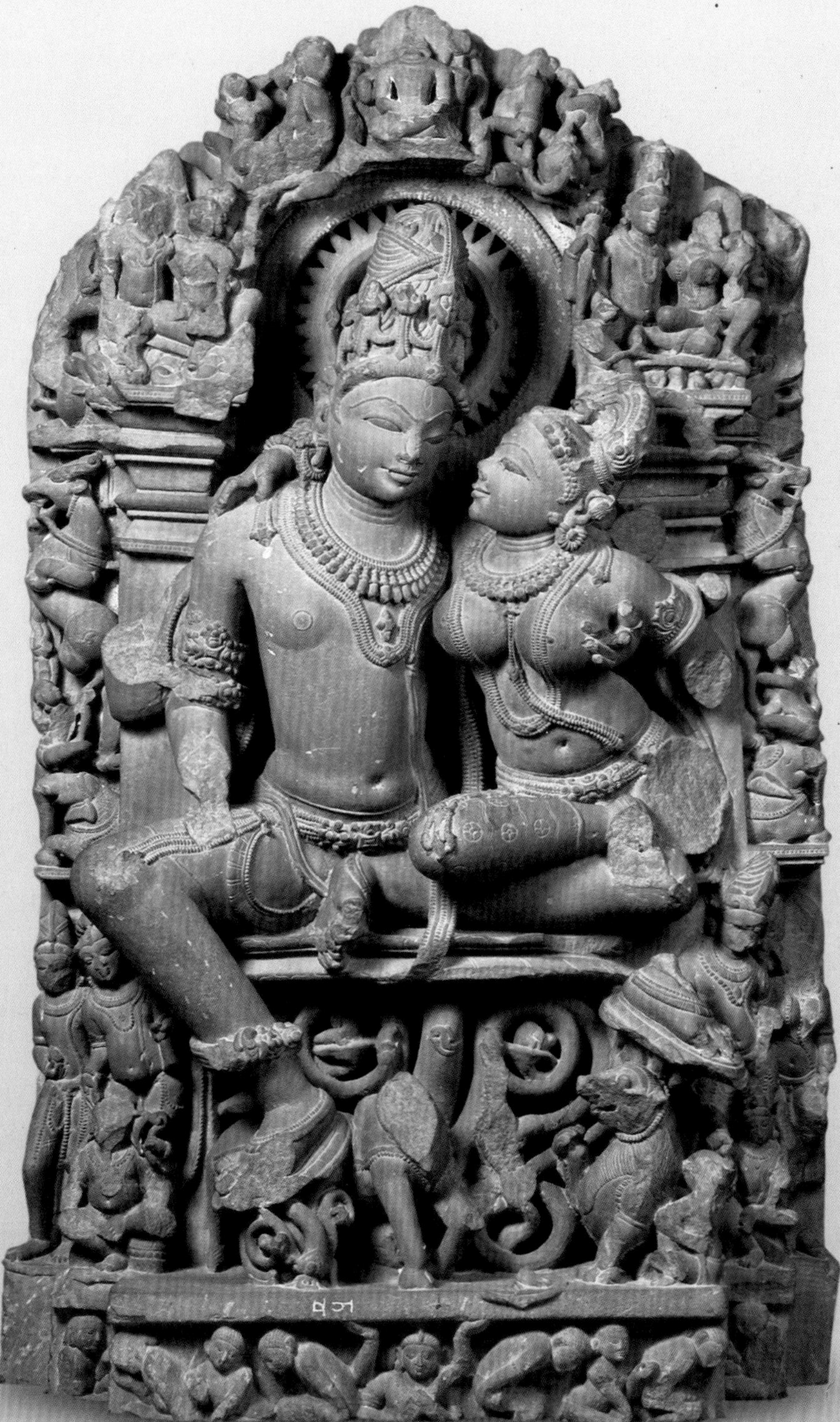

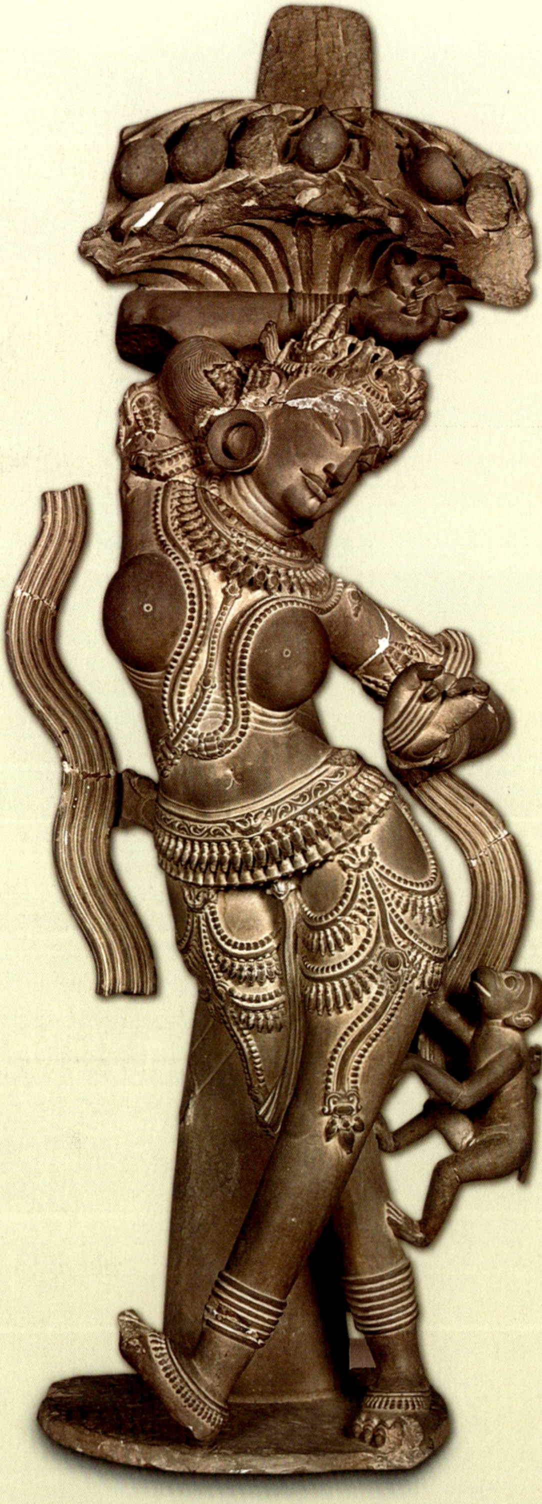

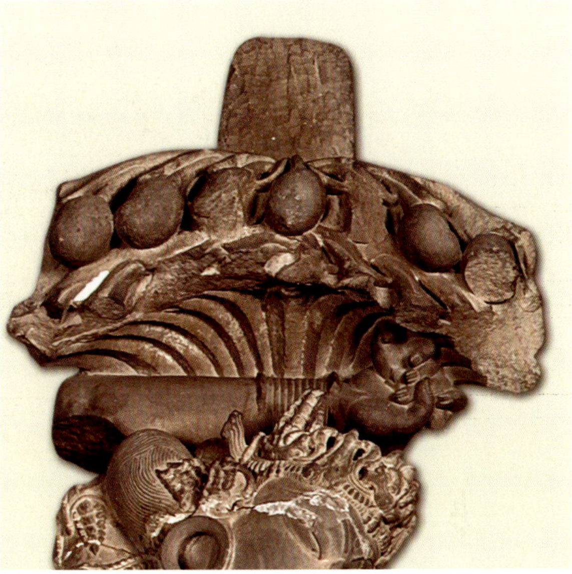

DANCING DAMSEL IN BRACKET FIGURE

A bracket female figure is shown standing on a lotus pedestal under a mango tree in a dancing posture. A monkey is seen clambering up her crossed legs. While she holds the branch of the tree with her upraised right hand, her left hand is raised in a gesture to drive the animal away. The branches and fruits of the tree form a serpent-hood canopy. She wears an elaborated crown consisting of three large triangular plaques composed of *kirttimukhas,* alternating with three smaller ones, large circular earrings, rows of bangles, necklaces, girdle with diamond shaped pendants and *urujalakas*. A tenon is visible on the top. The object might have been studded in the ceiling of the temple.

Provenance: Jamsot, Allahabad, Uttar Pradesh
Material: Buff Sandstone
Date: 12th century CE
Dimension: 118 x 34.5 cm
Acc. No.: AM-SCL-1042

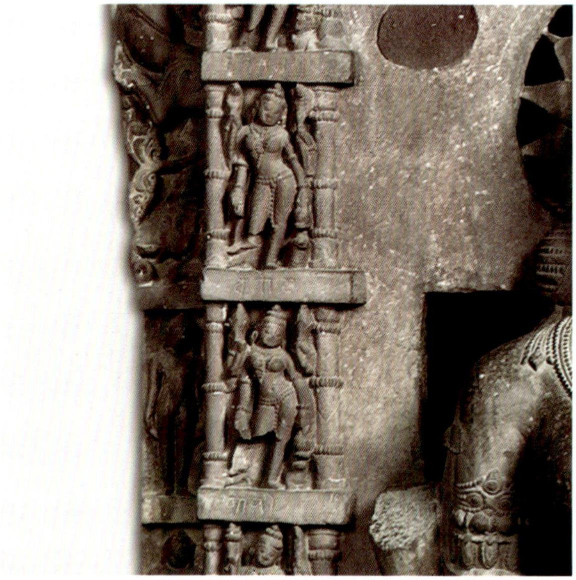

AMBIKA, THE ATTENDANT YAKSI OF NEMINATHA

A black stone stele showing the standing image of Jain Goddess Ambika at the centre. All her four arms are mutilated. She is attended by two youths. The one to her right is Deepankar, riding a lion, and the other is Shubhankar, waving a flywhisk or *chauri*. The pilasters flanking the Goddess are divided into several compartments i.e., niches, and are filled with standing *jinas* and Goddesses. Every Goddess is carved in a separate niche and has been inscribed with her name in early Devnagari script. On the top, in the central niche is the image of seated Neminath, identified by the conch, carved below his legs. A lotus flower, flanked by a four-armed deity and a worshiper is shown on the rectangular pedestal. Name of the deities flanking the main image are carved below the compartments.

Provenance: Satna, Madhya Pradesh
Material: Wine-coloured Sandstone
Date: 11th century CE
Dimensions: 170 x 99 cm
Acc. No.: AM-SCL-293

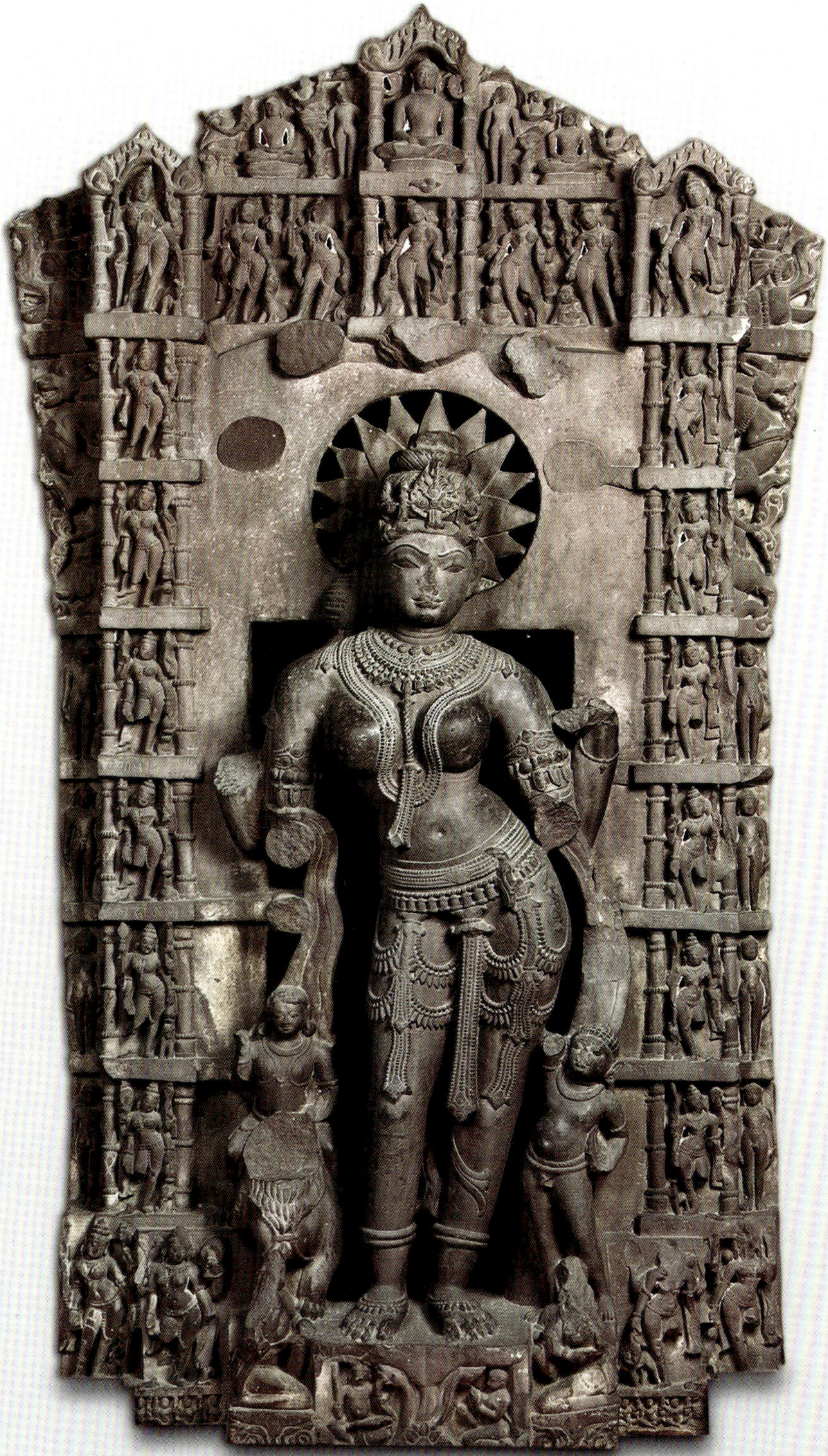

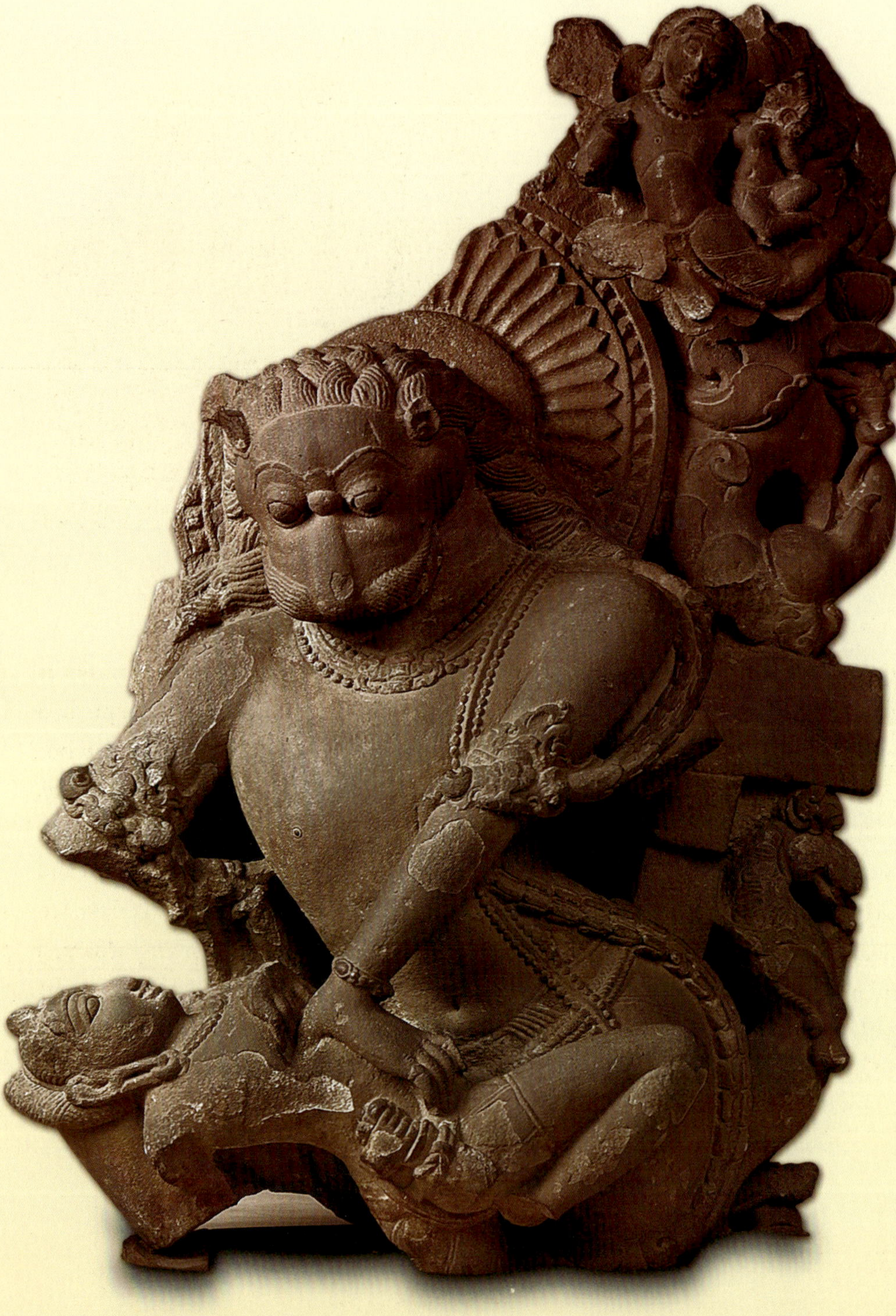

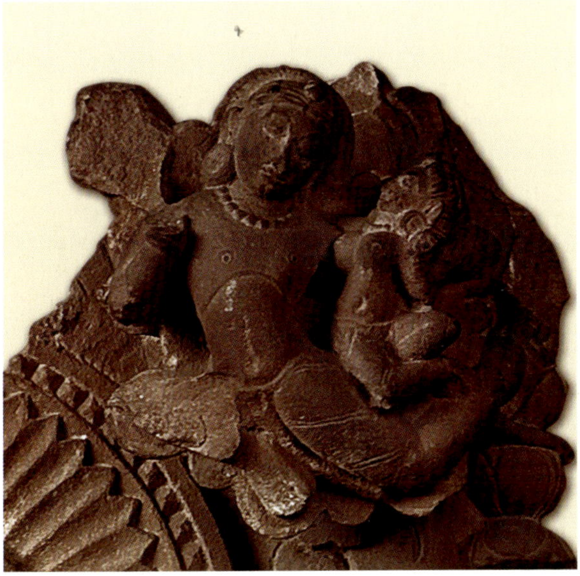

NARASIMHA SLAYING THE DEMON HIRANYAKASIPU

The statue is one of the ten *avatars* (incarnations) of lord Vishnu—Narasimha Avatara. In Brahmanical mythology, the *rakshasa* (demon) Hiranyakashipu had received a powerful boon from Brahma that he can be killed by neither a human nor an animal, inside or outside the palace, in day time or night, on earth or in the sky, with any weapon at all. This made him invisible and he declared himself a God. The lord Vishnu then descended on earth in a composite body of a lion and a man and used his claws to disembowel the rakshasa at the threshold of his house, at dusk, on his thighs. Left and lower portion of the statue is missing. A flying Vidyadhara, a divine couple has been carved against the clouds on the top of the figure. A rampart *vyala* (a composite animal), and traces of an attendant figure can be seen on the right side, just below the cross bar.

Provenance: Unchadiha, Allahabad, Uttar Pradesh
Material: Sandstone
Date: c. 9th century CE
Dimension: 95.5 x 48.5 cm
Acc. No.: AM-SCL-465

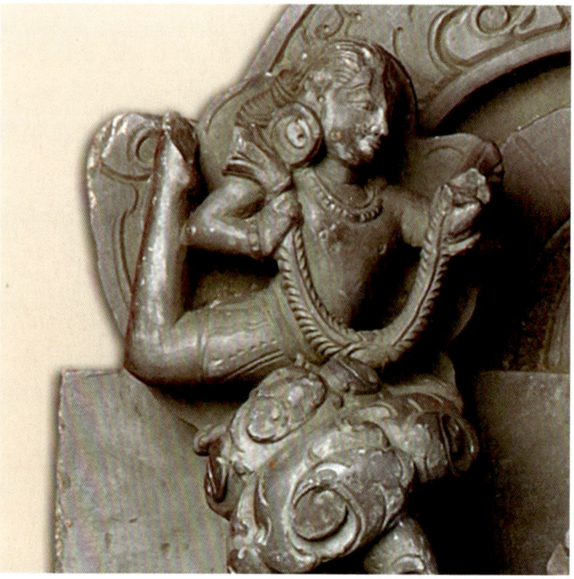

STANDING PARVATI

The stele contains a four-armed figure of Parvati, standing on a lotus. A lotus halo *prabhamandala*, with a border of a creeper is carved behind her head. There is a male garland bearer on either side, near her head. There are also two female attendants and a lion on either of side, near her legs. The Goddess holds a lotus and a *trisula* in her upper right and left hands respectively, while the lower hands are held in *abhayamudra*. Her hair is dressed upwards and held by a flat decorative band above the forehead. Her long necklace reaches her waist. She wears a lower garment, covering up to the feet. It is carved in black stone. She wears a *jatamukuta*, *kundalas*, torque, necklace, wristlets, and anklets and is draped in a sari and scarf, which winds round both her arms. This is a typical early medieval Katyuri Art of the Himalayan region, characterised by metallic finish, elongation of the figures, and an ornamental, arched canopy, crowning the image.

Provenance: Chandausi, Muradabad, Uttar Pradesh
Material: Black Stone
Date: 12th century CE
Dimensions: 42 x 25 cm
Acc. No.: AM-SCL-1070

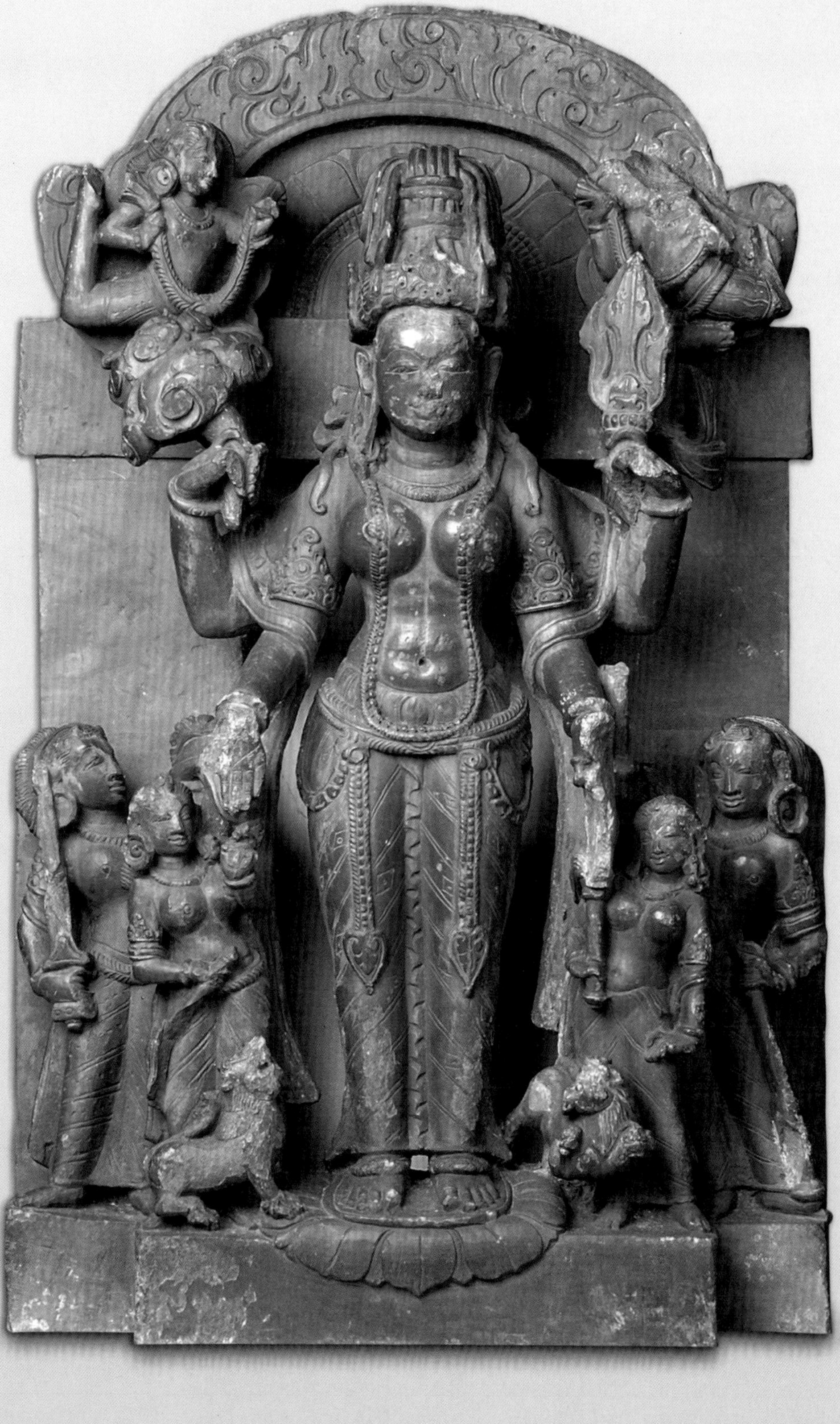

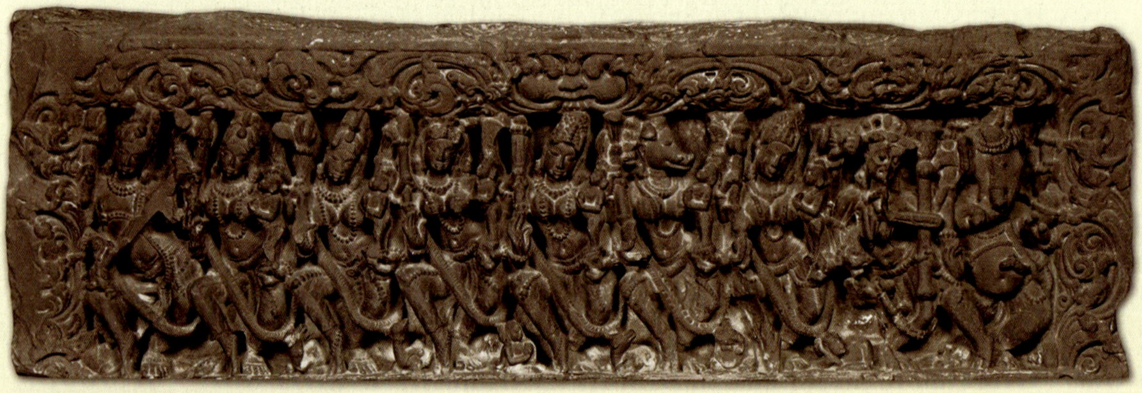

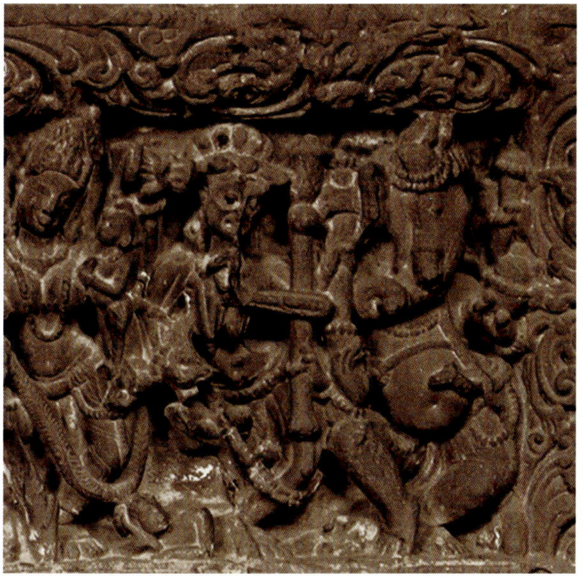

SAPTAMATRIKA PANEL

Matrika(s) or mother goddesses is a group of Brahmanical goddesses who are always shown together. Since they are usually depicted as seven mothers, they are called *saptamatrika*(s). The seven matrikas or goddesses are Brahmani, Vaishnavi, Maheshvari, Indrani, Kaumari, Varahi, Chamunda, and Narasimhi—the female counterparts of Brahma, Vishnu, Shiva, Indra, Kaumara or Kartikeya, Varaha, the boar incarnation of Vishnu, Vairabha, the ferocious form of Shiva, and the lion incarnation of Vishnu. The Saptamatrika panel contains floral border on sides. All the goddesses are shown with their attributes and vehicles. On the extreme left side there is a carved figure of Shiva, and on the extreme right is four armed Ganesha. On the upper side there is a *kirttimukha* (swallowing fierce monster face, a benevolent symbol of protection) in the centre.

Provenance: Gurgi, Rewa, Madhya Pradesh
Material: Grey Sandstone
Date: 10th century CE
Dimension: 40.7 x 125.7 cm
Acc. No.: AM-SCL-967

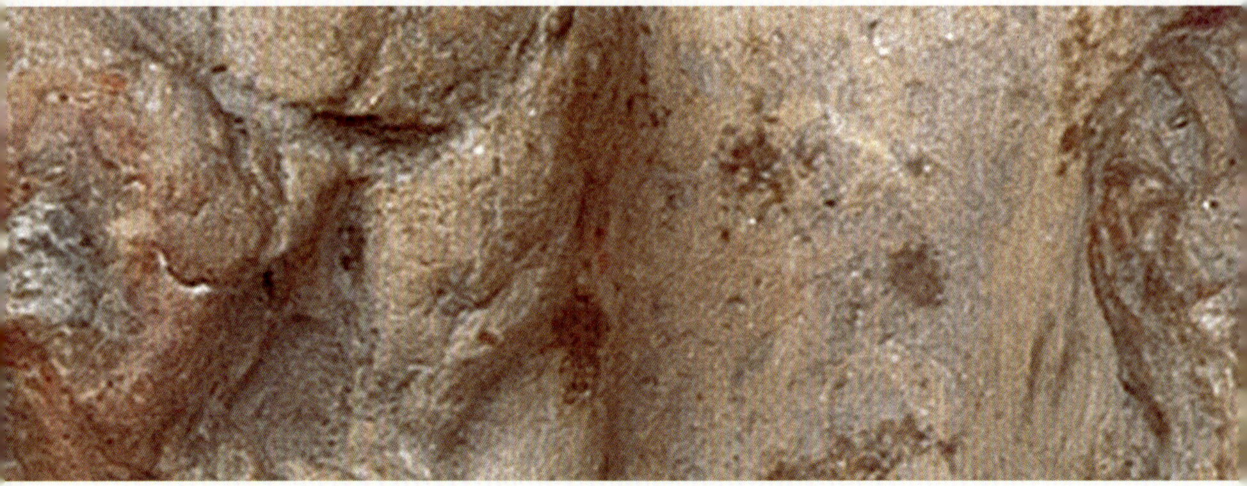

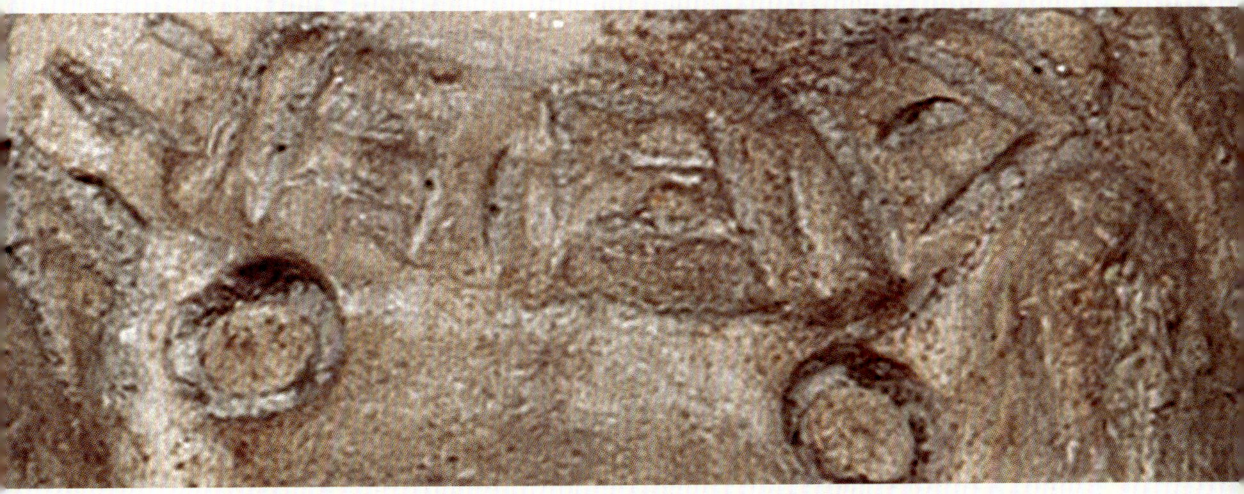

TERRACOTTA
GALLERY

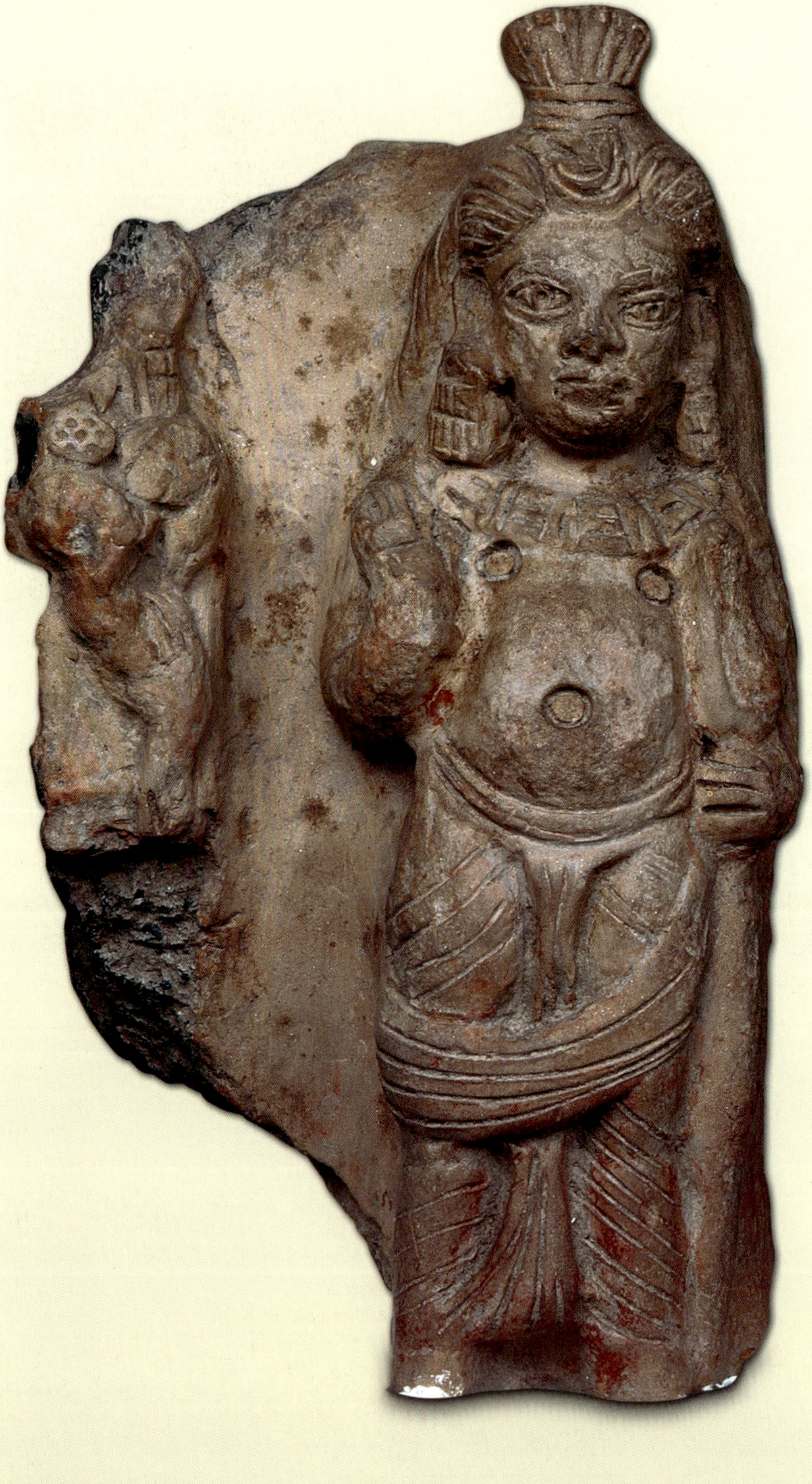

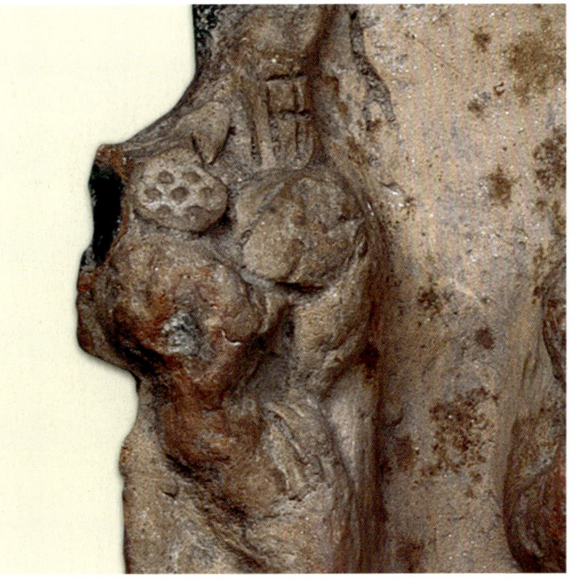

IMAGE OF A BODHISATTVA

The terracotta relief is a standing male figure who is shown holding a spear-like object in his left hand with his raised right hand in *abhayamudra.* He wears a dhoti resembling a bodhisattva image of the Kushana period in the 1st century CE. The coiffeur of the image has been stylistically depicted with an *ushnish* (a bun-shaped hairstyle), which is an identifiable sign of a bodhisattva. In the same terracotta, another small unidentifiable female figurine is shown standing on the right side of the main image.

Provenance: Bhita, Allahabad, Uttar Pradesh
Material: Terracotta
Date: c. 1st–3rd century CE
Dimension: 26.5 x 14 x 5.5 cm
Acc. No.: AM-TC-K220

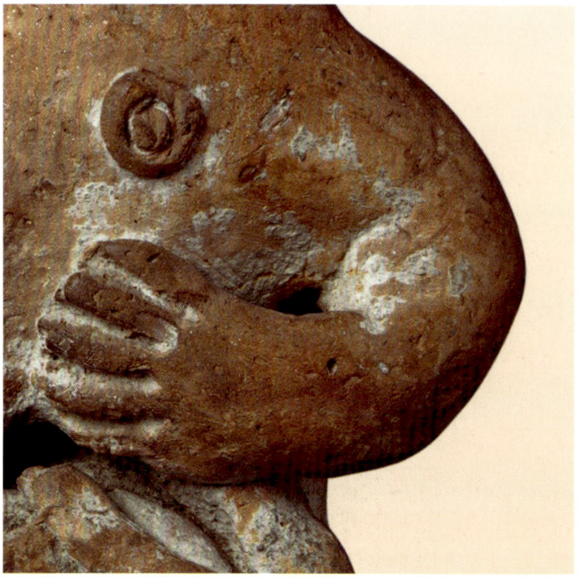

ABDOMEN OF A MALE FIGURE

The cynosure of all eyes, this is a curious terracotta image of an abdomen of a male figure where the exposure of the large intestine can be noticed. It is an internal organ in which the major part of the digestion of food occurs, a pear-shaped enlargement of the alimentary canal linking the oesophagus to the small intestine.

This terracotta piece was possibly used as a model for demonstration to medical students in ancient times. Indian surgery had reached its pinnacle in ancient times as can be substantiated by the great works of surgery by Sushruta, in his work *Sushruta.* This piece is believed to be the first of its kind, depicting the internal organs of the human body in terracotta.

Provenance: Kaushambi, Uttar Pradesh
Material: Terracotta
Date: c. 2nd century CE
Dimension: 13.5 x 10 cm
Acc. No.: AM-TC-K3179

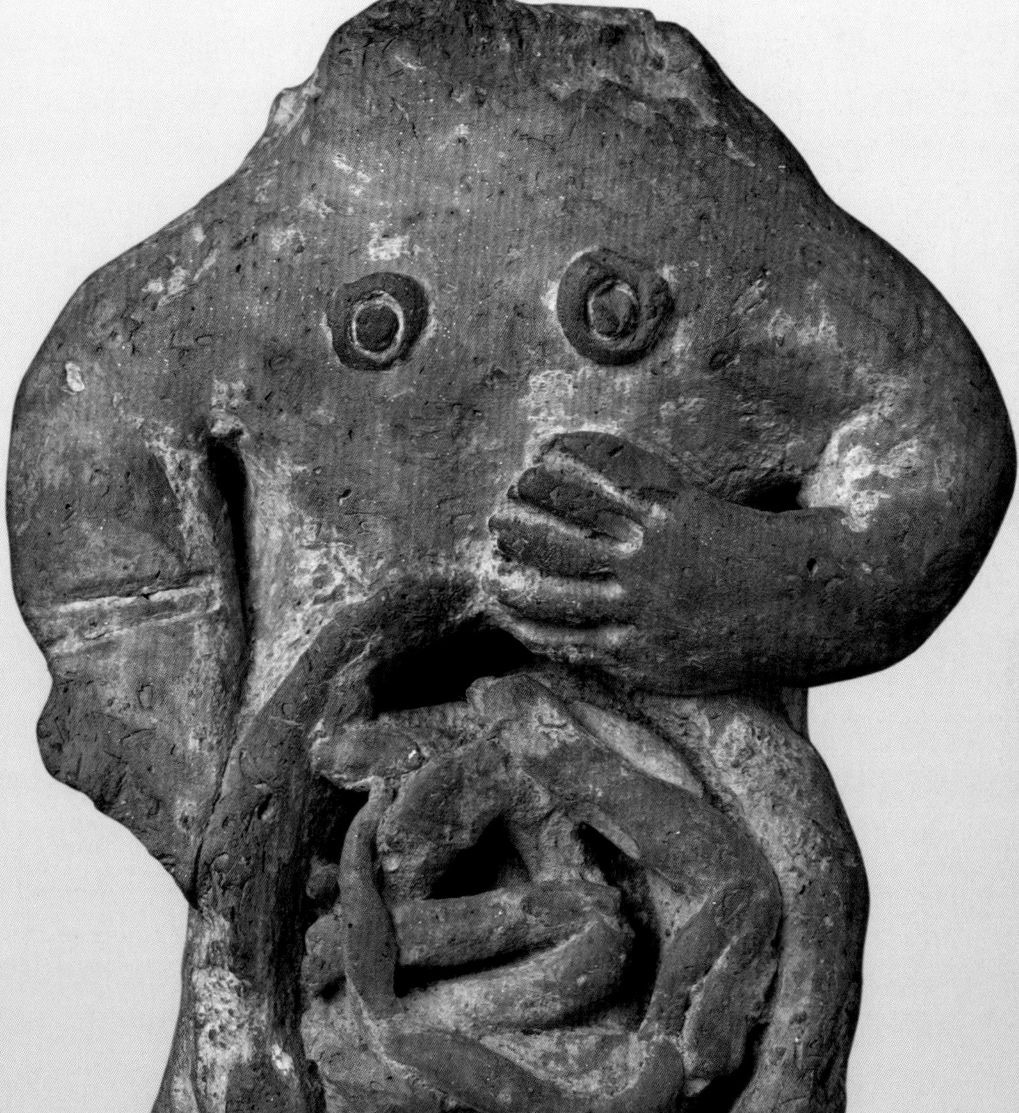

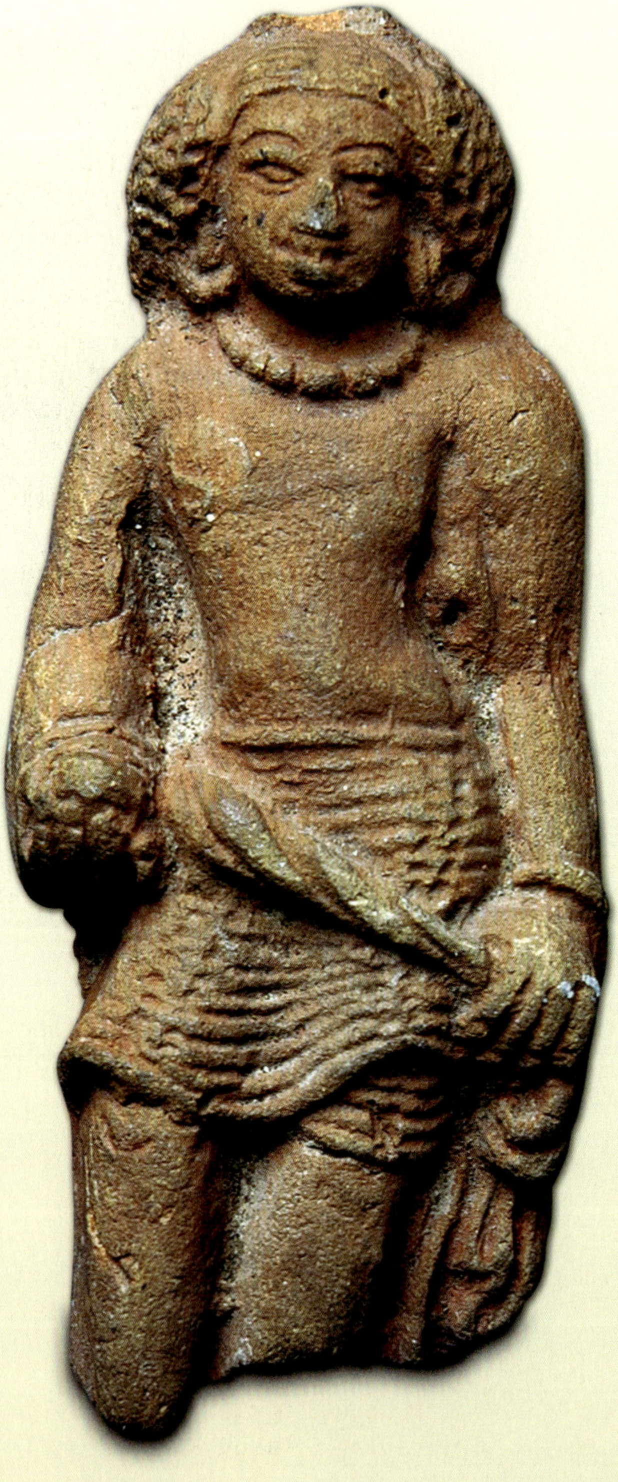

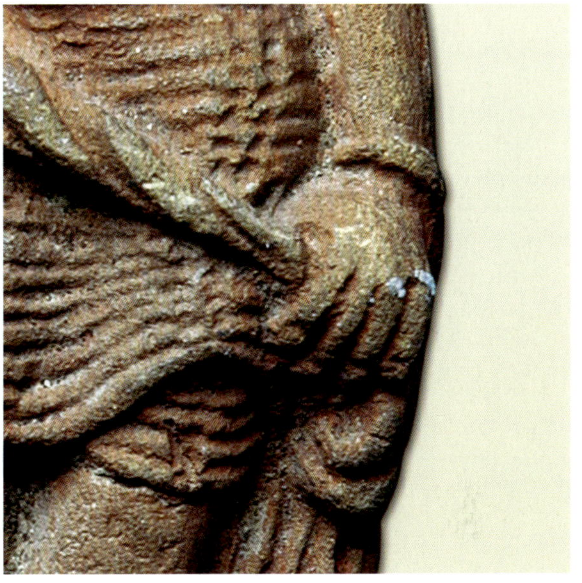

STANDING MALE FIGURE

A standing male figure, wearing *kundala* (earrings) and a beaded necklace. What is noticeable in the figure is a turban-like coiffeur on his head. He is shown wearing a dhoti up to the knee. His right hand holds a fruit-like object, and his left hand, a piece of cloth, as if he is squeezing a part of his wet dhoti. The lower part of the cloth is hanging below his hand.

Provenance: Bhita, Allahabad, Uttar Pradesh
Material: Terracotta
Date: 1st–3rd century CE
Dimension: 26.5 x 14 x 5.5 cm
Acc. No.: AM-TC-R2105

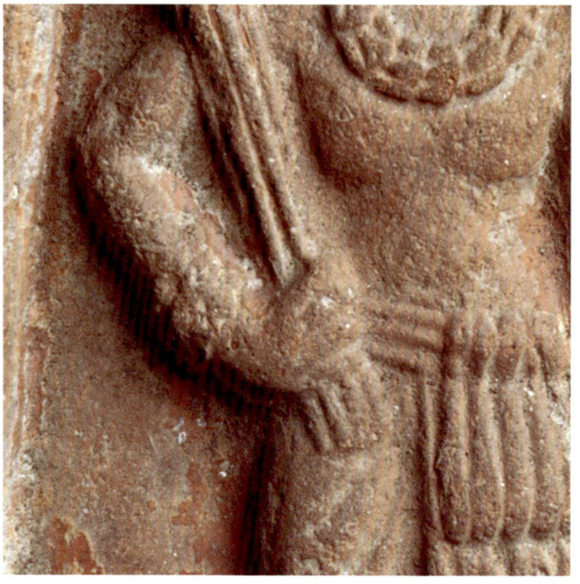

KAMADEVA

The terracotta plaque, a standing male figure holding bow in his left hand and arrows in the right, has been identified as the Kamadeva, the God of Love or Cupid. In Brahmanical mythology, Kamadeva is known as the son of Goddess Sri. He is also identified as Pradyumana, reincarnated and born as the son of Krishna. Here he is shown wearing a dhoti, his feet slightly mutilated. Usually Kamadeva is depicted iconographically as a young and handsome man with wings, green skin, holding a bow made of sugarcane, with a string of honeybees and arrows decorated with five kinds of fragrant flowers.

Provenance: Mathura, Uttar Pradesh
Material: Terracotta
Date: c. 2nd–1st century BCE
Dimension: 11 x 7 cm
Acc. No.: AM-TC-M2434

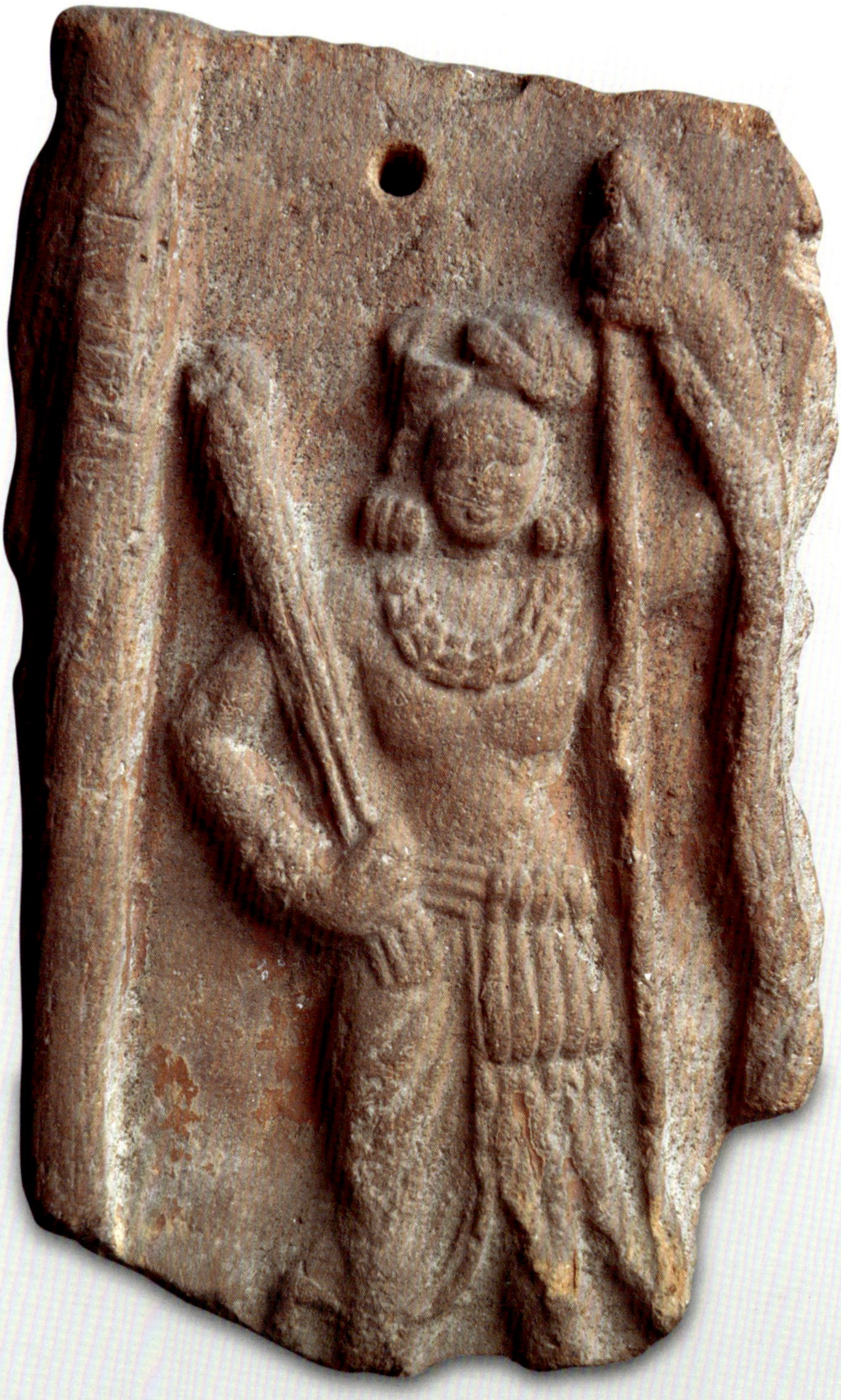

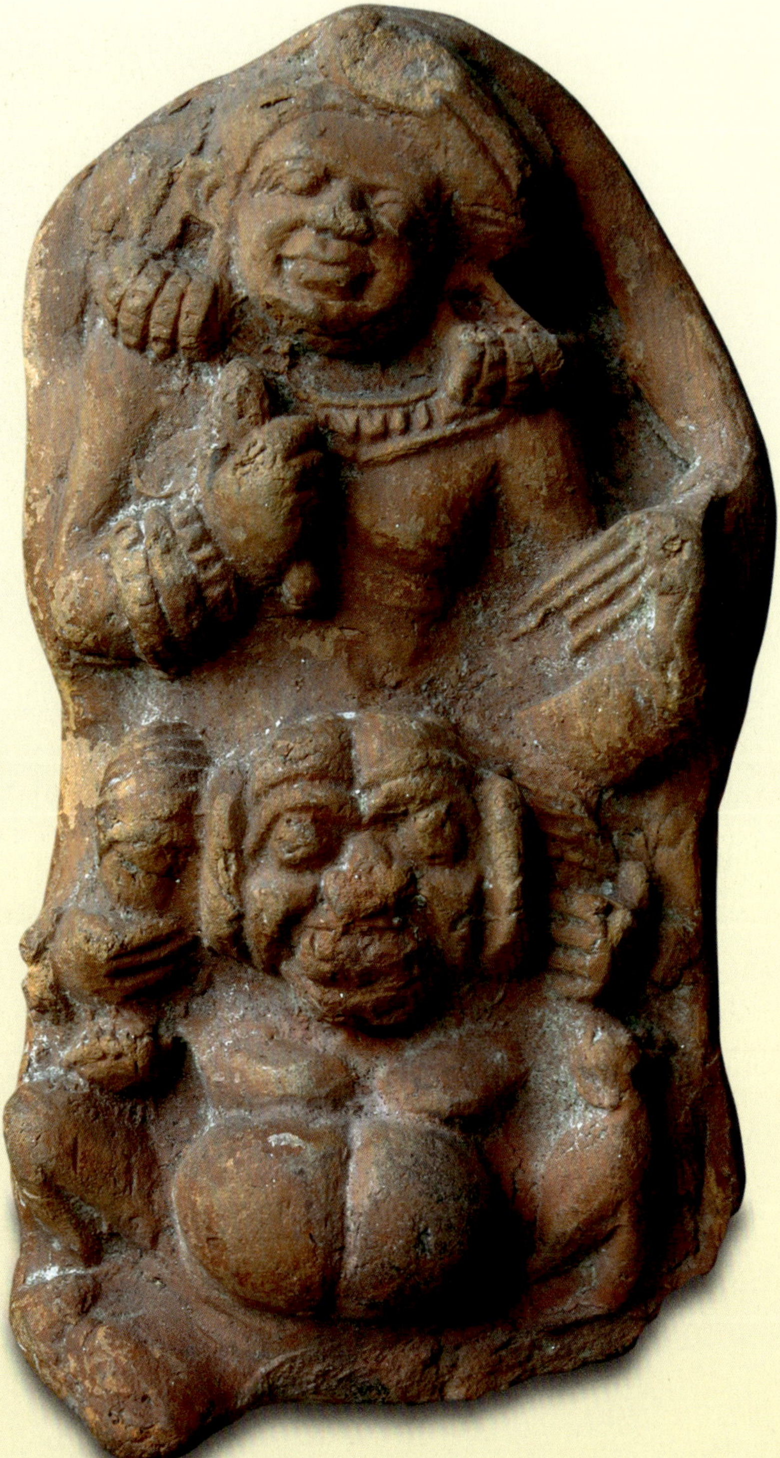

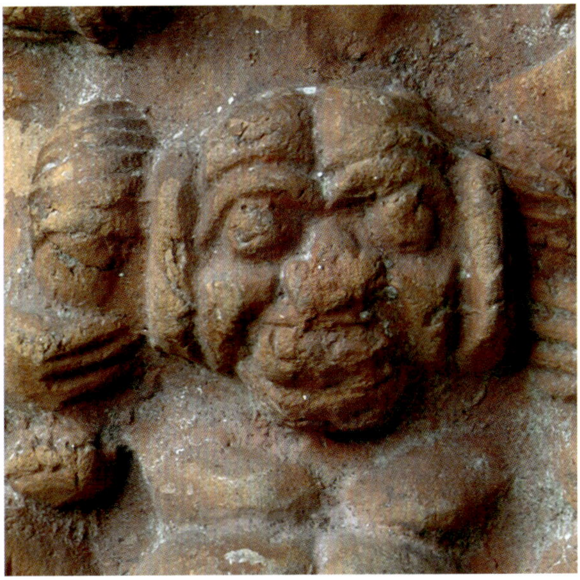

NAR-VAHAK KUBERA

Nara-vahak Kubera is a composite image. Kubera the Lord of the *yakshas,* is also identified as one of the *dikpalas* or guardians of the northern direction. He is carrying a man on his shoulder in this image, holding on his legs, and depicted as a pot-bellied, squatted figure. He has a ferocious look on his face, a broad nose and thick eyebrows. The image on the top is wearing a dhoti and a broad necklace and big earrings. He is holding a purse, resembling a pomegranate, in his right hand, and a bowl in his left hand.

Provenance: Not known
Material: Terracotta
Date: c. 2nd century BCE
Dimension: 12.5 x 7 cm
Acc. No.: AM-TC-M2436

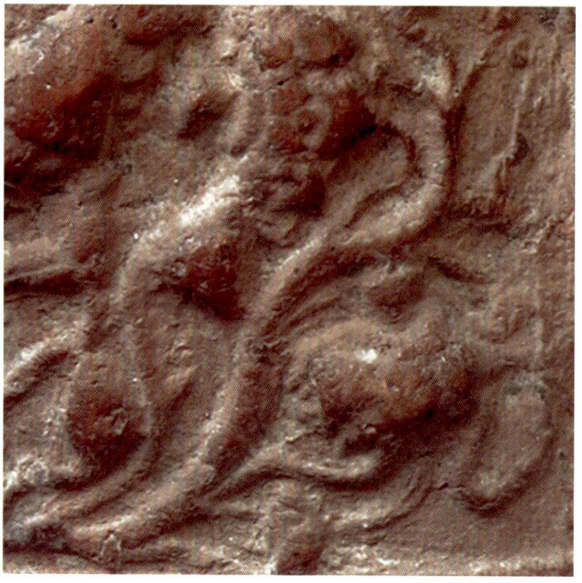

LAKSHMI STANDING ON LOTUS

A triangular-shaped mould, with traces of red paint, depicting Lakshmi, the Goddess of Wealth and Prosperity, is one of the beautiful terracotta figurines of the Museum. The Goddess standing on the petals of a fully bloomed lotus, its stalk emerging from the mud, with a few more lotus flowers and leaves around it. A wooden railing is seen at the bottom part of the plaque. Her right hand is raised towards the ear and left hand rests on the waist. She has an ornamental ribbon on her forehead and is wearing earrings with tiny lotus rosettes, a beaded necklace, a longer necklace, armlets, and bracelets.

Provenance: Not Known
Material: Terracotta
Date: c. 2nd century BCE
Dimension: 13.3 x 7 cm
Acc. No.: AM-TC-K2519

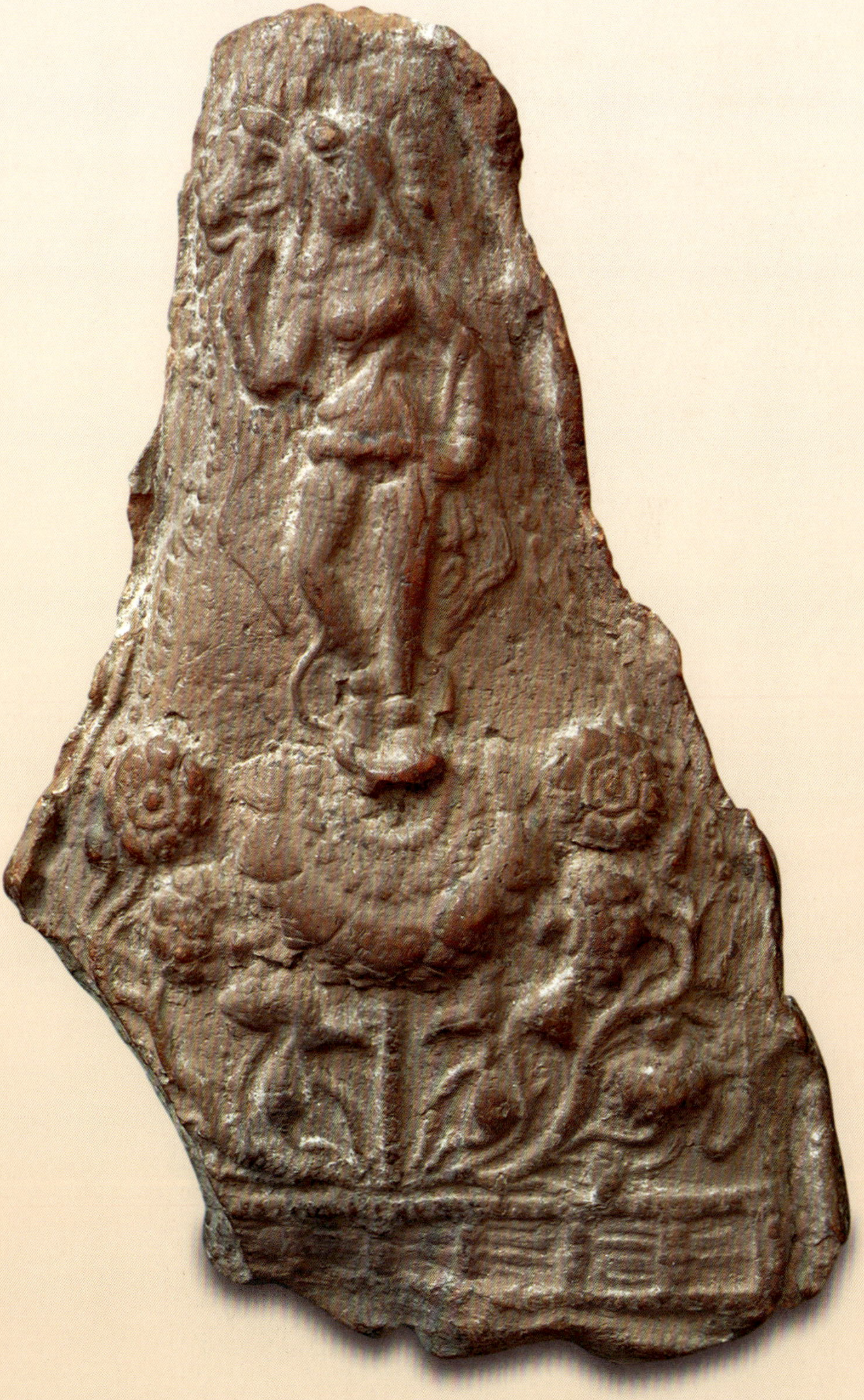

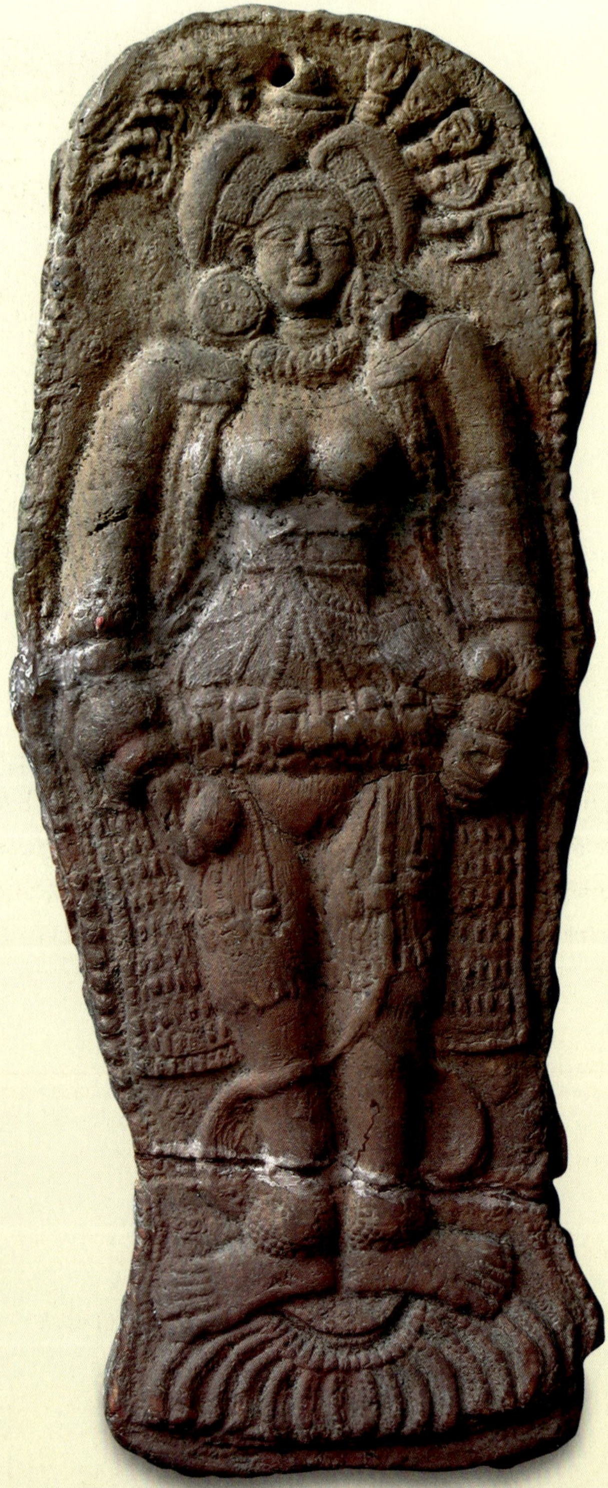

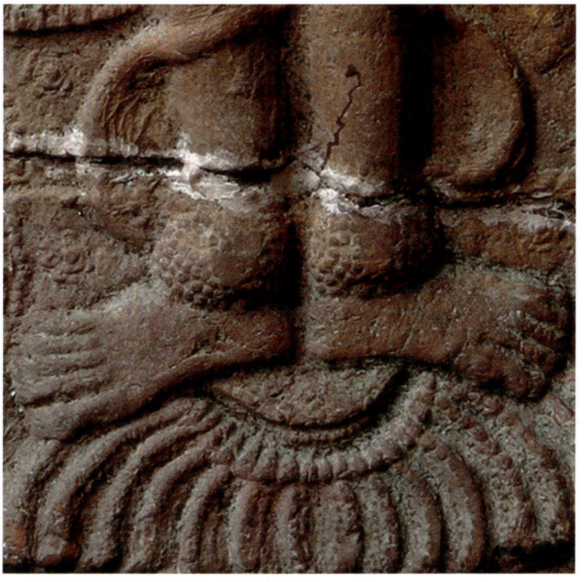

PANCHCHUDA (GODDESS LAKSHMI)

The figure is delicately moulded. Five auspicious symbols and five clusters of corns are set on the headdress. Her right hand is placed on her thigh. The braids of her hair fall on either side of her breasts. The plaque was broken in three pieces, which were later joined together. There are five sacred symbols on each side of her headdress, among them the *ankusa* (goad) and *parasu* (battle-axe) are distinct.

Provenance: Kaushambi, Uttar Pradesh
Material: Terracotta
Date: c. 2nd century BCE
Dimension: 25.5 x 10 cm
Acc. No.: AM-TC-K5158

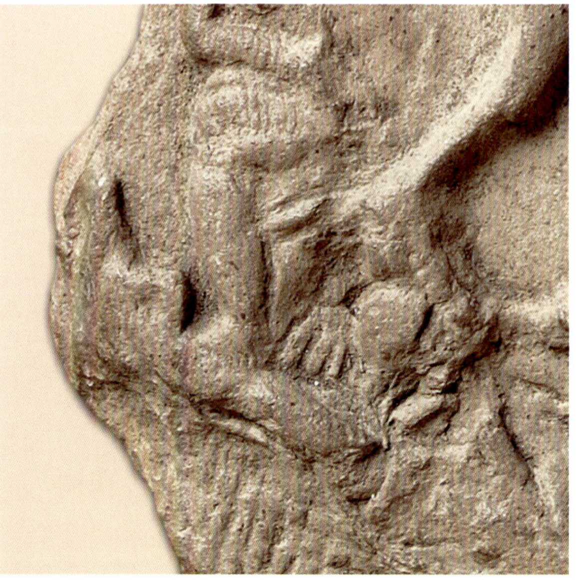

BACCHANALIAN SCENE

Thus oval-shaped terracotta plaque depicting a bacchanalian scene, recovered from Ahichchatra, is a very interesting piece of art indicating the Indo-Roman connection in Indian art. This is probably because of Indo-Roman trade that was noticed after the 1st and 2nd century BCE. In this piece of art the central figure is a bared bodied, tall, hefty male figure wearing a dhoti. He is wearing two large-sized *kundala* (earrings) and holding on to the two arms of a drunken lady, lifting her, perhaps to take her to the cot behind him. There are two ladies on his either side. While one is holding a wine jar, the other is holding the legs of the intoxicated lady.

Provenance: Ahichchhatra, Bareilly District, Uttar Pradesh
Material: Terracotta
Date: c. 2nd century BCE
Dimension: 11 x 9.5 cm
Acc. No.: AM-TC-AH4335

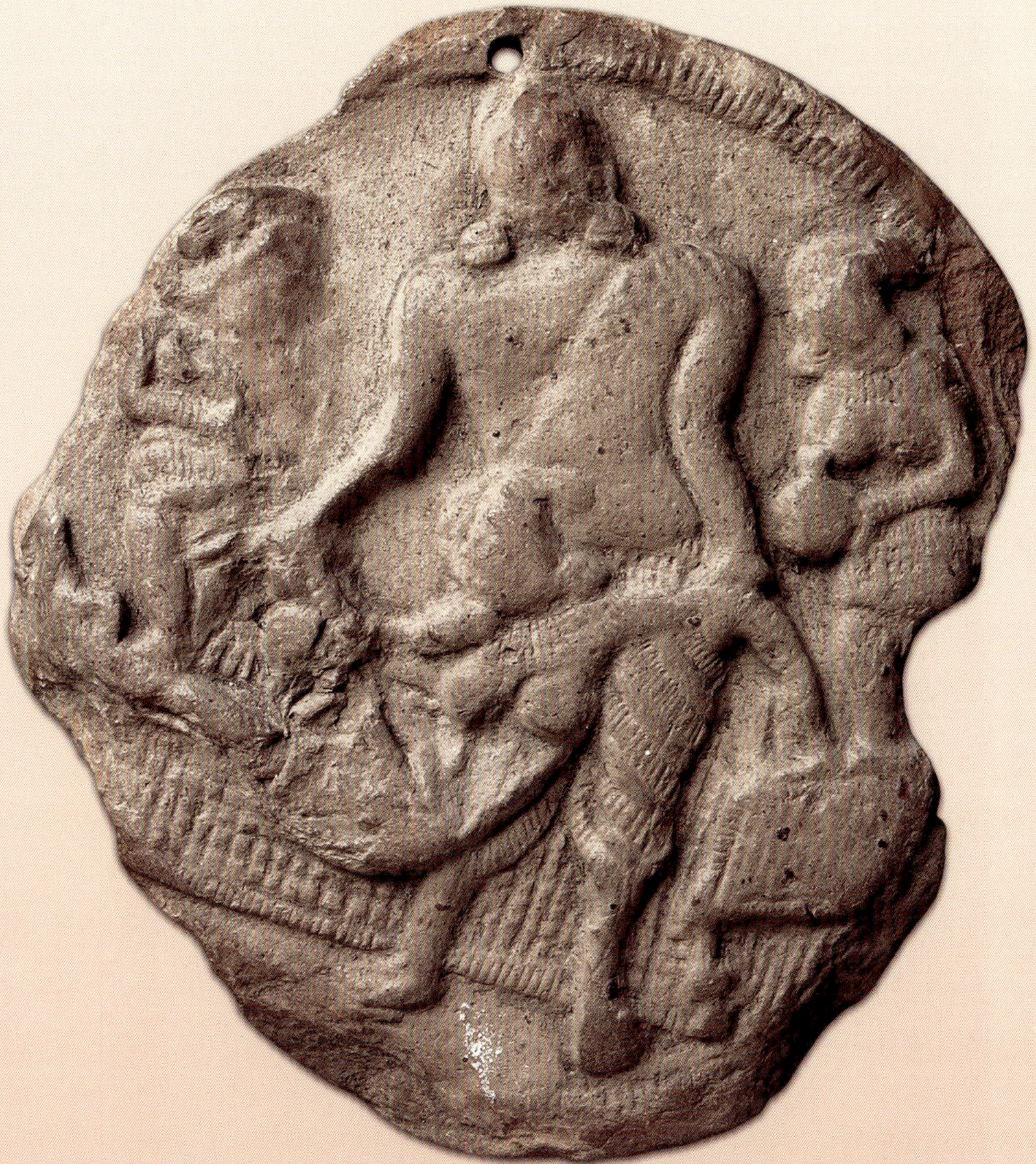

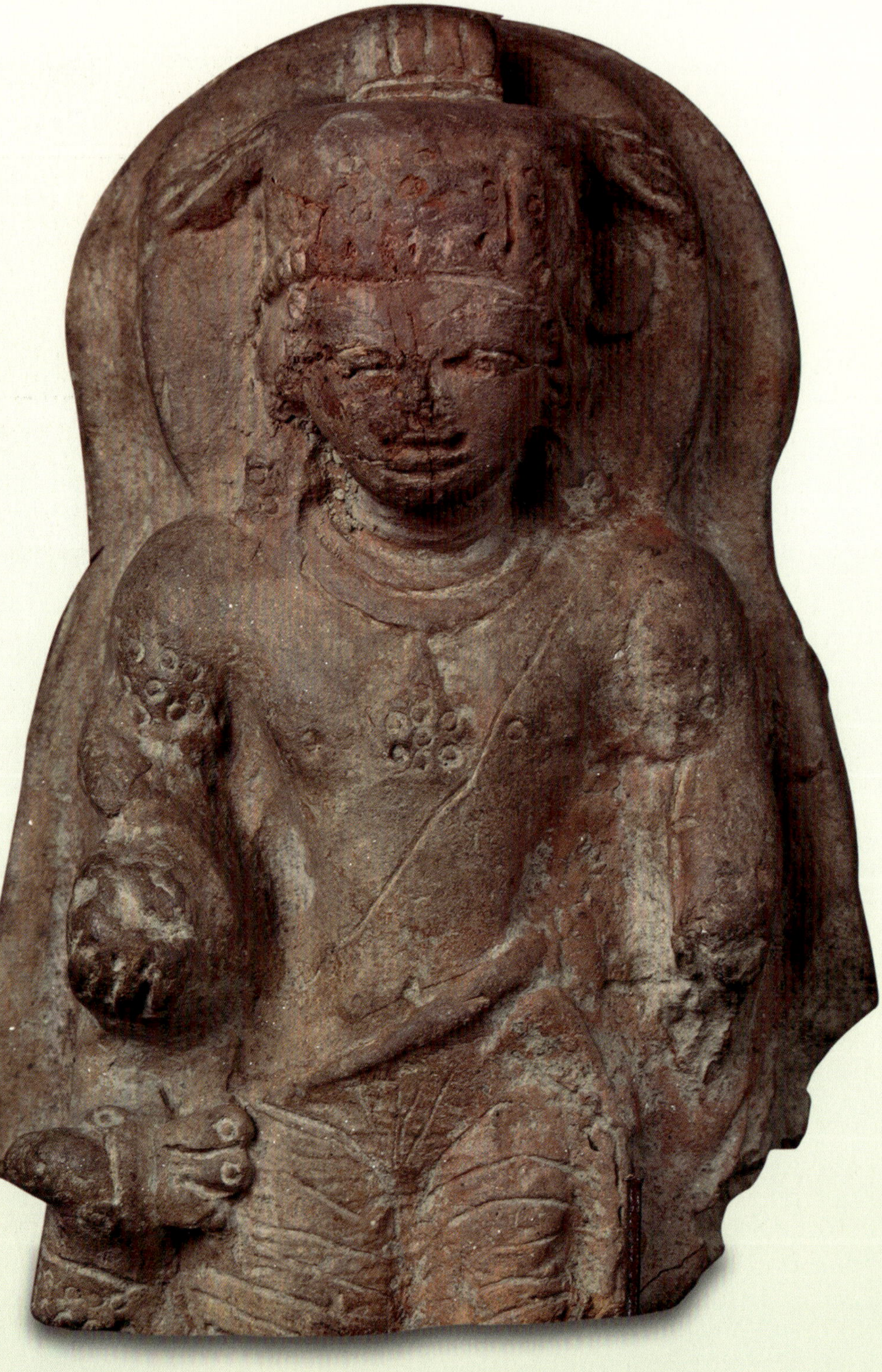

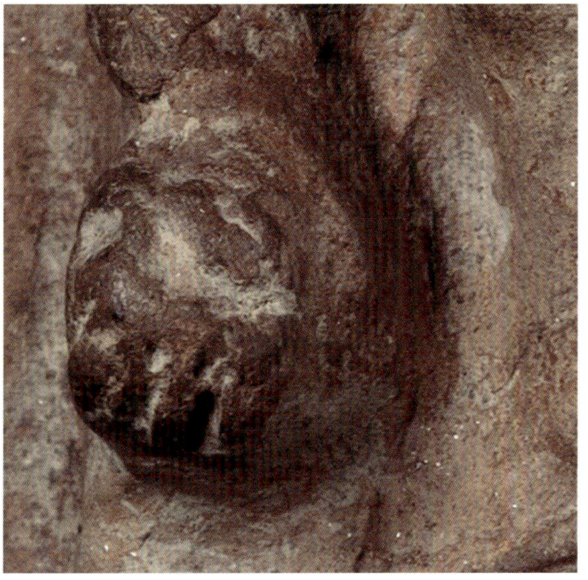

KARTIKEYA

Kartikeya, also known as Murugan, Skanda, Kumaran, Kumara Swami and Subramaniya, is the Hindu God of War. He is the commander-in-chief of the army of the devas and the son of Shiva and Parvati. This terracotta figure represents the standing image of Kartikeya wearing a crown on the head. He holds some circular object in his right hand. There is a plain halo behind the head of deity. His left hand is partly broken and the lower part of the figurine has been lost.

Provenance: Ahichchhatra, Bareilly District, Uttar Pradesh
Material: Terracotta
Date: c. 4th–6th century CE
Dimension: 15.5 x 10 cm
Acc. No.: AM-TC-AH4896

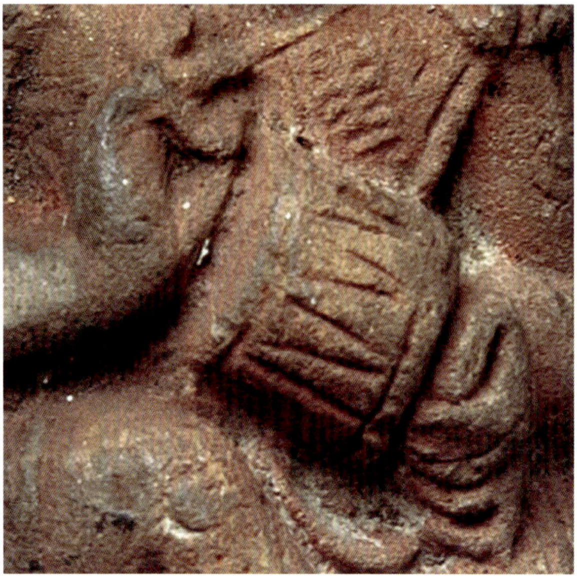

DRUMMER

A male figure, probably a young boy, sitting cross-legged in a dhoti, and beating a drum or a *mardangika,* with his fingers and singing to its beats. The art historians have identified that such figures usually come from Rajghat, in Uttar Pradesh.

Provenance:	Rajghat, Varanasi District, Uttar Pradesh
Material:	Terracotta
Date:	c. 4th–6th century CE
Dimension:	5 x 2.4 cm
Acc. No.:	AM-TC-R2107

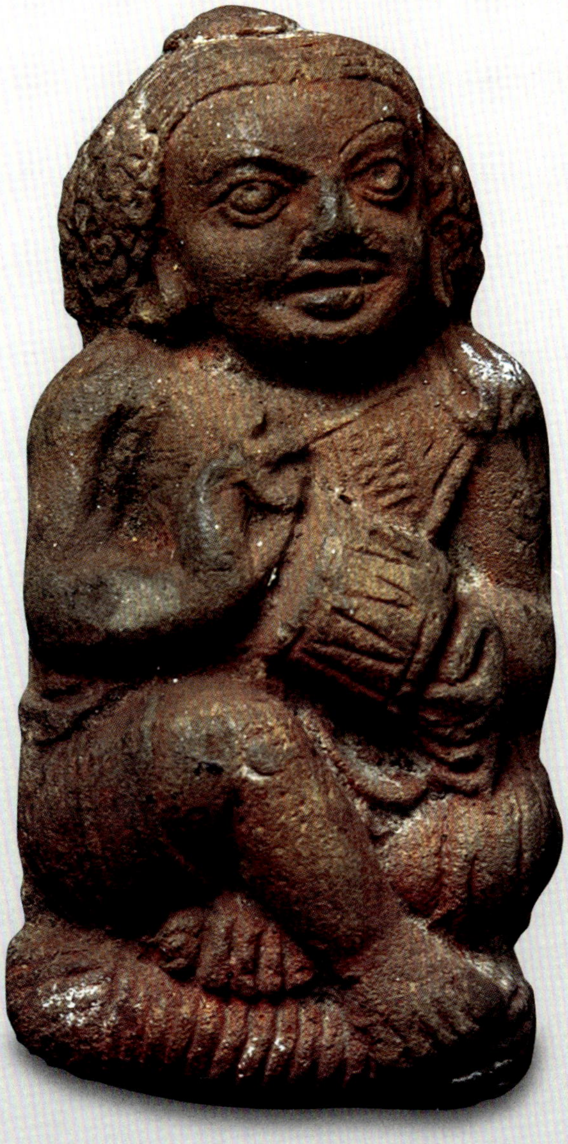

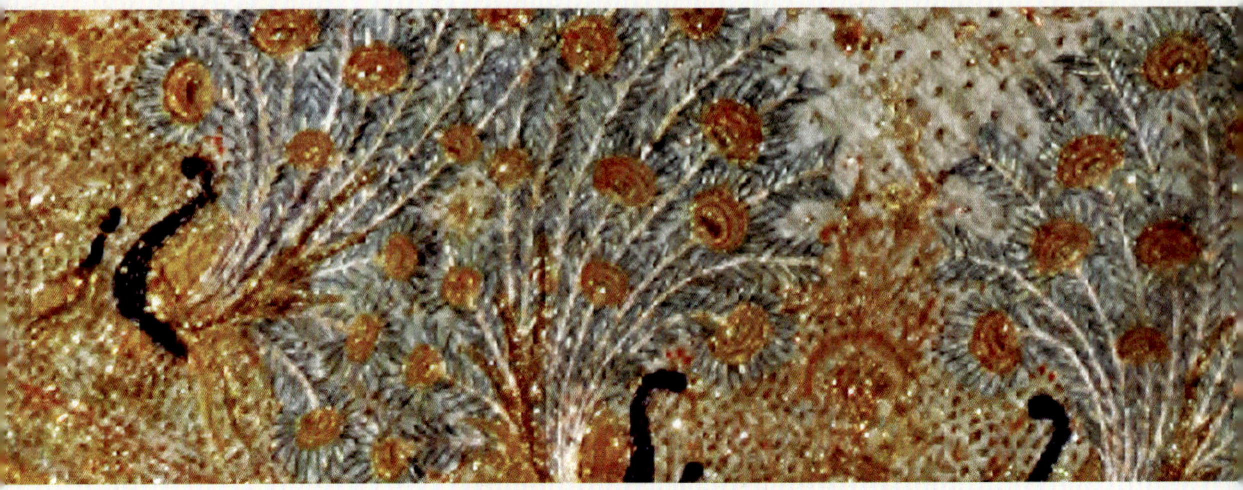

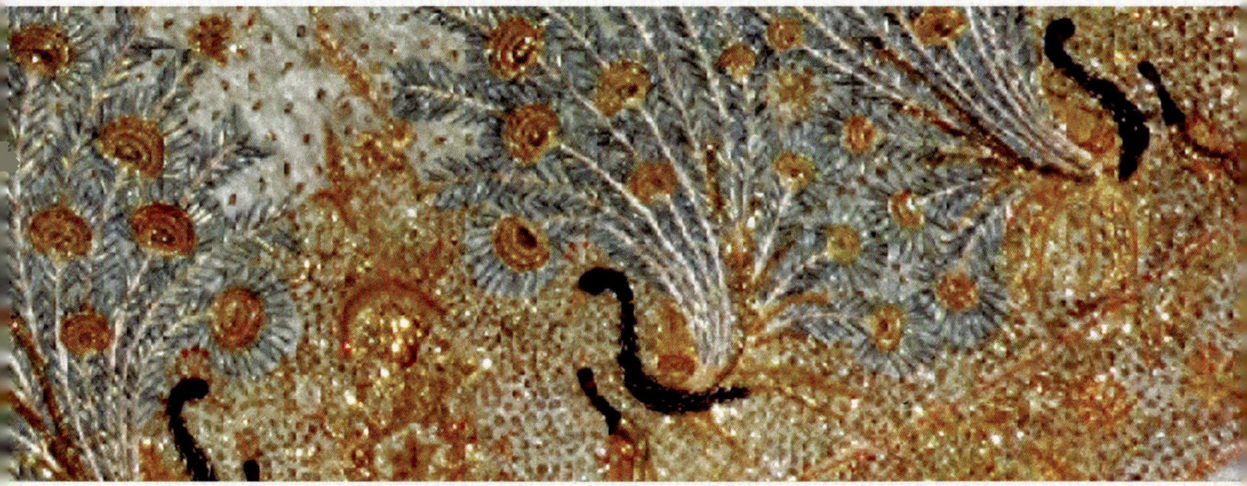

DECORATIVE ART
GALLERY

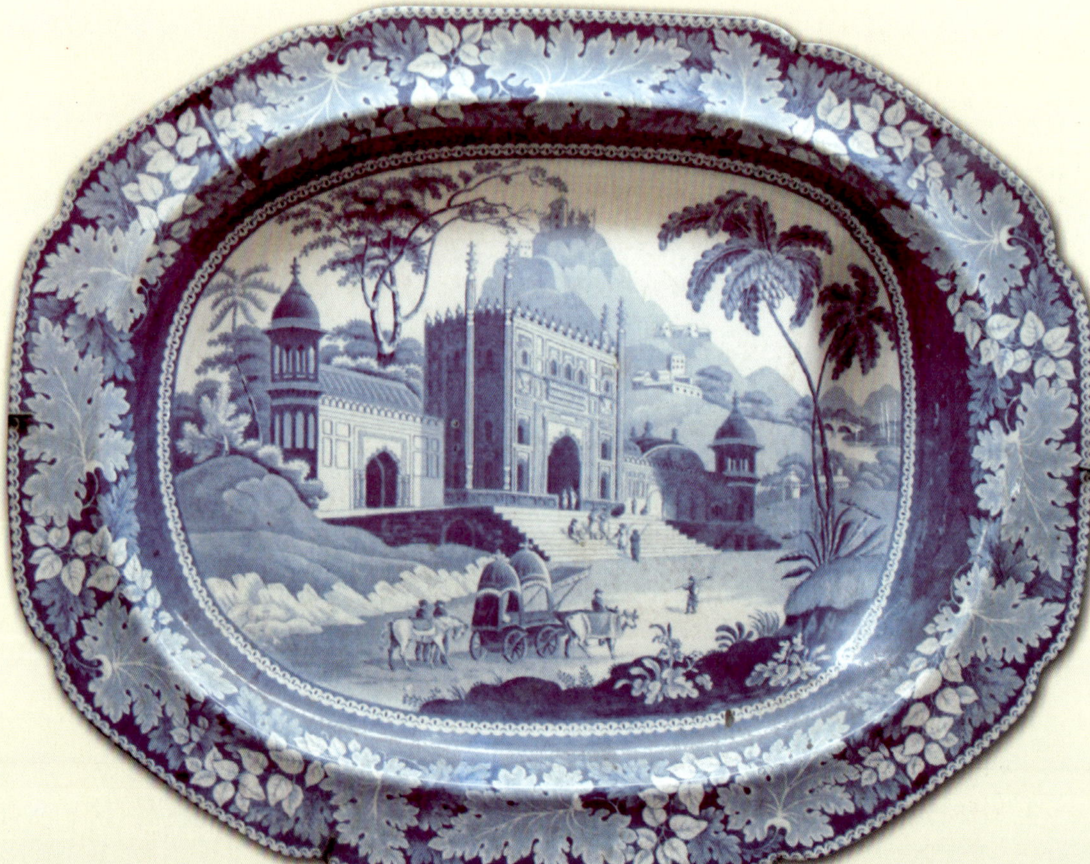

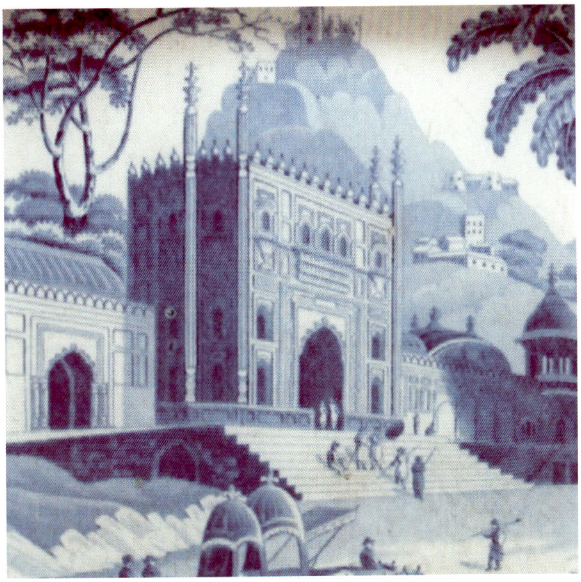

PORCELAIN DISH WITH PILIBHIT MOSQUE

The gateway of a mosque at Pilibhit on porcelain or a delftware. This tells the story of how the lithograph of a painting, published in England in 1801 CE, was transformed by a porcelain potter in Holland, and later bought by an Indian art connoisseur, Hamid Ali, who donated the Delft ware to the Allahabad Museum. This octagonal porcelain dish shows the facade of a mosque founded by Hafiz Rahmat Khan, the Afghan Rohilla leader, whose estates included Pilibhit and Bareilly (Uttar Pradesh), where he was buried later. The gateway of the mosque was built later. The gateway depicted in this delftware is a transformed version of a painting by Thomas and William Daniel, who documented Indian monuments in the 19th century CE.

Provenance: Not known
Material: Porcelain
Date: 18th century CE
Dimension: 47 x 37 cm
Acc. No.: AM-DA-602

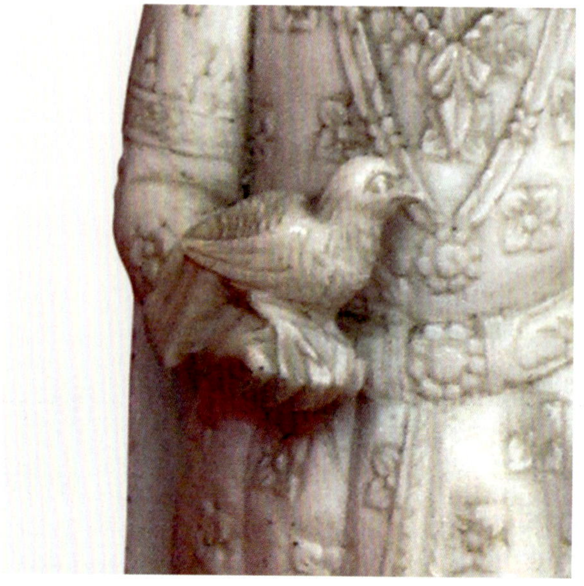

AKBAR HOLDING BIRD

The figure of the Akbar the Great, carved in ivory, has him standing on a round pedestal, wearing a royal robe, with small embroidered flowers on it, and an ornamental belt and pyjamas. He holds a sword in his left hand and a bird on his right hand. He has a calm but firm countenance.

Provenance: Not known
Material: Ivory
Date: Not known
Dimension: 15.9 x 4.6 cm
Acc. No.: AM-DA-709

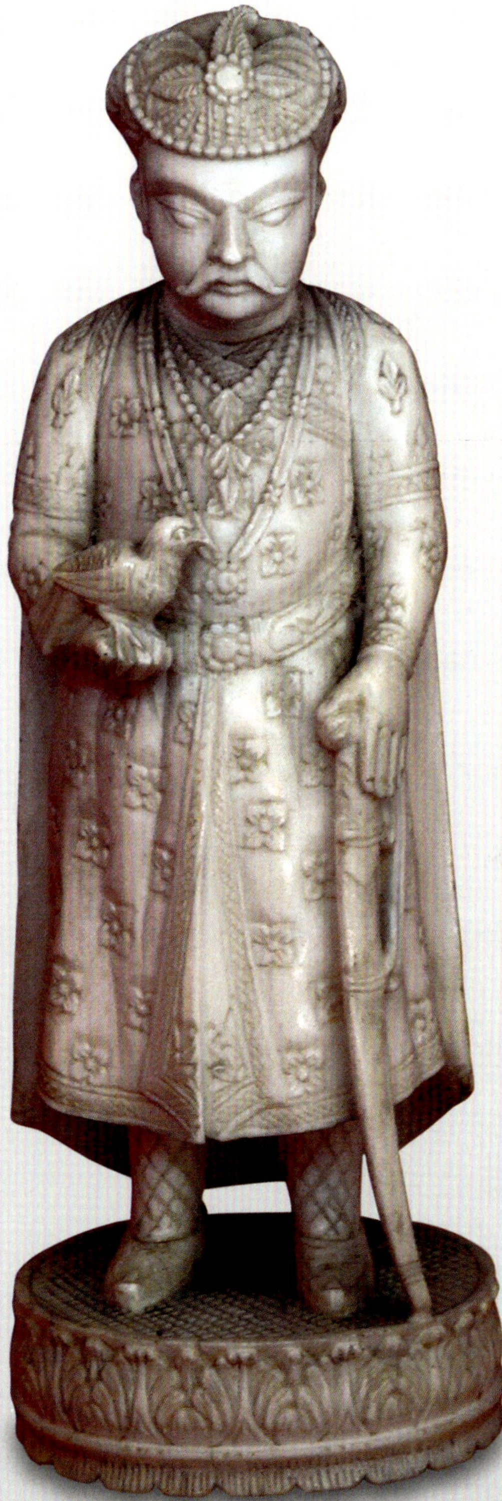

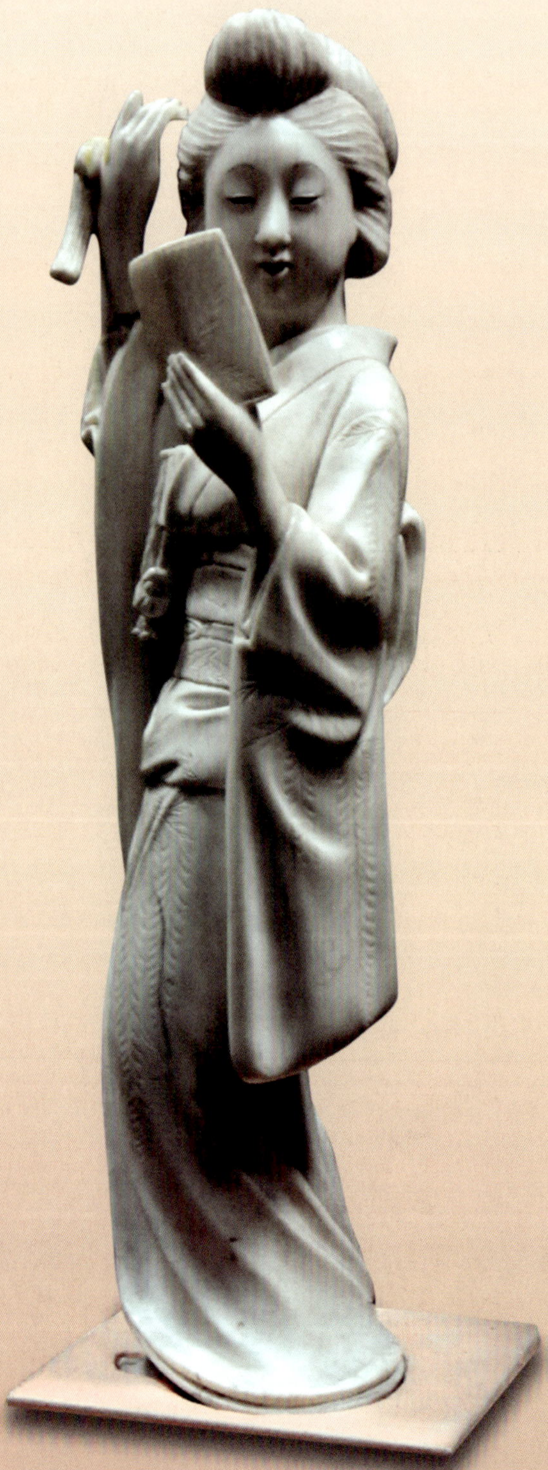

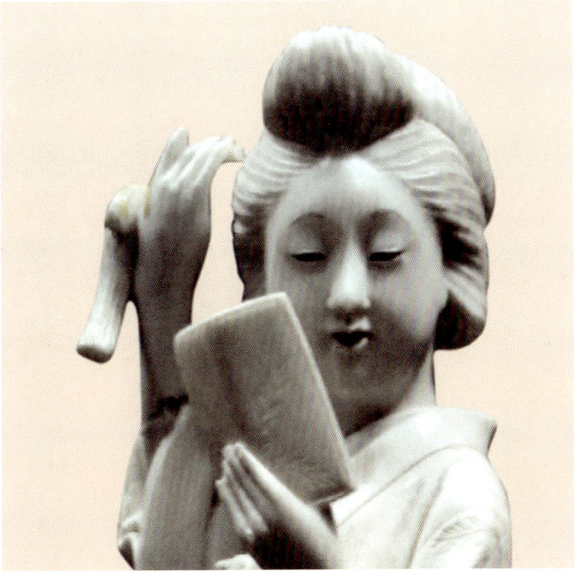

JAPANESE QUEEN IN IVORY

The image of a Japanese queen, carved with great precision on ivory. She holds a mirror in her left hand and is seen dressing up her hair with a beautifully designed comb in her right hand. She is slender, beautiful, and regal and wears a long kimono with light embroidery work.

Provenance: Not Known
Material: Ivory
Date: 19th century CE
Dimension: 18 x 8 x 4.8 cm
Acc. No.: AM-DA-597

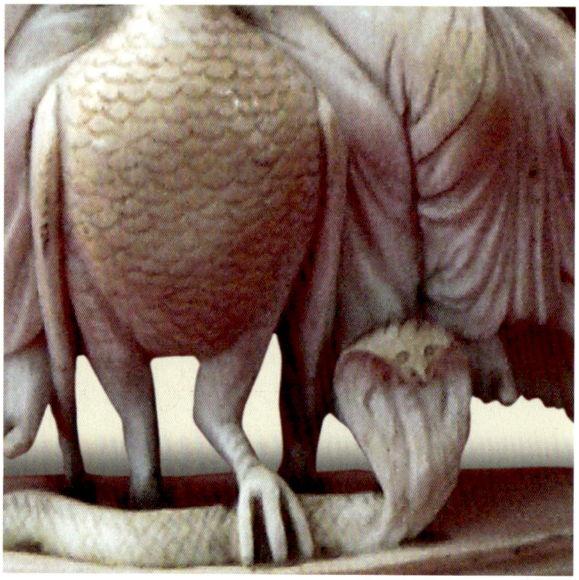

SKANDA IN IVORY

The image of Kartikeya, also known as Skanda, has been beautifully carved on ivory. The deity is shown with six heads and twelve hands. He is seated on a peacock with two goddesses (*matrikas*) in *alinganamudra*. They all wear high crowns and bead garlands. Skanda, the commander-in-chief of the *devtas,* is shown with all his weapons or *ayudha*s, but his right hand is raised in *abhayamudra*, a gesture assuring safety. He is seated on his *vahana*, the peacock, which has a snake captured in its claws.

Provenance: Not known
Material: Ivory
Date: Not known
Dimension: 11 x 9.5 cm
Acc. No.: AM-DA-705

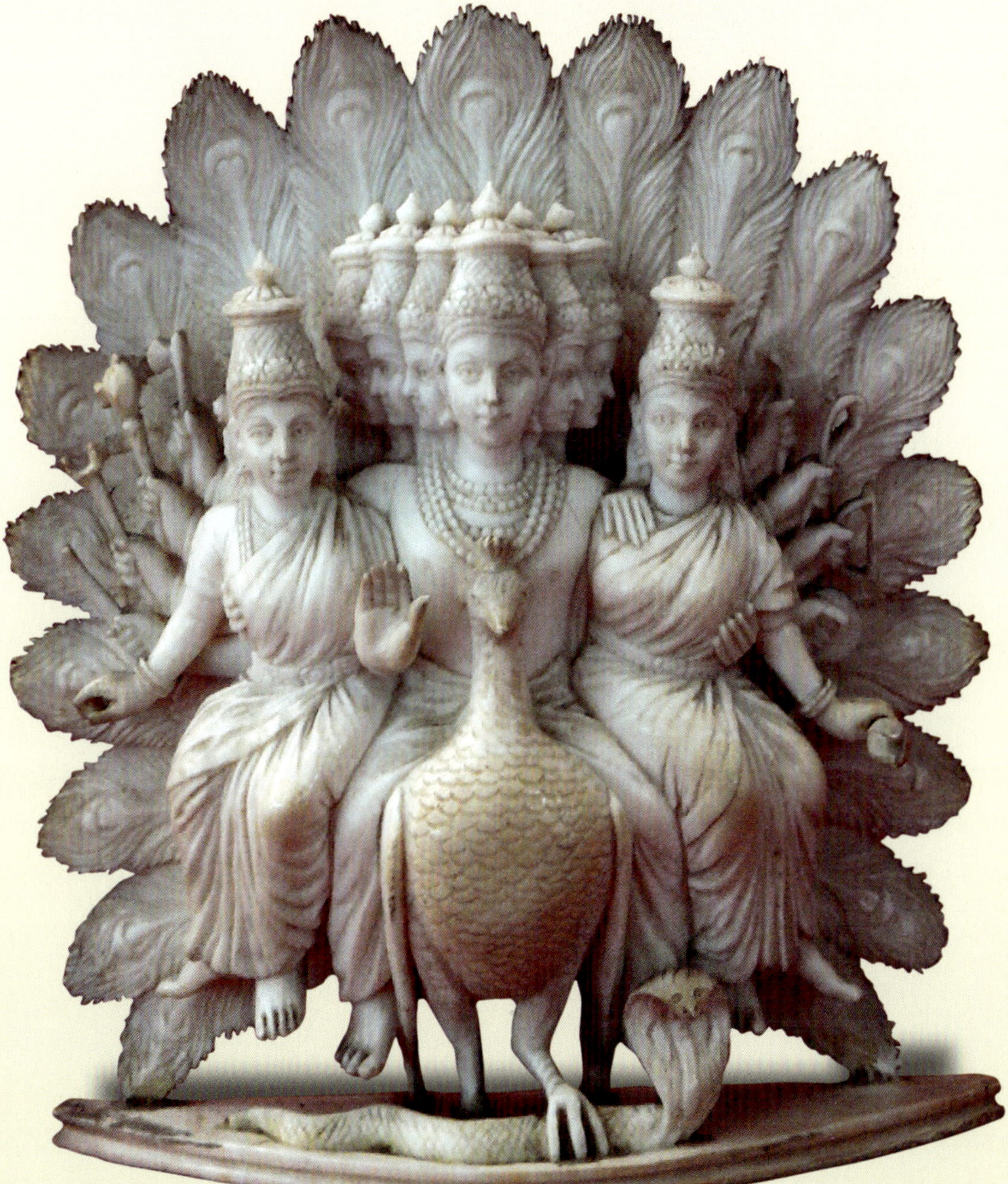

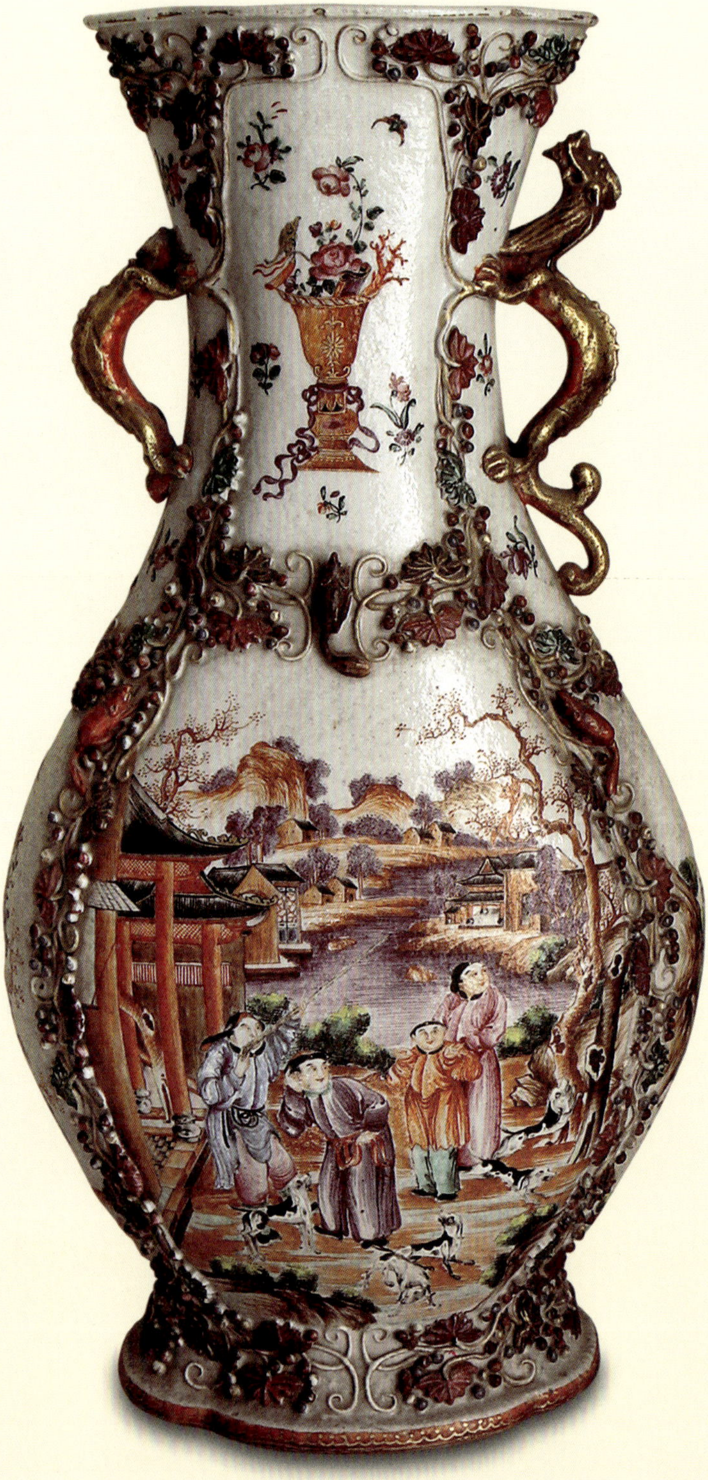

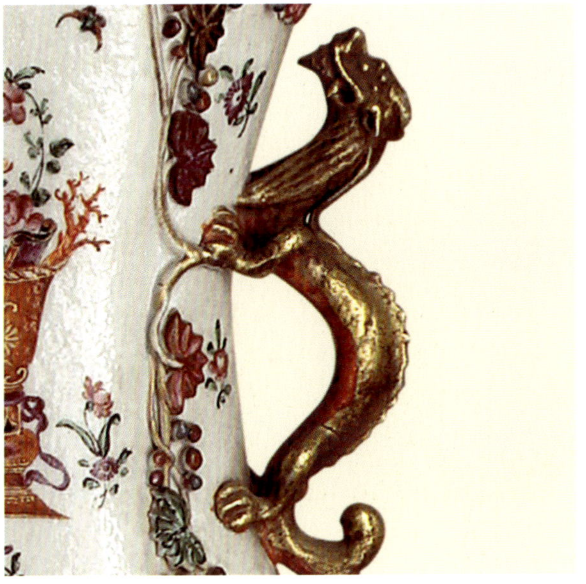

PORCELAIN FLOWER VASE

A beautiful porcelain flower vase with an applique design on it. Both the handles of the vase bear representations of dragons; one of them is broken and painted with golden and red colour. Wine creepers and leaves along with the fruits have been carved all over the body of the vase. There are three mice, along the creepers, moving in upward direction. In the centre of the vase, four men and five dogs are shown on a river side. One of them is with a rifle assisted by other three people. A fox-like animal is shown hanging from the branch of a tree. In the background, is a beautiful landscape—forest resorts, a natural scene of a Chinese village, and a series of houses (Pagoda Style) are seen on the bank of the river.

Provenance: Not known
Material: Porcelain
Date: Not known
Dimension: 40.8 x 20.5 cm
Acc. No.: AM-DA-1116

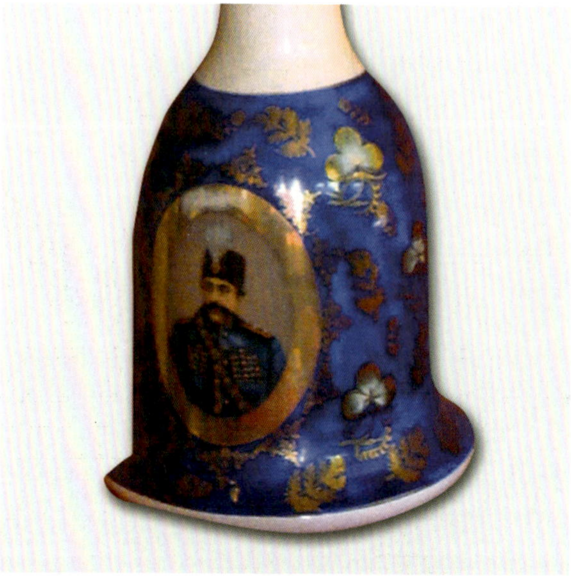

PERSIAN HOOKAH

A Persian hookah made of porcelain with a wooden smoking pipe. It is painted in blue and decorated with golden leaves and small flower sticks. Tri-petal flowers are prominently painted in golden and turquoise colour. In the centre there is a portrait of a Persian royal, wearing a coat with a cross belt and twenty-one medals on his chest. He has three stars on his epaulettes and a hat on his head and a stately demeanour. The royal figure, in a miniature form, appears towards the top of the hookah as well.

Provenance: Not known
Material: Wood and Bronze
Date: c. 20th century CE
Dimension: 68 x 45 cm
Acc. No.: AM-DA-606

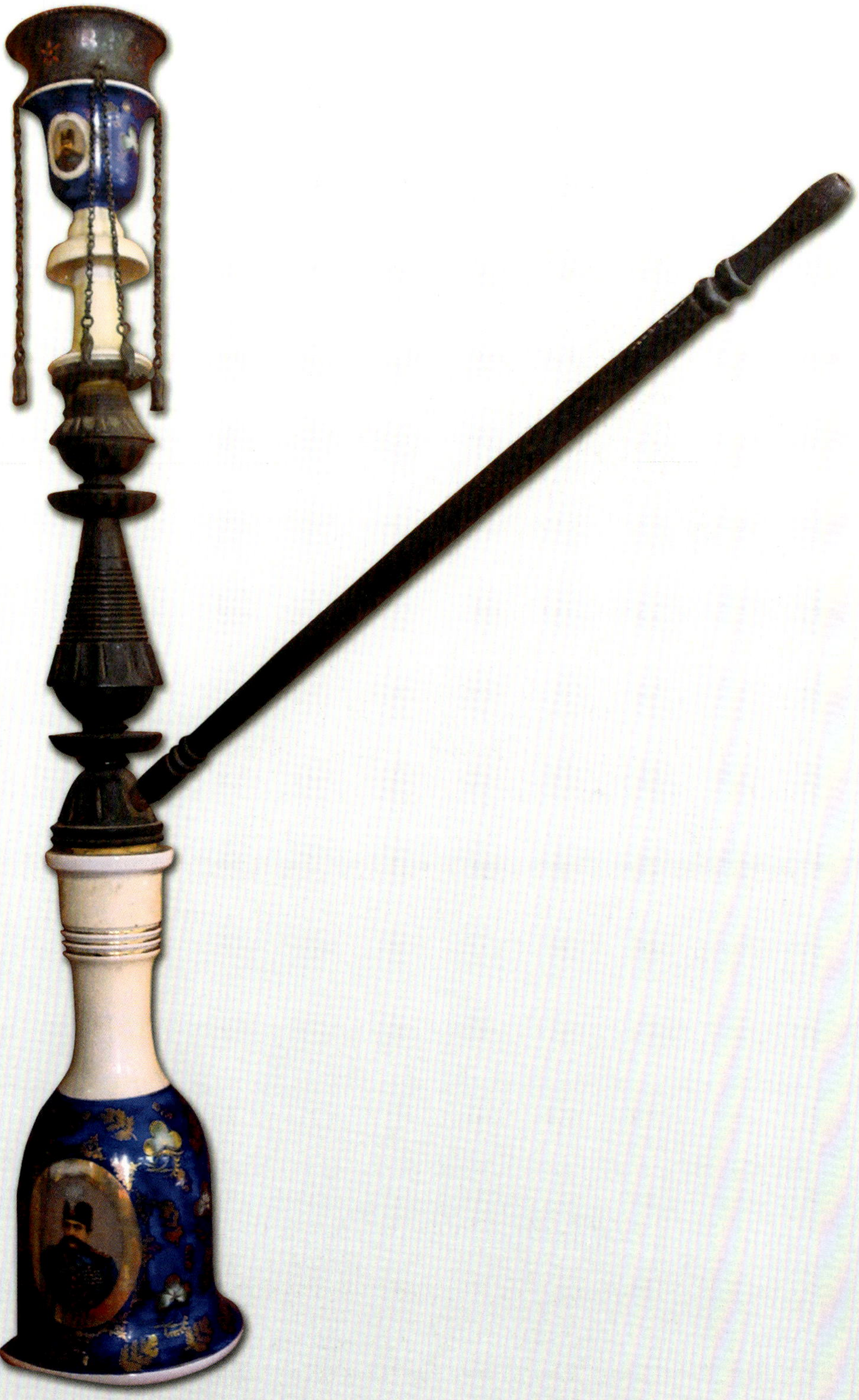

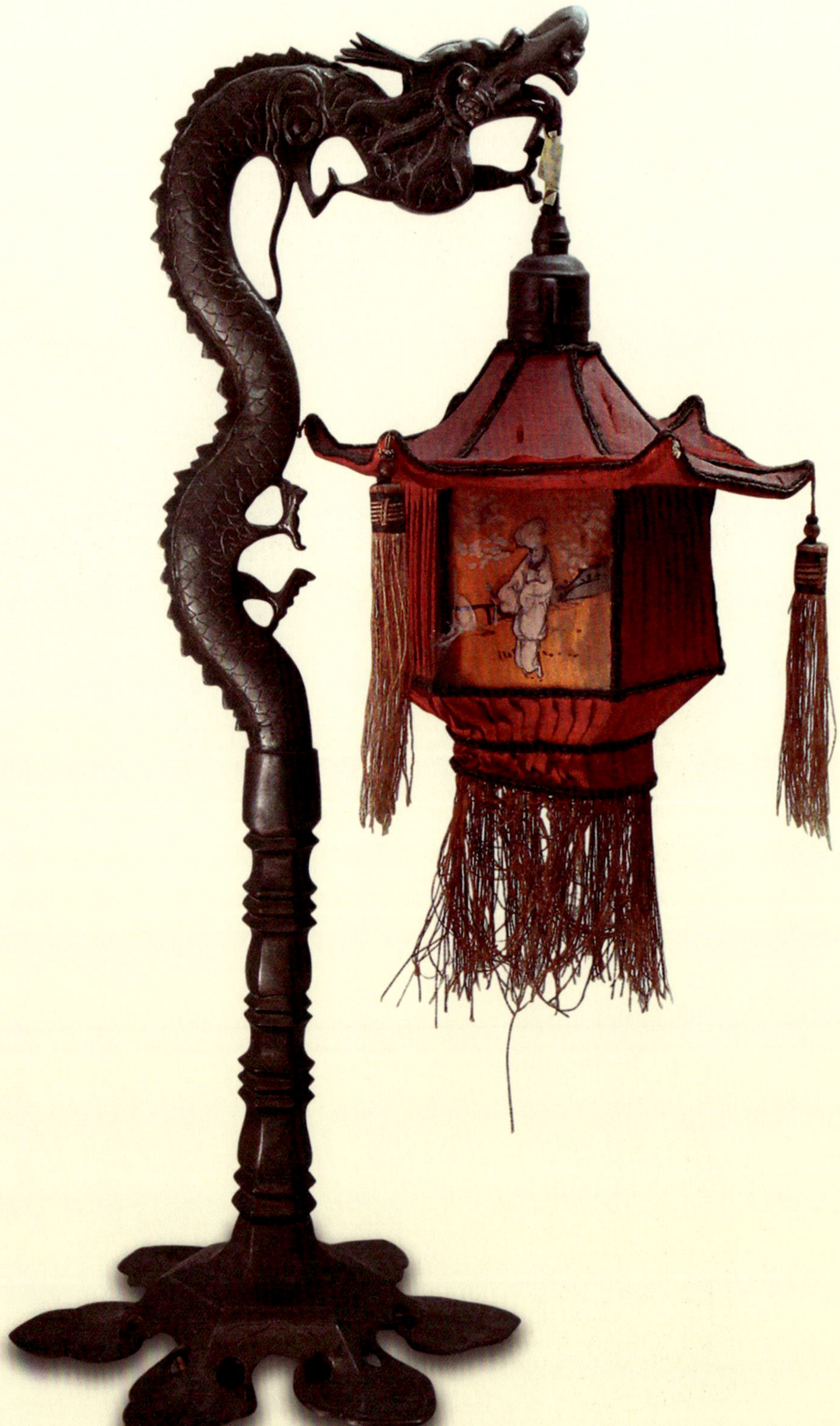

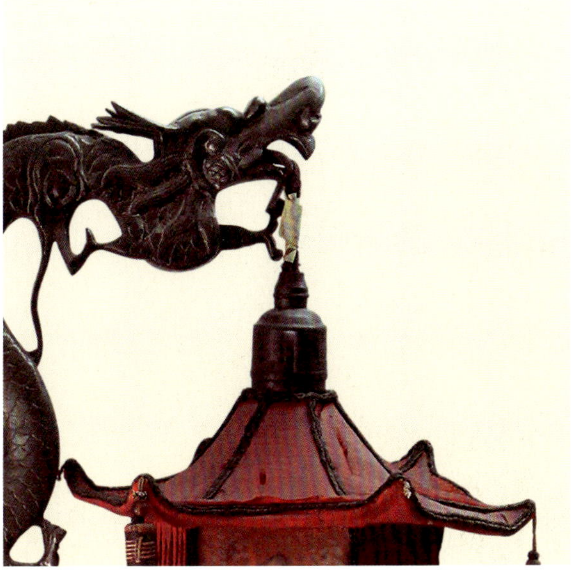

CHINESE LAMP WITH DRAGON

It shows a lamp string emerging from a dragon's mouth. The dragon looks fierce with its tail fixed on a stand. The dragon, the stand, and the holder of the lamp are all made of brass. The base of lamp holder has a red cloth with a pagoda design on it. Three Chinese figures can be seen on the outer surface.

Provenance:	Not known
Material:	Bronze, Cloth
Date:	c. 20th century CE
Dimension:	57.5 x 23.5 cm
Acc. No.:	AM-DA-607

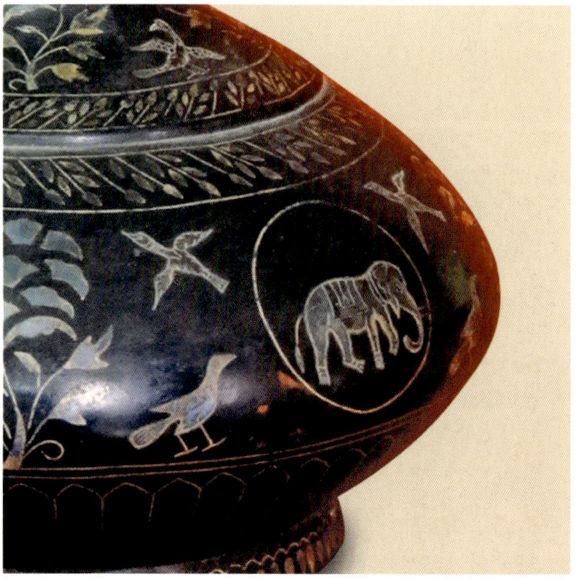

BIDRIWARE

It is a vase-like container having a thick circular base. The ware is decorated with white leaves, plants, birds, and animals on a black surface. There are three different parts in this ware. The bottom is a pot-bellied container with an elongated neck. The neck has a circular ridge at the bottom to resemble a surahi, and it culminates with a finial or a lid on the top. The entire ware is profusely decorated with floral and faunal figures, such as a tiger and an elephant, within a circle. Four different birds and a bouquet of flowers can be seen on the belly portion.

Bidriware is a metal handicraft originated in Bidar, Karnataka, during the rule of the Bahamani Sultans in the 14th century CE. With striking inlay artwork, Bidriware is a kind of metal casting from an alloy of copper and zinc. The zinc content gives the alloy a deep black colour.

Provenance: Not known
Material: Copper
Date: Not known
Dimension: 22.9 x 9.2 cm
Acc. No.: AM-DA-805

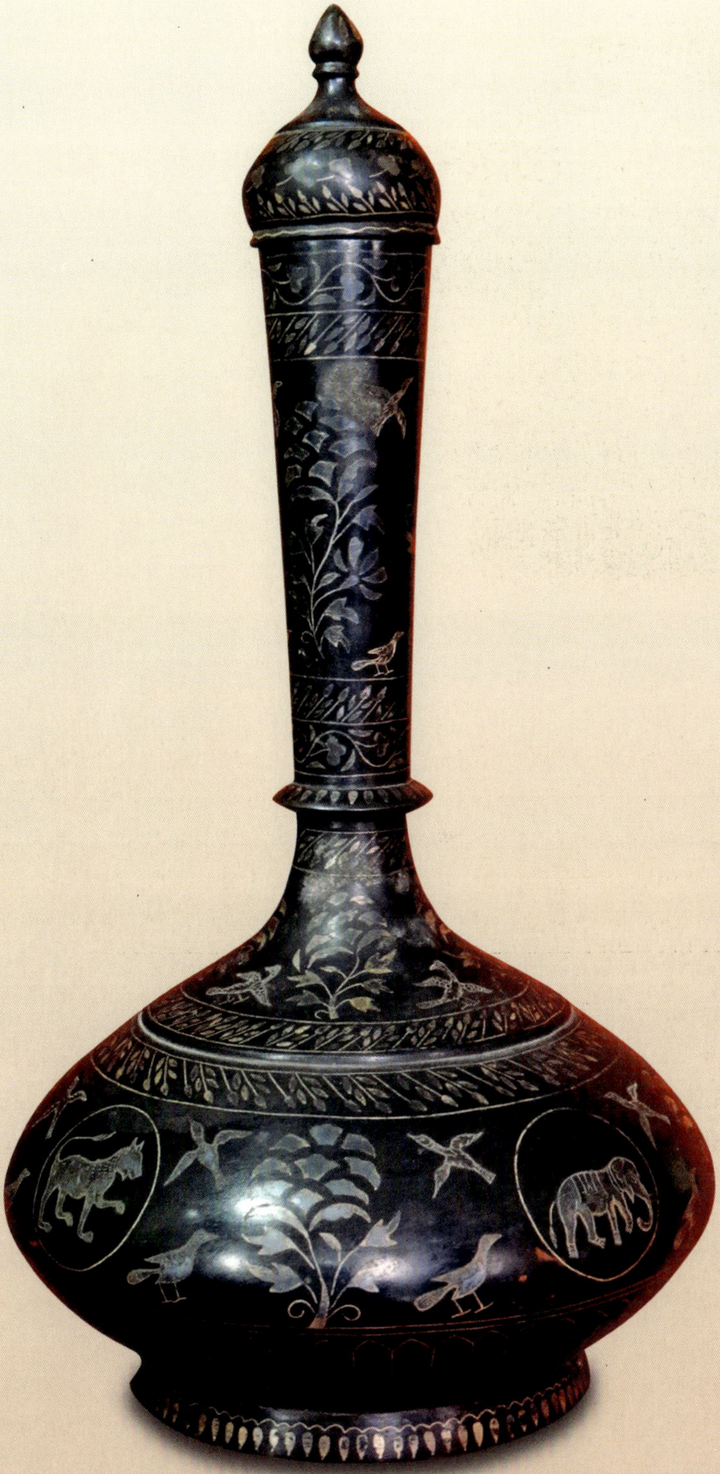

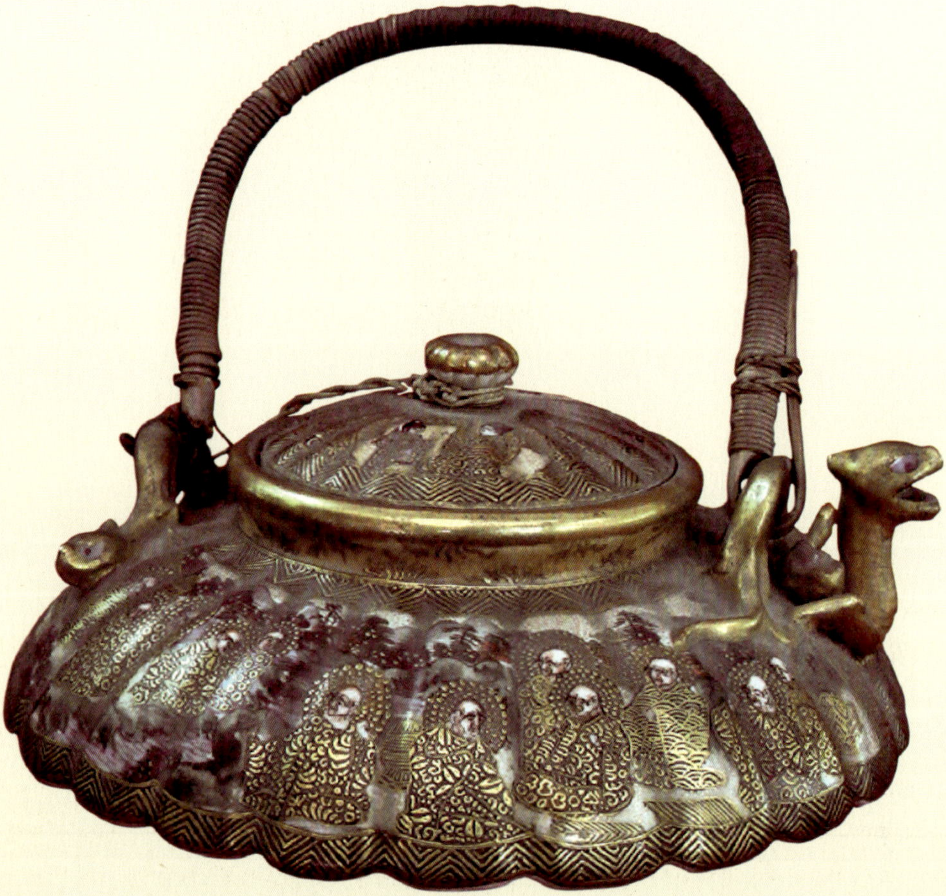

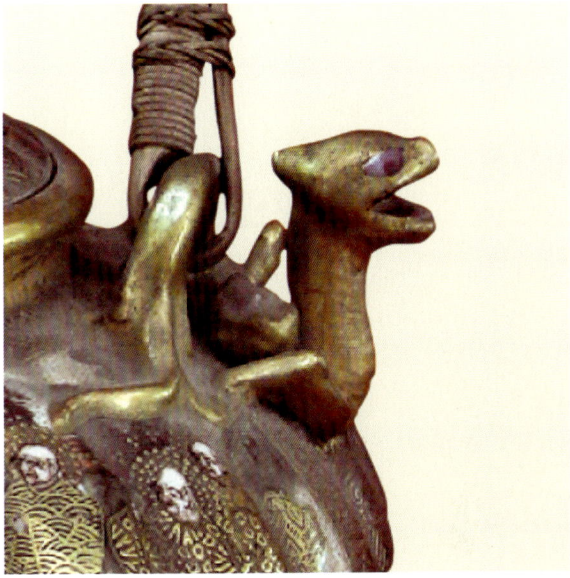

SATSUMA

Japanese ceramics from the Satsuma province, from the island of Kyushu, are elaborately decorated enamel-glazed wares. They range from simple dark clay earthenware of the 17th century CE to the ivory-crafted pieces created for exporting to Europe in the later period.

This Satsuma kettle has the shape of an inverted lotus-petal. On either sides of the kettle, two crocodile-like aquatic animals are attached, and it has a lion-shaped mouth for pouring tea. The belly portion of the kettle is beautifully decorated in two parts. On one side, there are rows of seated monks facing the chief priest. Behind the head of the monks, is the *abhamandala*, a bright circle, which indicates their divine association. They are assumed to be Buddhist *arhat*s or divine beings. Natural landscape of hills, trees, and small houses and Buddhist temples form the background. The other side and the lid are, likewise, decorated with Japanese figures.

Provenance: Not known
Material: Brass
Date: c. 19th century CE
Dimension: 15 x 7.7 cm
Acc. No.: AM-DA-596

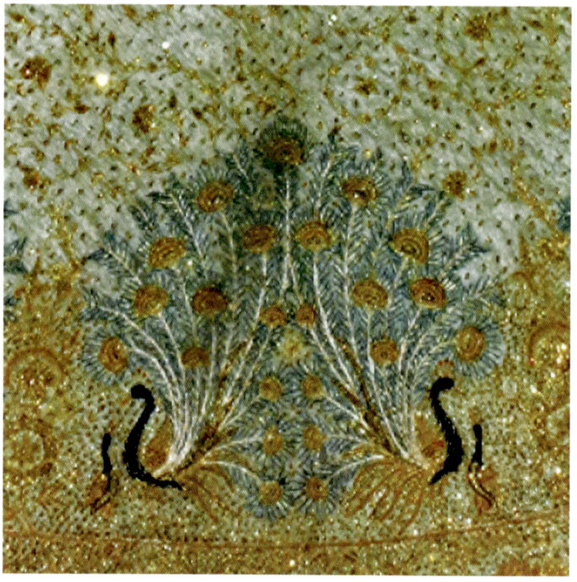

ZARDOZI WORK ON A LEHENGA

Lehenga is an embroidered long skirt, worn as a lower garment in Rajasthan. Similar skirts are also worn by other tribal communities in India and known by different names. In North India and Pakistan, a zardozi or silver embroidery is done on a lehenga for festivals and weddings. This is one such lehenga decorated with peacock designs.

Provenance: Not known
Material: Silk
Date: 20th century CE
Dimension: NA
Acc. No.: AM-TXT-657

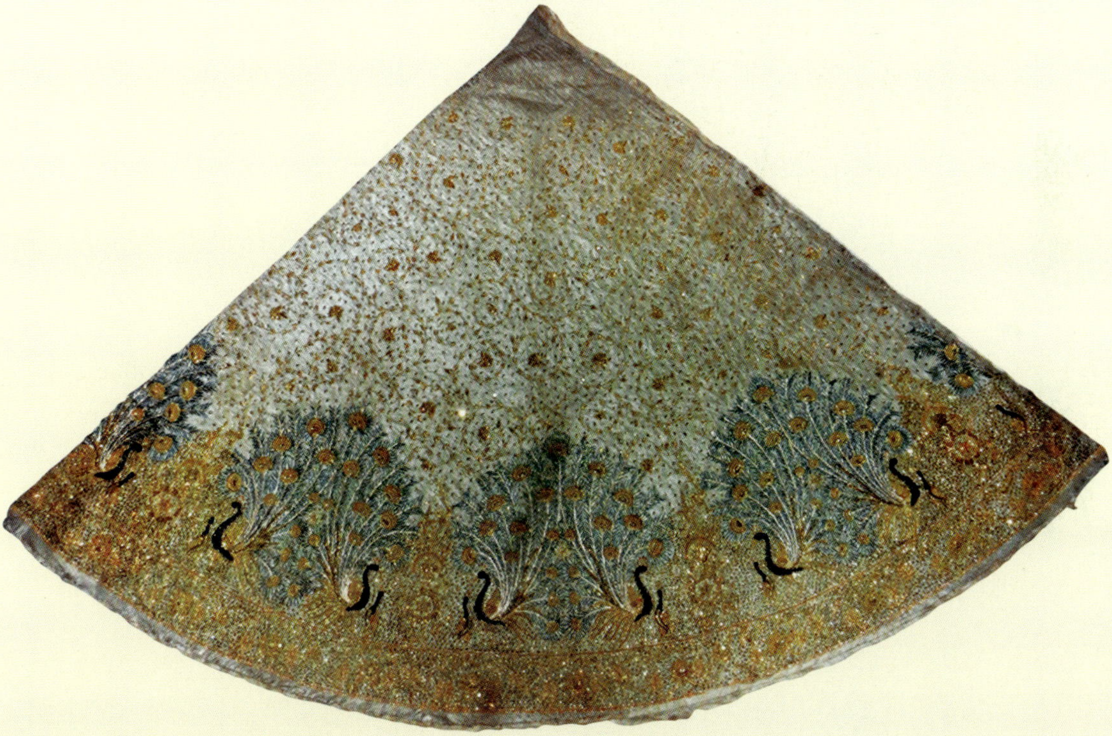

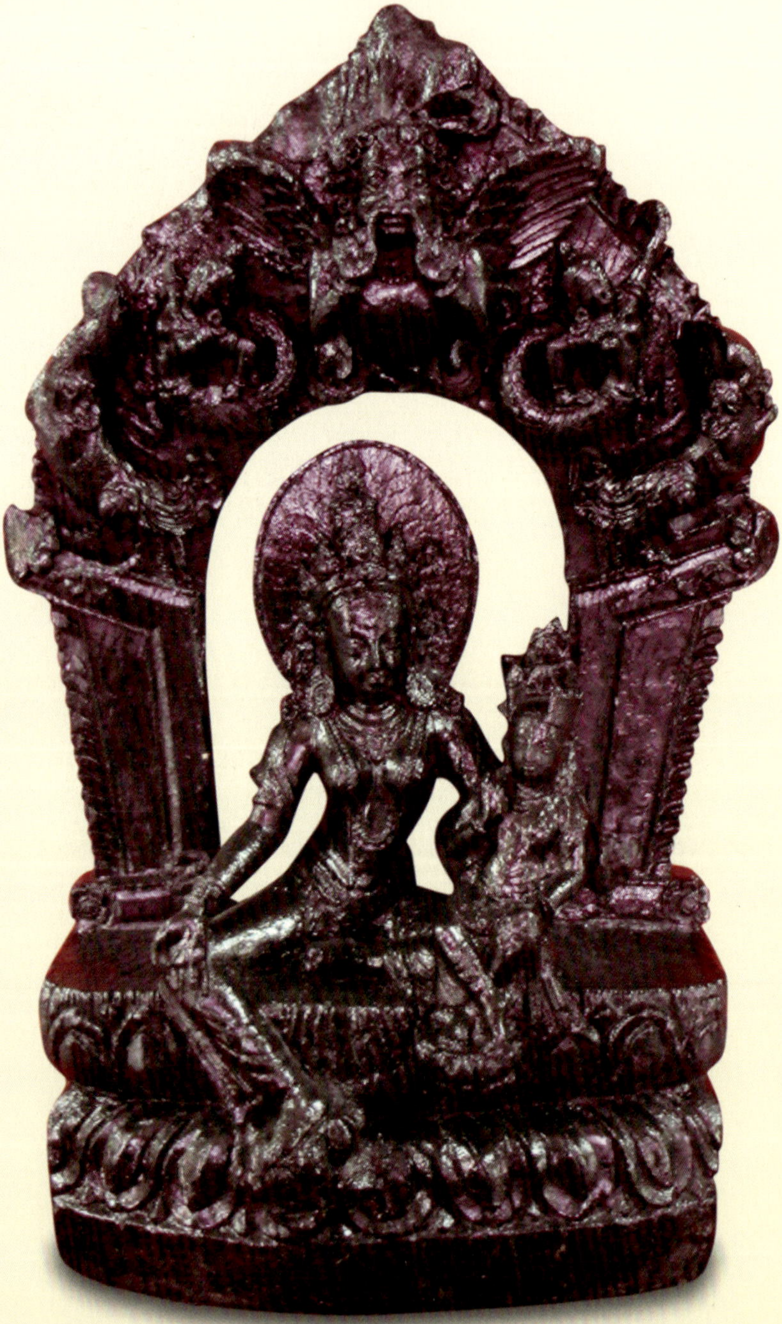

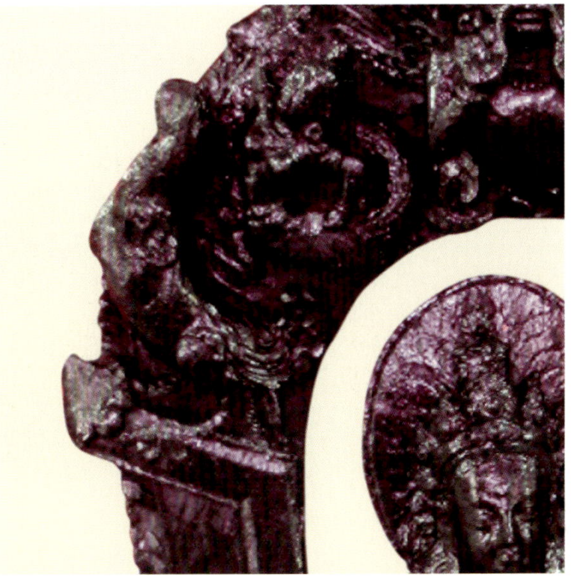

WOODEN FIGURE OF A BUDDHIST GODDESS

The Goddess is seated on a lotus throne with right foot resting on a lotus footrest rising from the bottom of the throne. A male child sits on her lap. There is a plain oval halo behind the head of the Goddess. She wears a beautiful crown, embedded with precious stone. Circular earrings resembling rosettes, armlet, bangles, necklace, and garlands decorate her. The upper part of the wooden stele is cut in a triangular shape. The apex of the triangle has a winged demonic male figure, holding his long drooping moustaches with his hands. On either side, there is a female figure flying in the opposite direction. These women seem to be emerging from the body of a *naga*. The image is a fine example of Nepal Art.

Provenance: Not known
Material: Wood
Date: 20th century CE
Dimension: 53 x 33 cm
Acc. No.: AM-WA-735

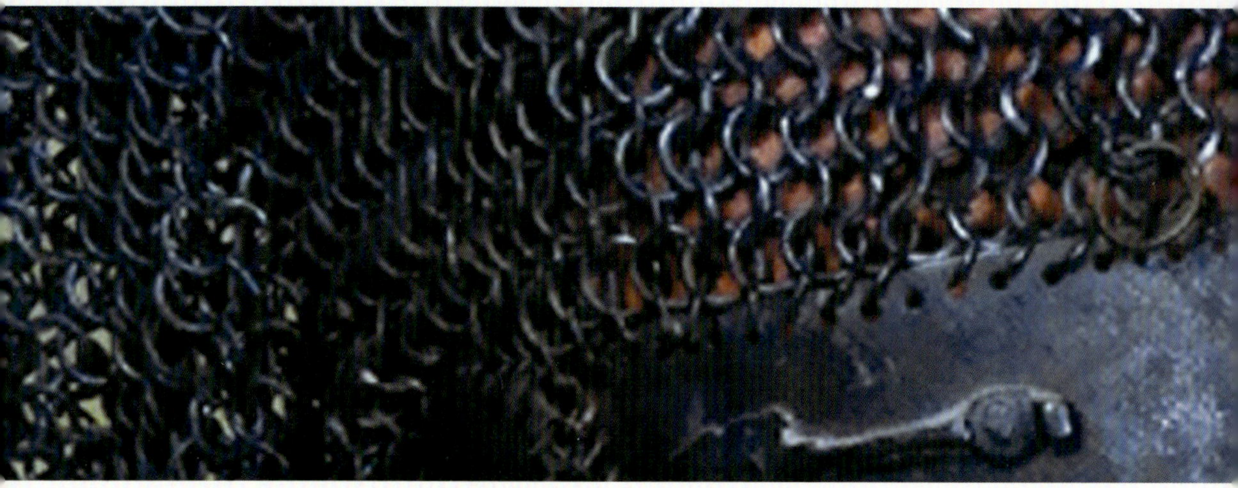

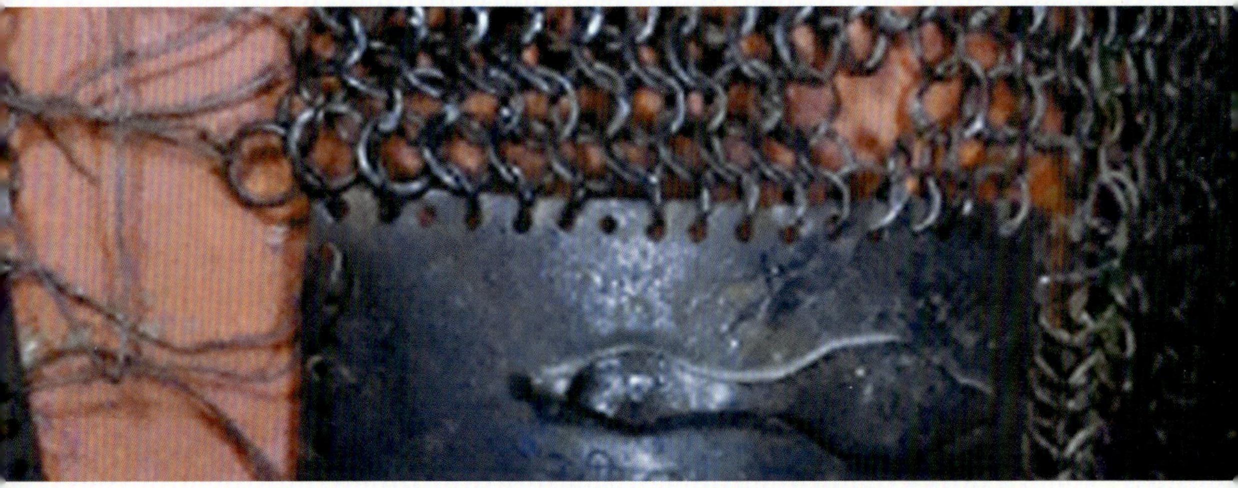

ARMS AND ARMOUR

GALLERY

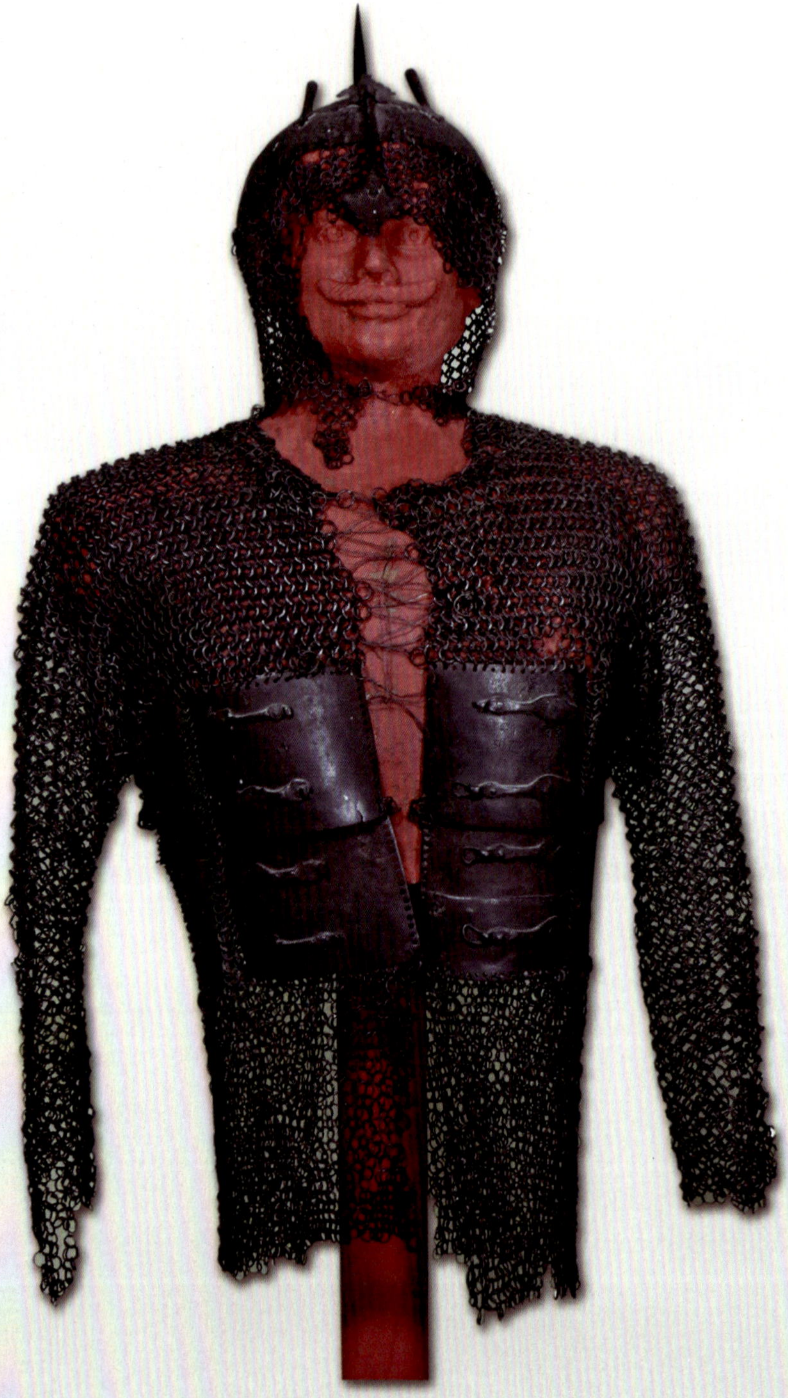

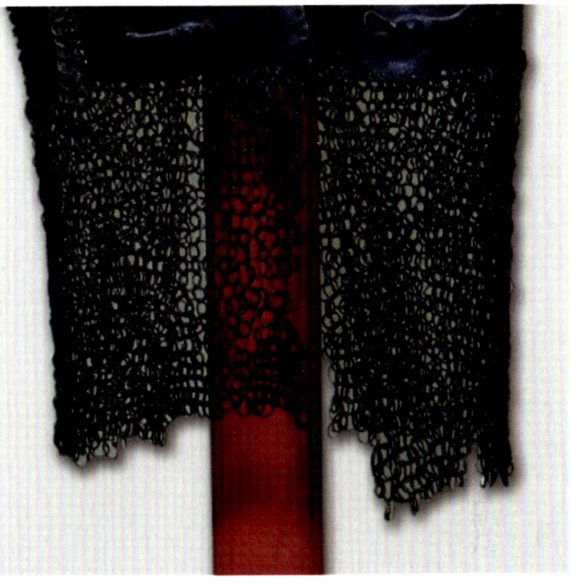

ARMOUR

This chain-mail armour is part of a body defence that probably began in pre-historic times, used with leather shields, and continues to be in vogue in modern times in a transformed fashion as bullet proofs vests. Chain mail provided some safety from sword blade and arrow tips but also allowed flexibility for the limbs. The Mughal-style helmet continued to be in use in the 19th century CE. With the advent of fire arms, chain mail fell out of use. The helmet is made of iron plate, having a pointed nail or sharp iron spike. Armour consists of small metal rings linked together in a pattern to form a mesh. The chain armour interlink with iron rings and cover the upper part of the body and both hands. Four iron plates protect the stomach. It belongs to 17th century CE.

Provenance: Not known
Materi al: Iron
Date: 17th century CE
Dimension: 140 x 115 cm
Acc. No.: AM-ARM-659

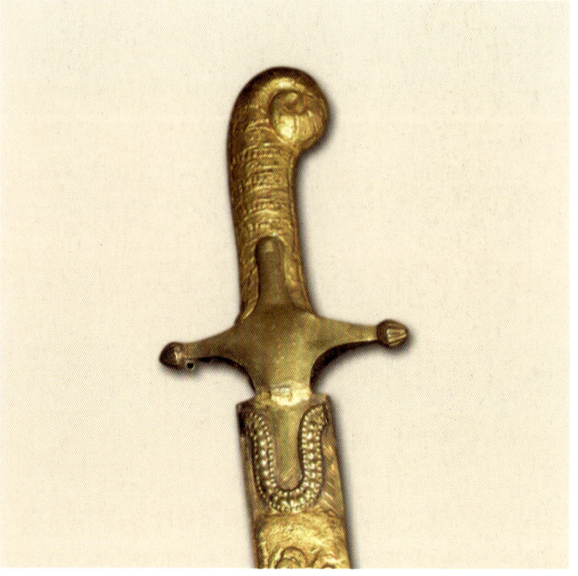

GOLDEN SCABBARD

Shah of United Arab Emirates gifted a golden scabbard to Governor House, which Shri B.L. Joshi Governor of Uttar Pradesh further donated to the Allahabad Museum.

Provenance: Not known
Material: Gold
Date: 18th–19th century CE
Weight: 397 gm
Acc. No.: AM-ARM-12.10

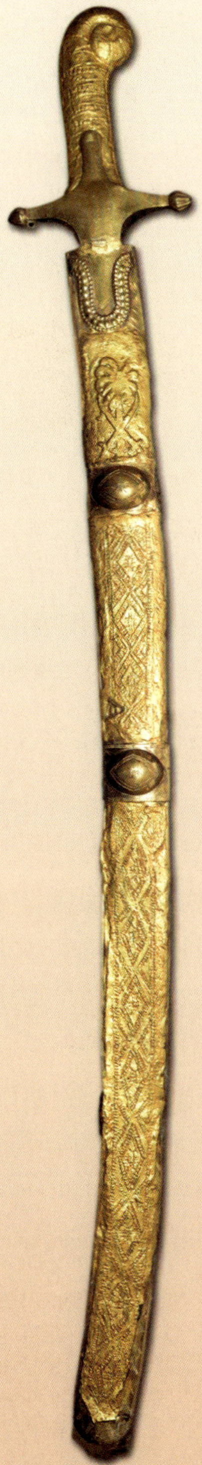

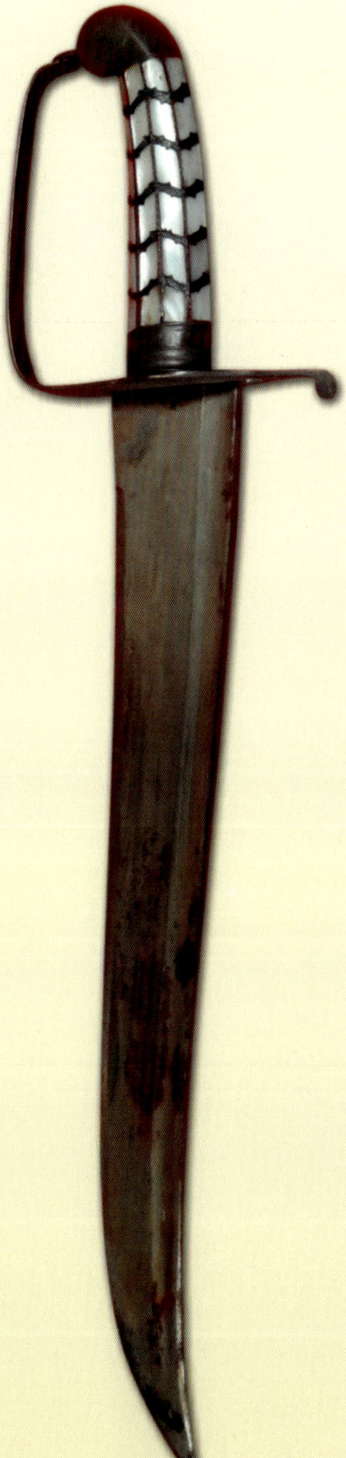

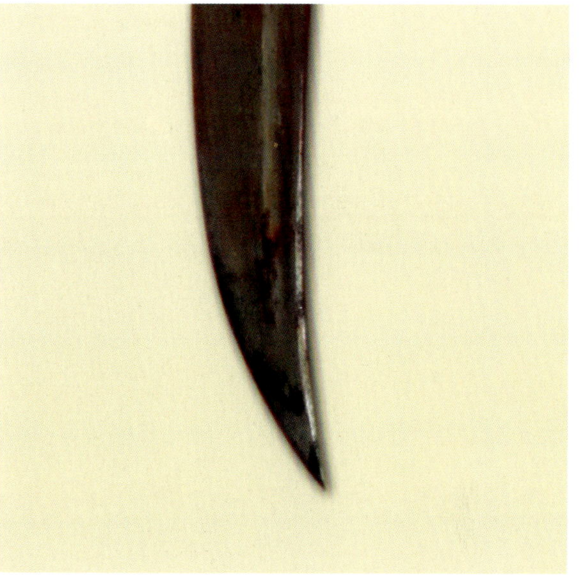

DAGGER

A single-edge, designed to be used as a thrusting or stabbing weapon, this has a flat blade with a pointed tip. The hilt is decorated with mother of pearl and has a finger guard. The grip is studded with pearls and an amber-like material for fixing the end of finger guard.

Provenance: Not known
Material: Iron
Date: 18th–19th century CE
Dimension: 14.5 x 4 cm
Acc. No.: AM-ARM-1460

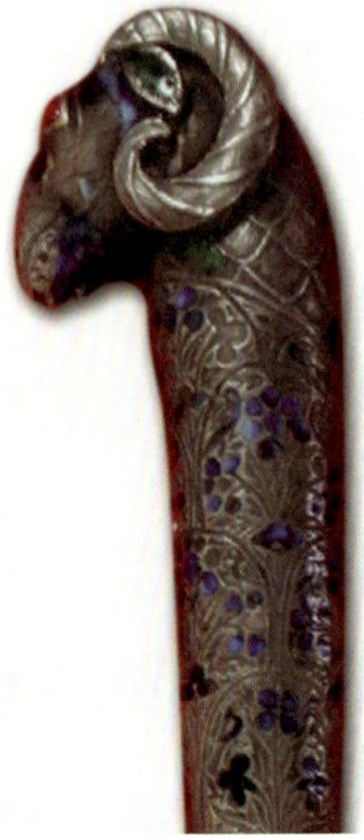

SWORD OF AKKA DEVI: CHALUKYA QUEEN

This Indo-Persian sword belongs to Akka Devi. She was a queen of the Chalukya Dynasty in the Kalyani kingdom in Karnataka. The blade of the sword has a sharp edge on one side and a golden border on the blunt side. The hilt also has a golden border up to the pommel. The sword had been presented to Late Smt. Indira Gandhi, former Prime Minister of India by the Chalukya family member, Sardar Appana, on 2 October 1966. Later, the sword was donated to the Allahabad Museum.

Provenance: NA
Material: Iron
Date: 19th–20th century CE
Dimension: 87 cm
Acc. No.: AM-ARM-1566

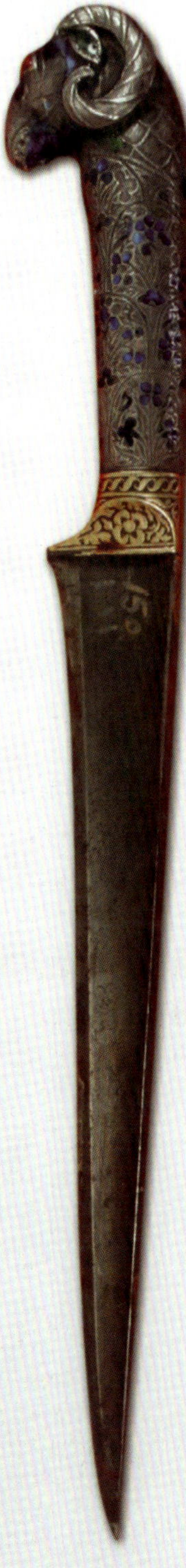

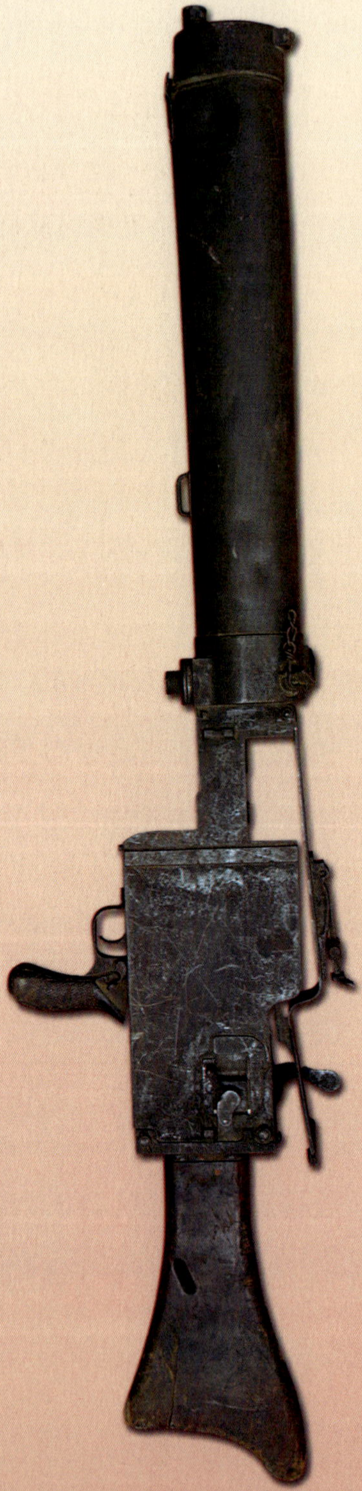

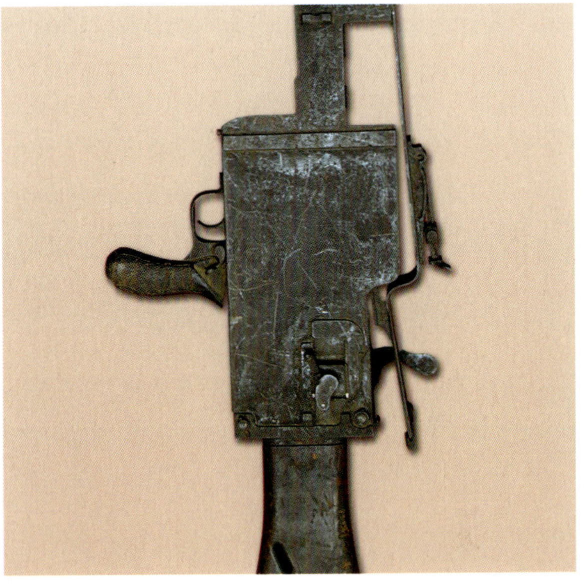

LIGHT MACHINE GUN

This light machine gun was used during First World War. The number MG08/15 LMG is displayed on the outer side, along with Harry Mark, 5895 SUH. It was manufactured in 1917.

Provenance: NA
Material: Iron
Date: 19th–20th century CE
Dimension: Length: 128 cm; Bore: 0.6 cm
Acc. No.: AM-ARM-1591

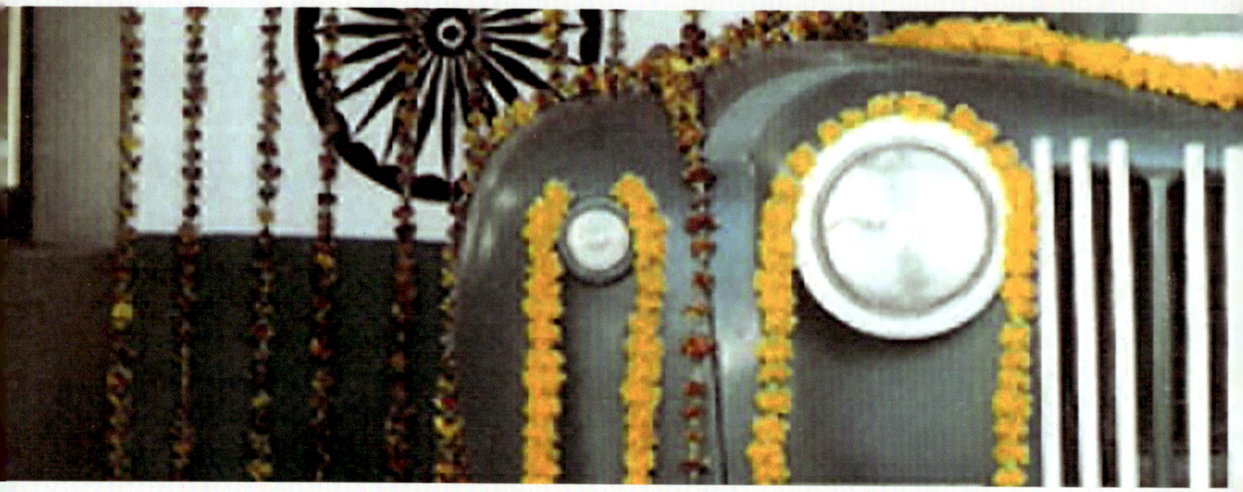

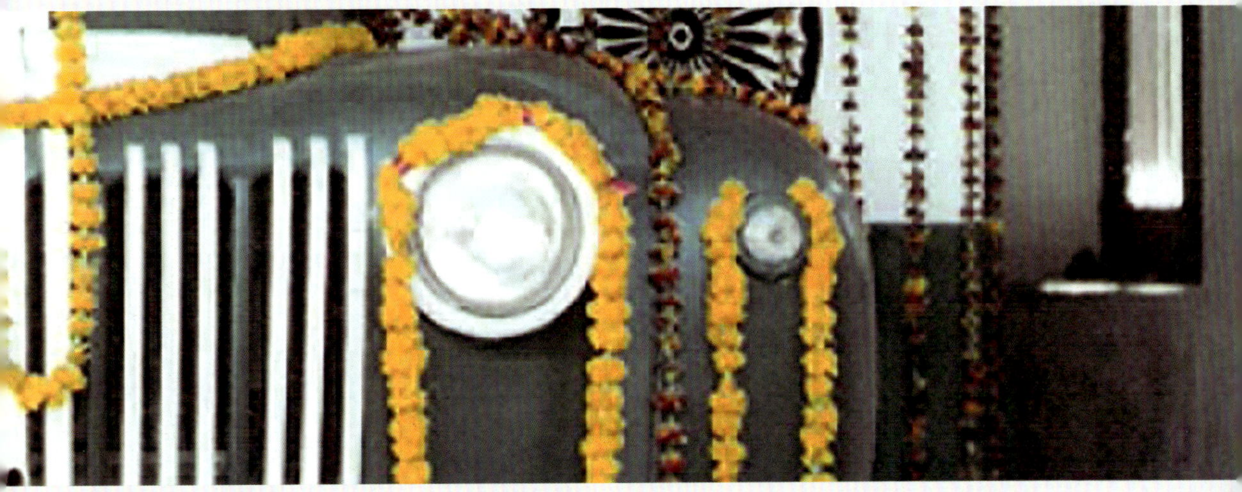

FREEDOM STRUGGLE
GALLERY

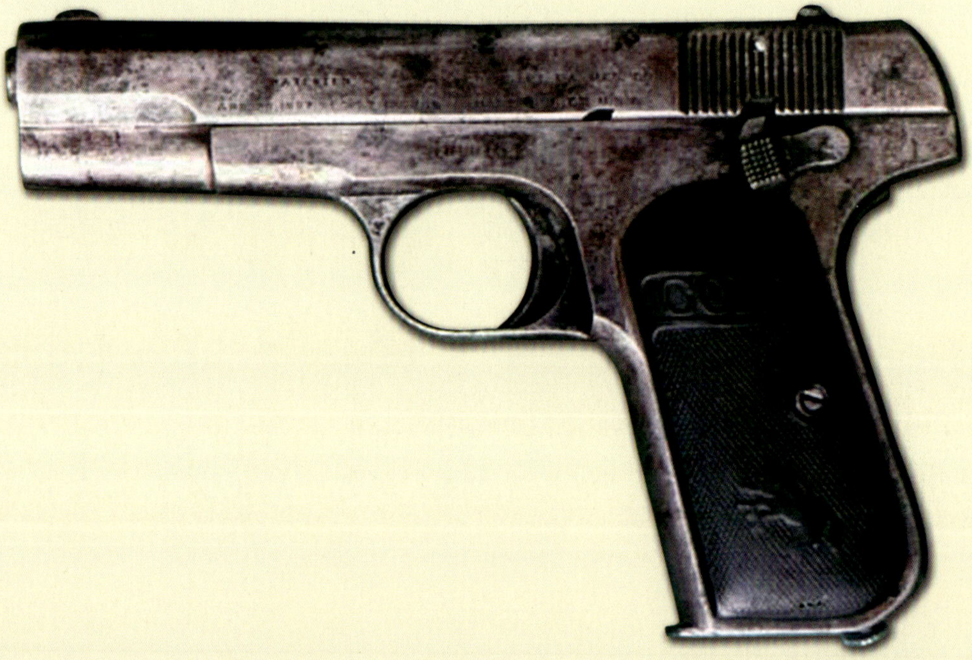

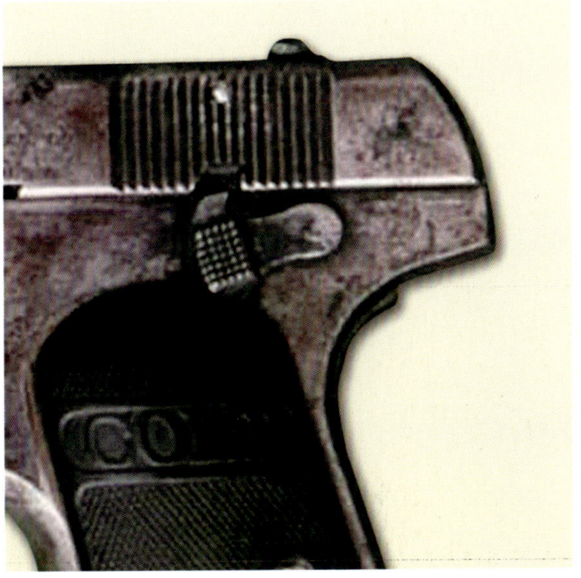

PISTOL OF CHANDRASHEKHAR AZAD

It is a Colt, automatic pistol of 0.32 bore/ caliber with a ten round magzine. It is rimless, smokeless and was patented on 20 April 1897. It was manufactured by Colt Hart Fort CT USA on 22 December 1903. This pistol was used by Chandrashekhar Azad while he was fighting his last encounter with the British police in the erstwhile Alfred Park of Allahabad. This historic encounter took place on 27 February 1931 at Allahabad.

Provenance: NA
Material: Metal
Date: 1903 CE
Dimension: 16.8 x 11 cm
Acc. No.: AM-FS-9

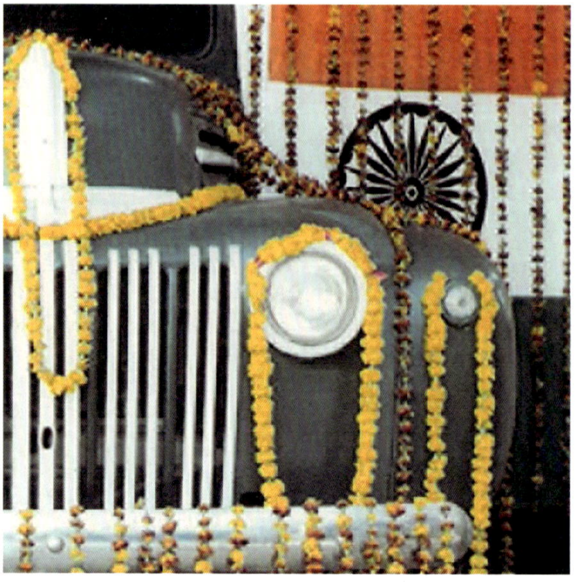

THE GANDHI MEMORIAL VEHICLE

The Gandhi Memorial Vehicle is a large lorry (V 8 1947, Ford Lorry) manufactured by Ford Corporation. 'The Gandhi Memorial Vehicle' was deliberately designed for a procession to be taken out for the immersion of the ashes of Mahatma Gandhi after his death. The ashes of Mahatma Gandhi were kept in a bronze casket, which was carried in this vehicle from the Allahabad Junction Railway Station to the sangam or confluence of Ganga and Yamuna rivers for immersion. The vehicle was handed over to the Allahabad Museum in 1954. All its parts were renovated and were replaced with the original Ford accessories in 2005 with the effort of Uttar Pradesh State Road Transport Corporation. Now, it is in running condition. It is taken out every year on 12 February, the day Mahatma Gandhi's ashes were brought to the Triveni Sangam at Allahabad.

Provenance: Ford Corporation Factory, US
Material: Metal
Date: 20th century CE
Dimension: Ford Style
Acc. No.: AM-FS-10

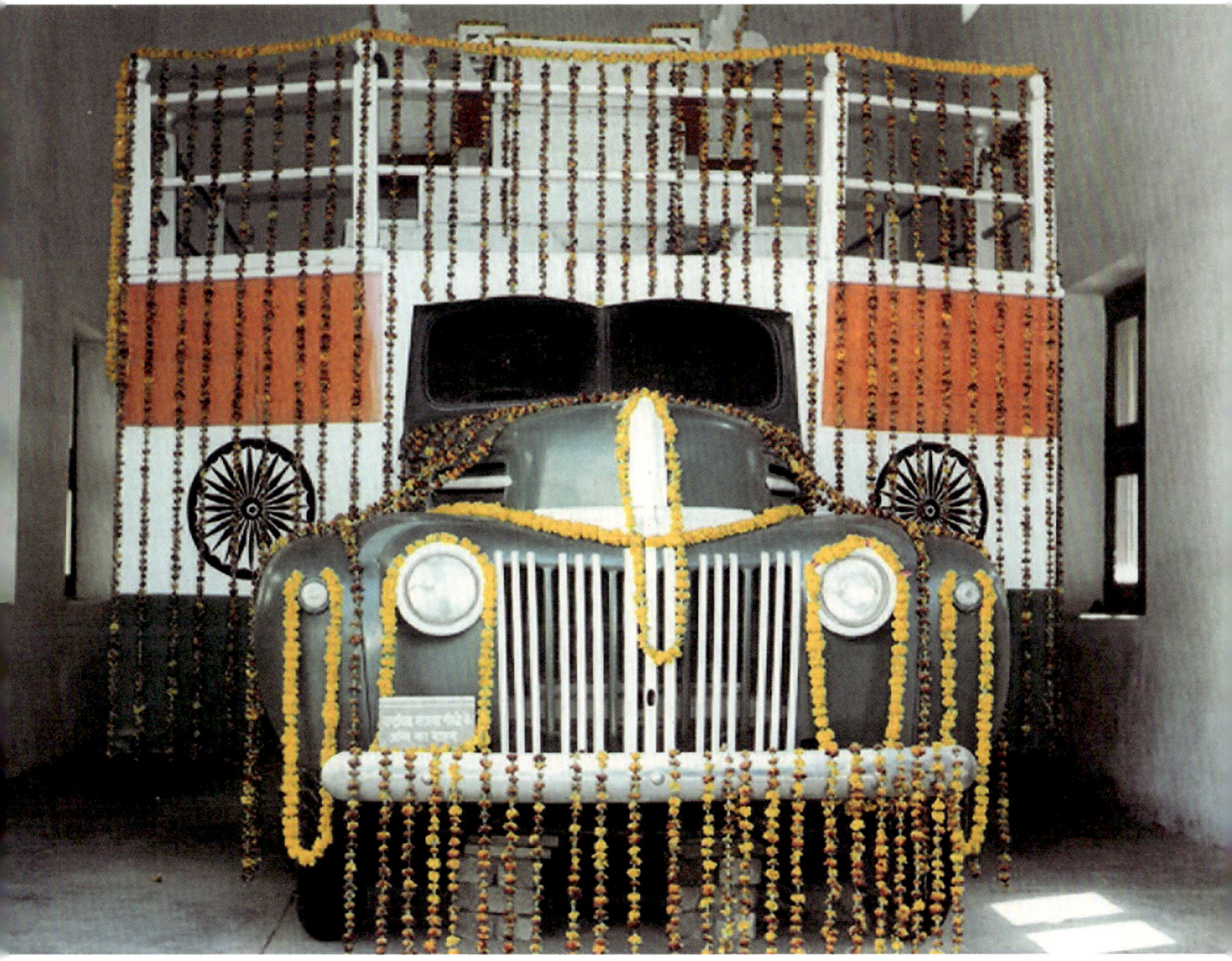

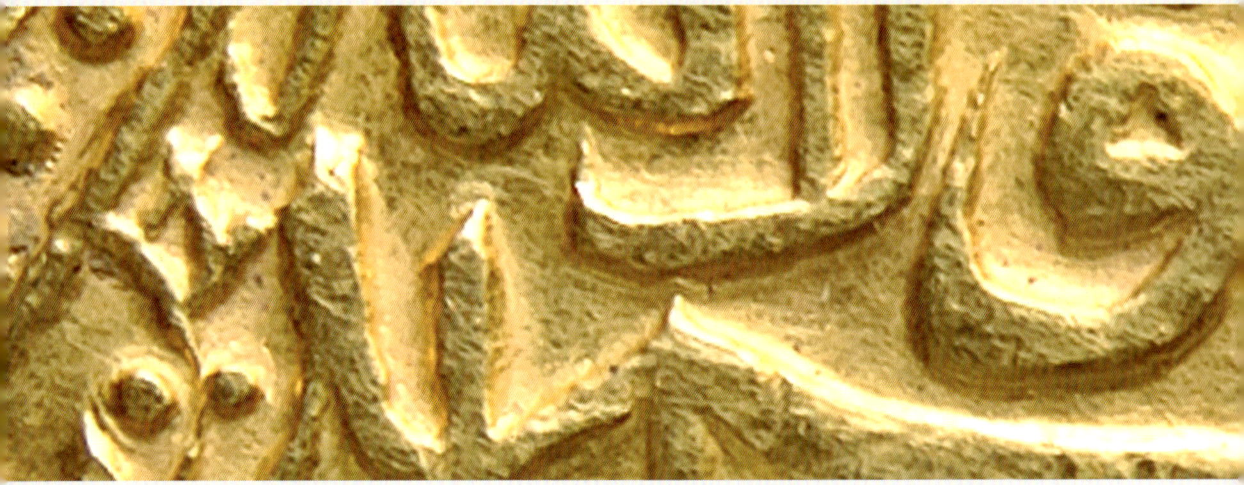

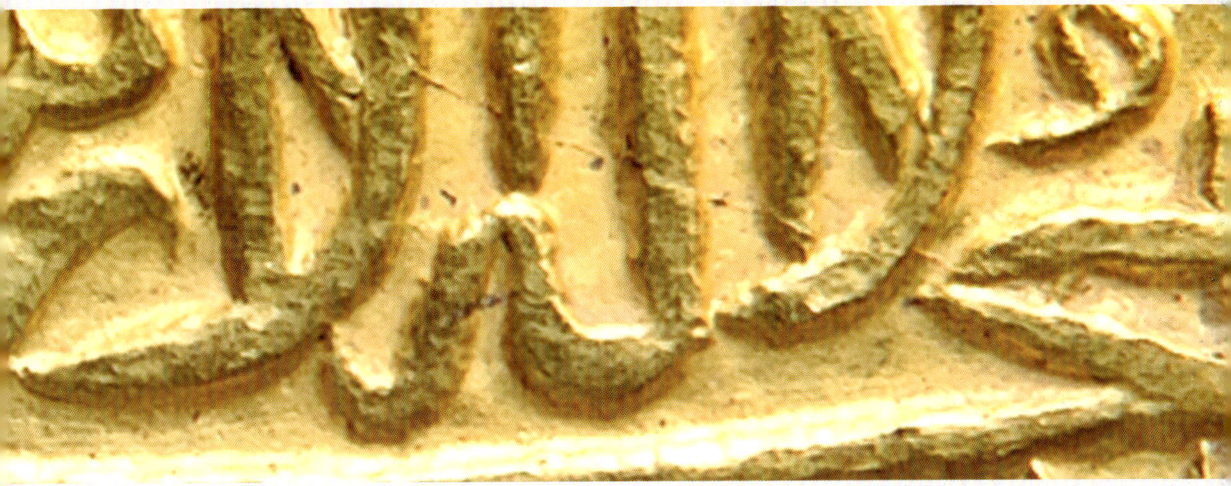

ARCHAEOLOGICAL
GALLERY

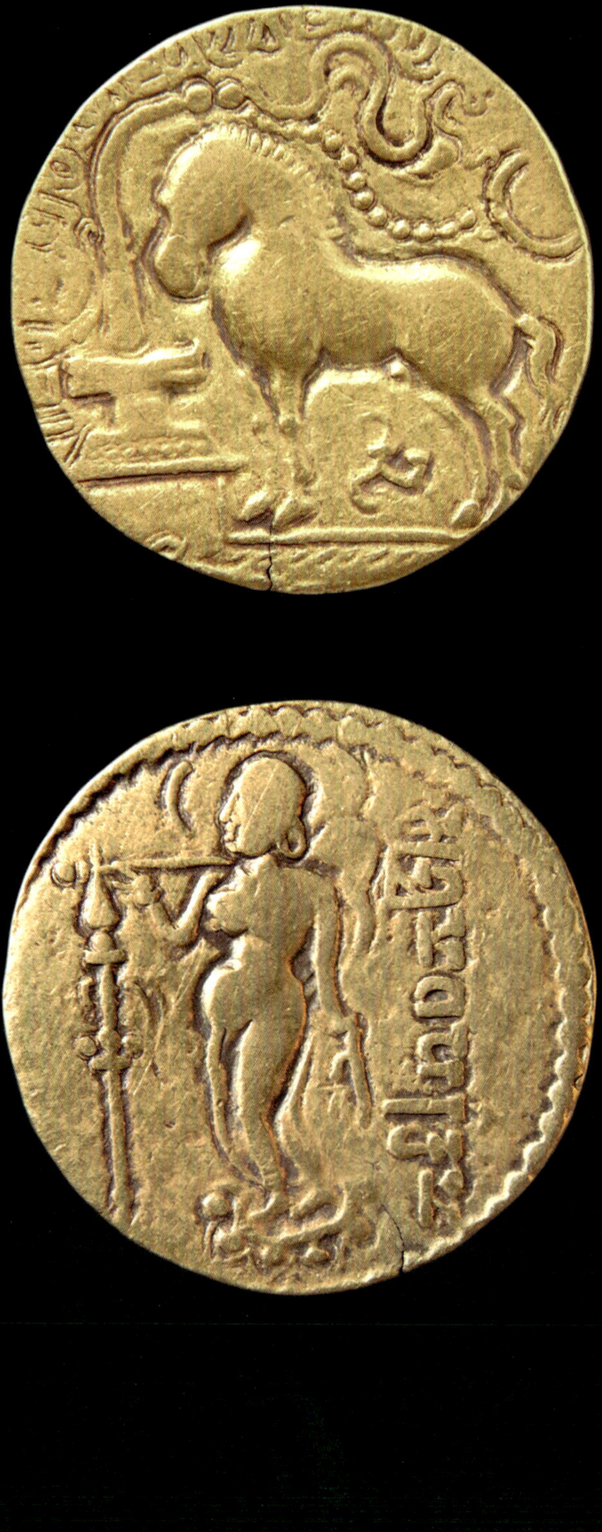

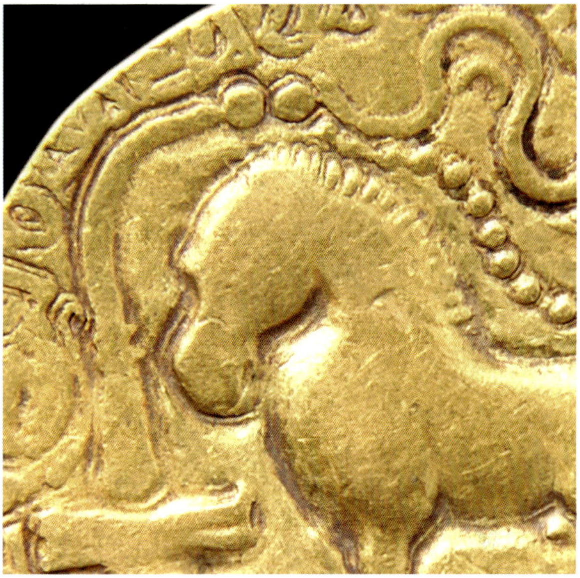

GOLD COIN OF SAMUDRAGUPTA

After extensive conquests over twelve south Indian states and six northern tribal states, Samudragupta, the emperor of Gupta Dynasty (350–370 CE), issued Ashwamedhika gold coins, as a mark of his victory and valour, after performing the *ashwamedha yajna*.

OBVERSE: A string of beads above the head and back of the horse. The legend in Gupta Brahmi letters is: *Rajadharaja prithavamavatva dava jayatya.* Around the circular part of the coin, a *yupa* (flag post) is shown on the coin. Some part of the legend is missing.

REVERSE: Queen is standing on a bead-bordered mat, with a towel in her left hand, in front of an ornamental *suchi* or spear with a flywhisk over her right shoulder, and the legend reads: *Ashvamedhaparakramah.* The *suchi* has three circular attachments in the upper half and she is shown with a halo signifying her royalty.

Dynasty:	Gupta; Ruler: Samudragupta
Provenance:	Not known
Material:	Gold
Date:	4th century CE
Dimension:	Dia.: 2.2 cms; Wt: 7.3 gm
Acc. No.:	AM-GC-1

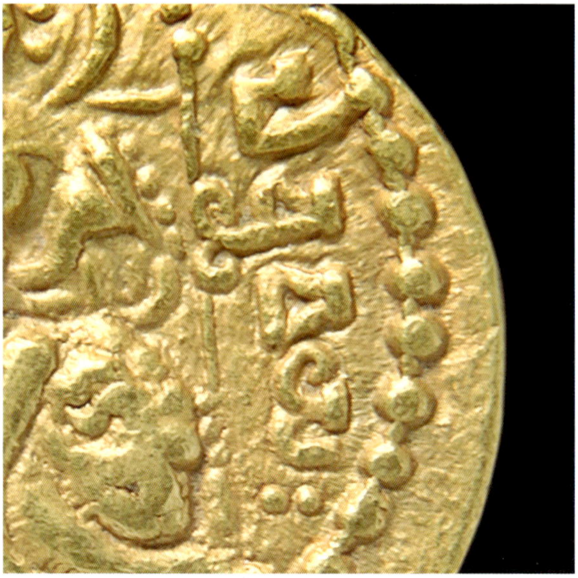

GOLD COIN OF CHANDRAGUPTA I

This coin was issued by Chandragupta I on the occasion of matrimonial relations with the Lichcchavis of Vaishali.

OBVERSE: Both king and queen are shown standing opposite each other. The king and the queen are adorned with *nimbate* (aura). The king is wearing close-fitted tailcoat and trousers, pearl-bordered headdress, earrings and armlets. The legend embossed is: *Cham gu dra pta* or *Cha gu ndra pta*.

REVERSE: The Goddess is sitting on the lion showing her knees in front. Back of the throne is clearly visible. A roughly drawn monogram is depicted on the left. The legend on the rights says: *Lachchhavayah.*

Dynasty:	Gupta; Ruler: Chandragupta I
Provenance:	Not known
Material:	Gold
Date:	4th century CE
Dimension:	Dia.: 1.9 cms; Wt: 7.56 gms
Acc. No.:	AM-GC-10

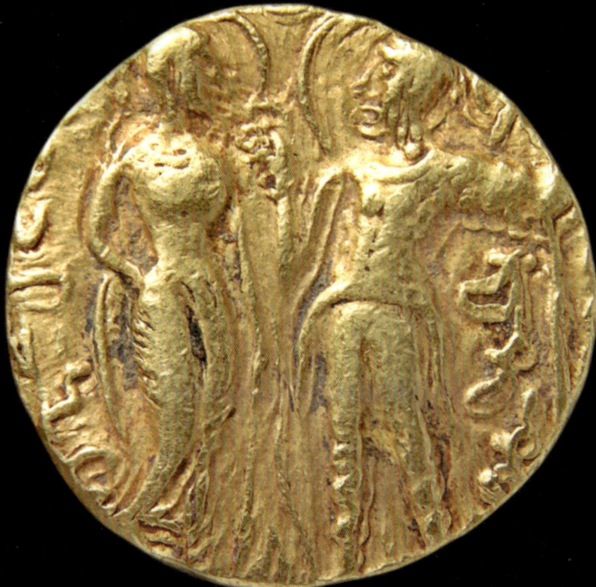

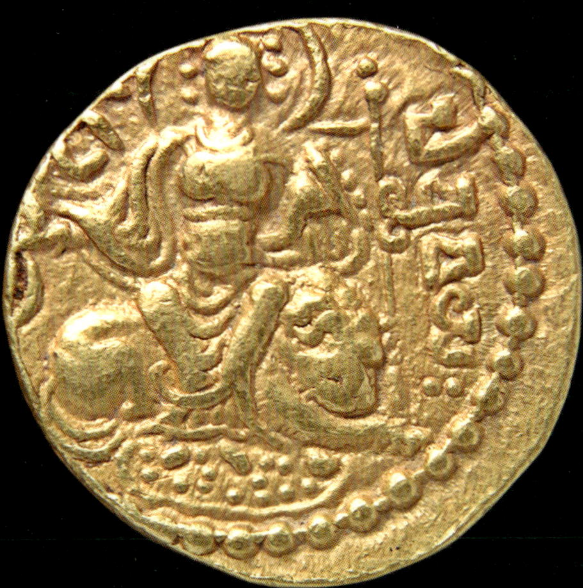

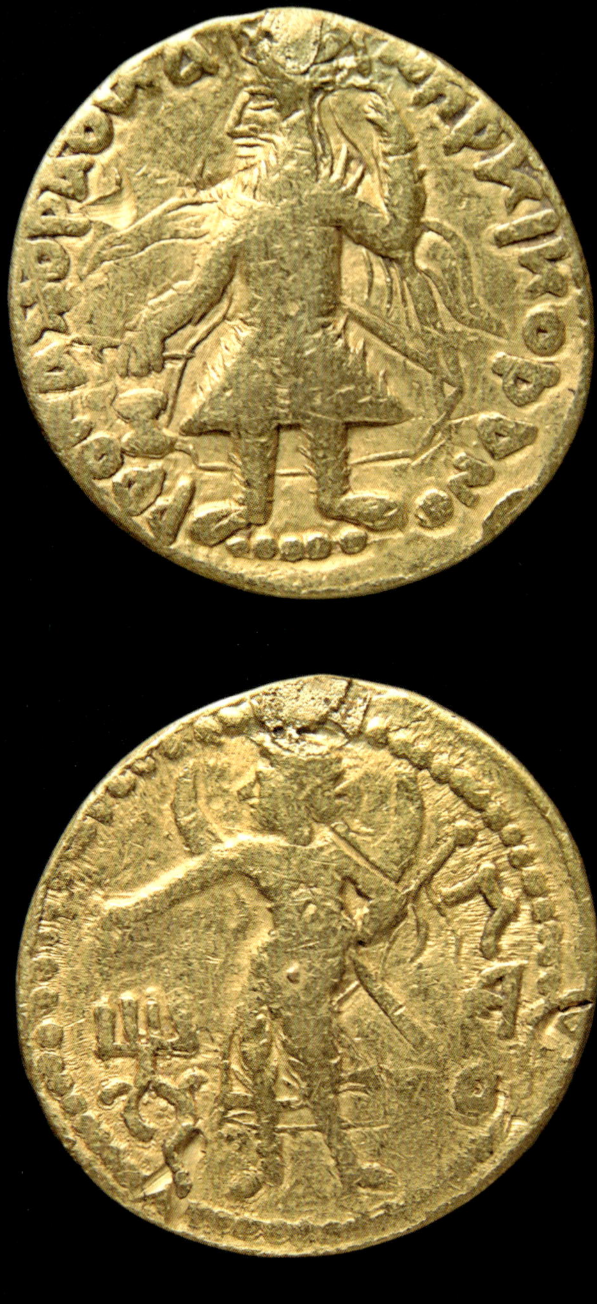

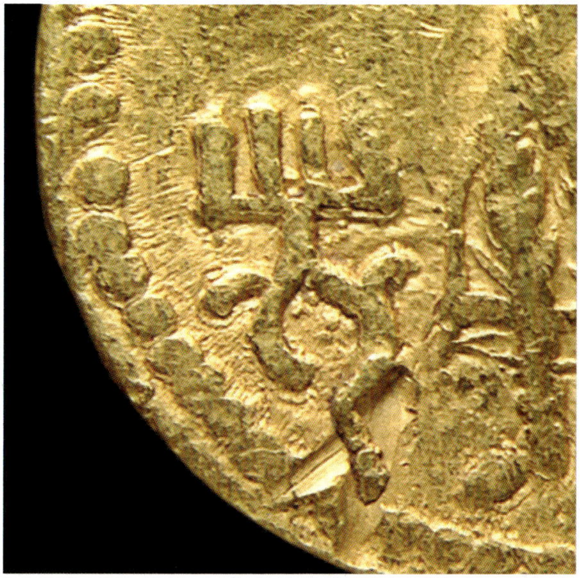

OLD COIN OF KANISHKA I

Kanishka (Kanishka I), considered the successor of Vima Kadphises, had issued coins in gold and copper with the same type of portrayal—him standing, dressed in a long tunic, salwar, mantle held by double clasp at the chest, and a low round cap; a sacrifice at an altar while he holds a spear in his left hand. The reverse side of his coins were not dedicated to any particular deity. Kanishka had ended the bilingual tradition of Greek and Kharoshthi and retained only Greek for a while and issued coins with the legend: *Basileos Basilion Kanishkou.*

OBVERSE: Bearded king standing on a circular mat, wearing peaked helmet, coat, trousers, holding in right hand an elephant-goad and sacrificing it over an altar with a spear; Bactrian legend: *Shaonano Shao Kaneshki Koshno.*

REVERSE: Moon God standing to left; Legend: Mao; Monogram on left.

Dynasty: Kushan; Ruler: Kanishka
Provenance: Not known
Material: Gold
Date: 1st century CE
Dimension: Dia.: 2.1 cms; Wt: 8.05 gms
Acc. No.: AM-GC-100

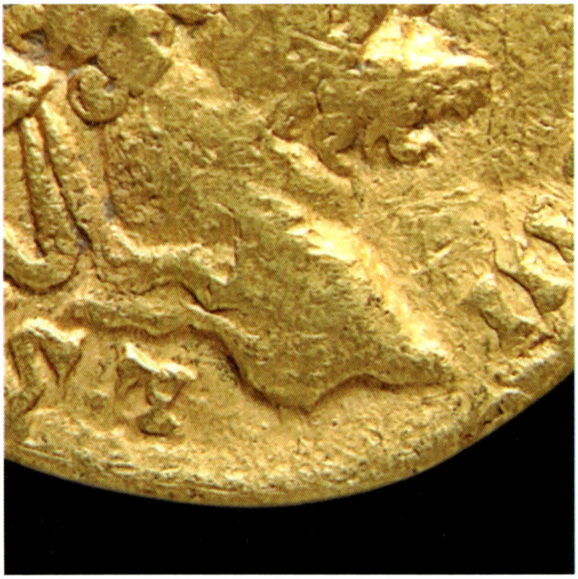

INDO-ROMAN GOLD COIN OF SEPTIMUS

This Roman gold coin was issued in the 2nd to 3rd centuries CE. It was minted in the name of the Roman Emperor Septimus Severus (193–211 CE). It may have been circulated in India for trade and commerce. Numerous hordes of Roman gold coins from the time of Augustus and emperors of the 1st and 2nd centuries CE have been found from India. His coins were found predominantly in the northern part of India.

OBVERSE: King faces to the right; head of Caesar; legend: SEPTSEV P II *RiAVg* iy PIII.

REVERSE: Winged human deity; legend: Vic TAVG, P II COS II.

Dynasty: Indo-Roman; Ruler: Septimus
Provenance: Not known
Material: Gold
Date: 2nd century CE
Dimension: Dia.: 2 cm; Wt: 6.98 gms
Acc. No.: AM-GC-105

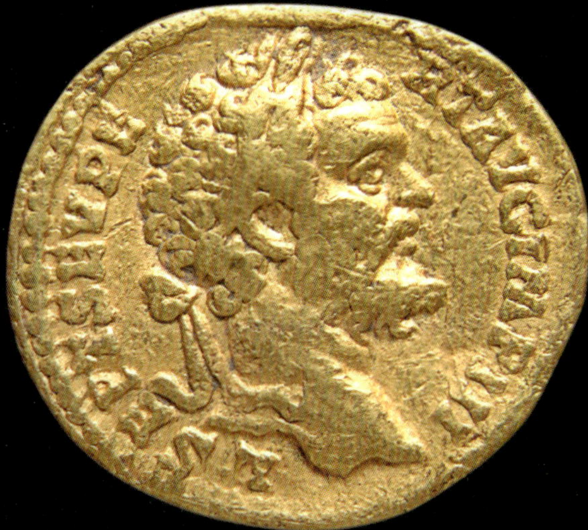

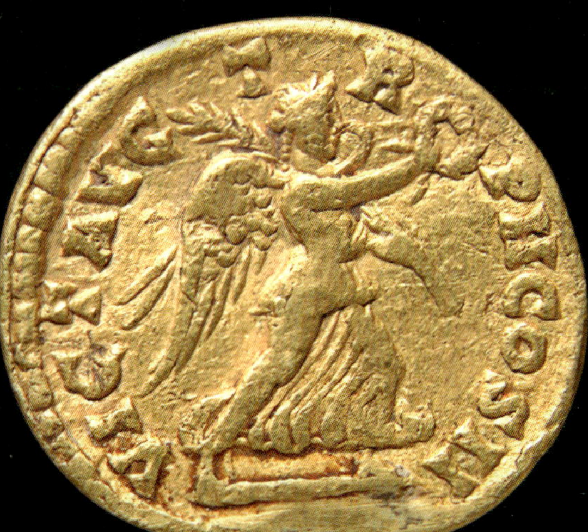

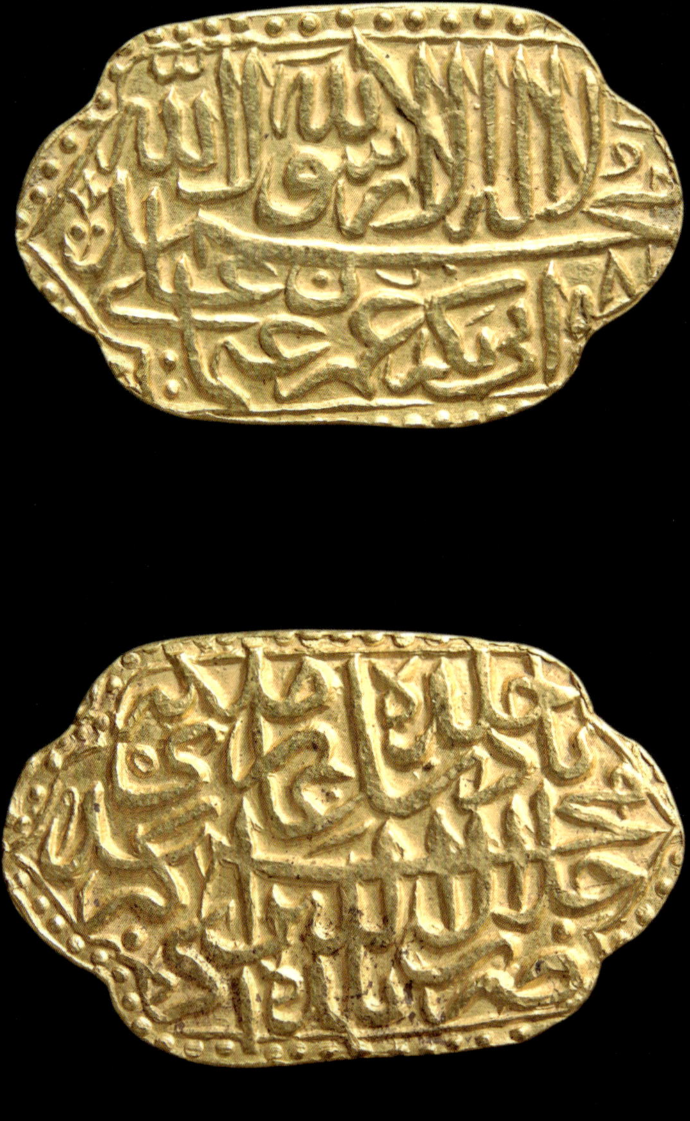

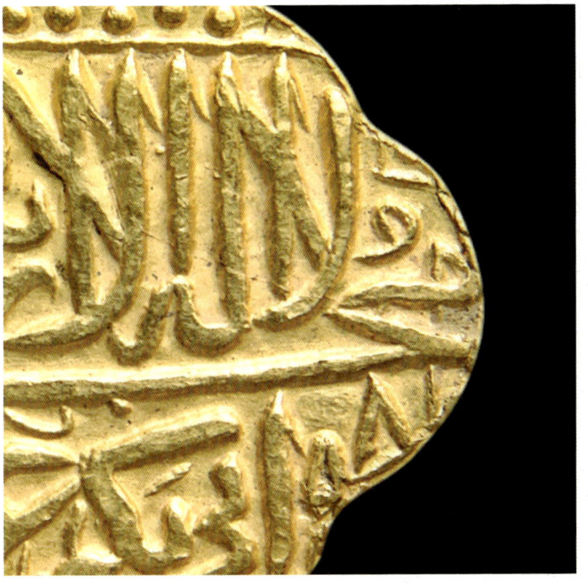

MEHARABI COIN OF AKBAR

Akbar had issued some gold coins in *mehrabi* shape (hexagonal with oblong upper and lower sides; left and right side in the shape of a dome) to commemorate important events, but they are extremely rare. The mehrabi held an important place in the imagery of the Mughal court, and is specifically mentioned in the court chronicles *Ain-e-Akbari* by the emperor's secretary Abu'l Fazl.

OBVERSE: Inside lozenge, is a *kalima*; legend: *Abu Bakr 'Umar 'Usman Ali.*

REVERSE: Inside lozenge legend: (1) *Khalad Mulkahu* (2) *Badshah Ghazi* (3) *Muhammad* (4) *Jalalud-din Akbar* (5) *Zarb Baldat Agra.*

Provenance: Not known
Material: Gold
Date: 16th century CE
Dimension: 2 x 3.1 cm
Acc. No.: AM-GC-69

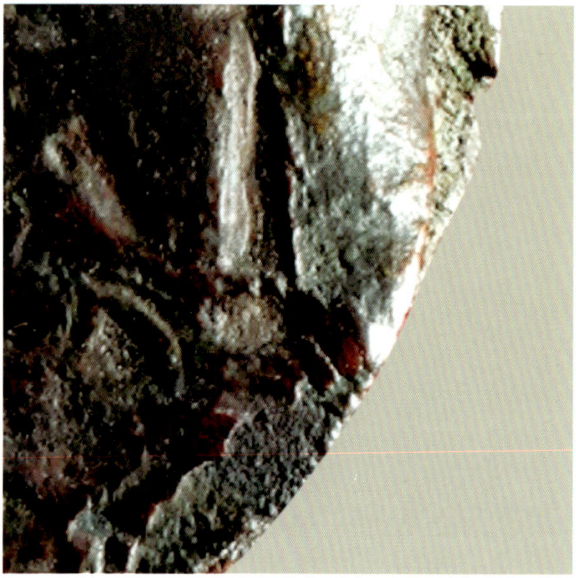

COPPER PLAQUE

This copper plaque bears an exquisitely carved scene on it. On the top surface there is a *chaitya* (prayer hall), resembling the stone chaityas of South India. A king is seen close to the chaitya. Perhaps he is going away after making offering. In the second compartment below, the king is shown riding a chariot drawn by horses and proceeding towards his palace. It is probably a Buddhist subject. Curiously enough the site of Jhusi has not yielded a single Buddhist object so far. It is possible that the plaque was imported to Jhusi from some other Buddhist centre.

Provenance: Jhusi, Allahabad, Uttar Pradesh
Material: Copper
Date: 2nd century BCE
Dimension: 2.5 x 1.9 cm
Acc. No.: AM-ARCH-101

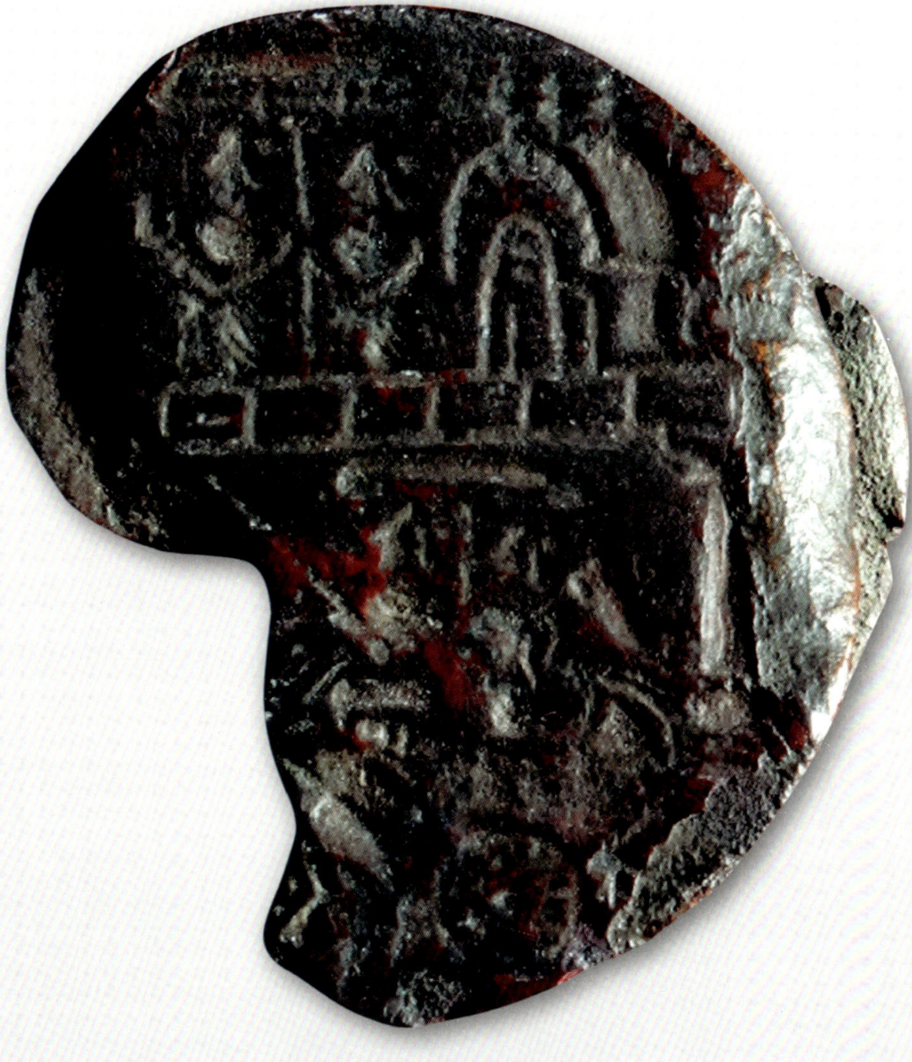

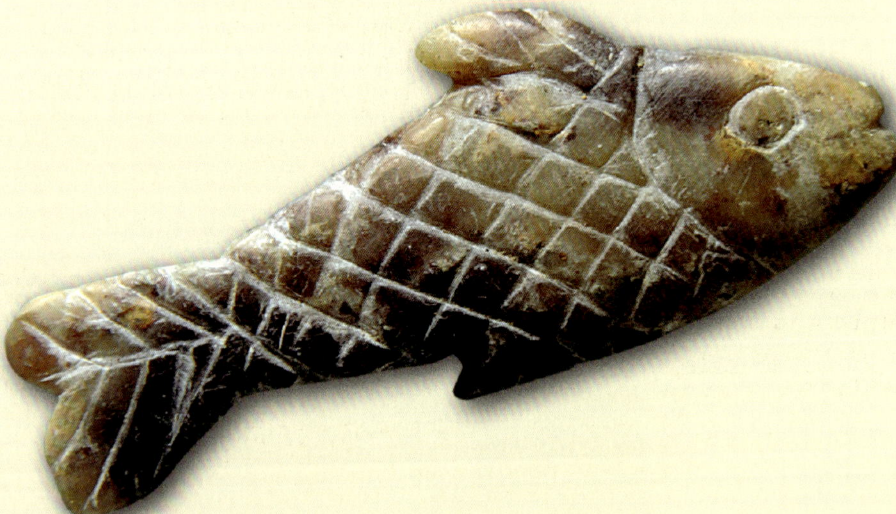

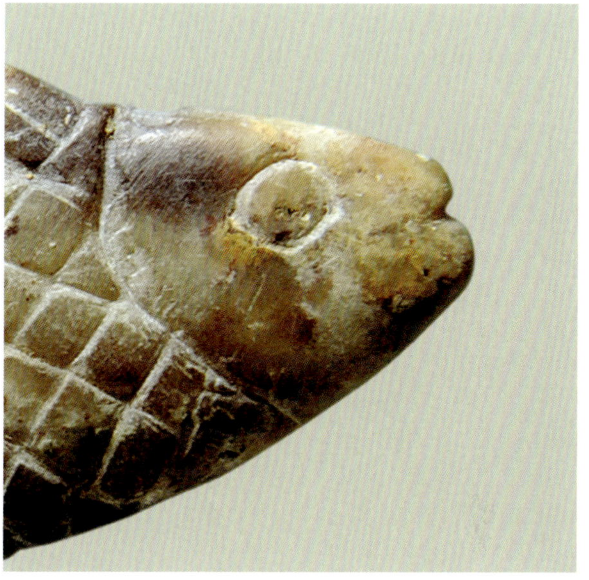

FIGURE OF A FISH

The fish-shaped figure may have been used as a bead because it has perforations to thread it in. It is made of soft stone. The fish is beautifully carved on both sides and polished to perfection.

Provenance: Kaushambi, Uttar Pradesh
Material: Soft stone
Date: Early Historic
Dimension: 3.2 x 1.3 x 1 cm
Acc. No.: AM-BED-02.101

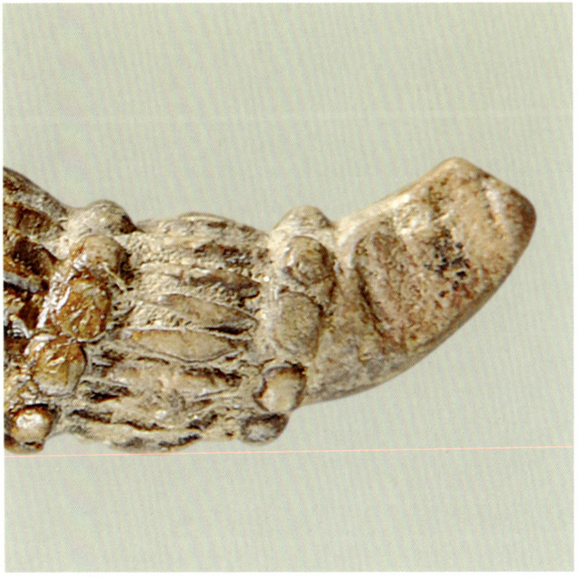

FIGURE OF A COMPOSITE ANIMAL

Compost figure of two animals (partially a lion and a crocodile) has been carved in a form of a bead. It is depicting a lion, charging. The colour of the object is buff.

Provenance: Kaushambi, Uttar Pradesh
Material: Soft stone
Date: Early Historic
Dimension: 3.3 x 1.7 cm
Acc. No.: AM-BED-182

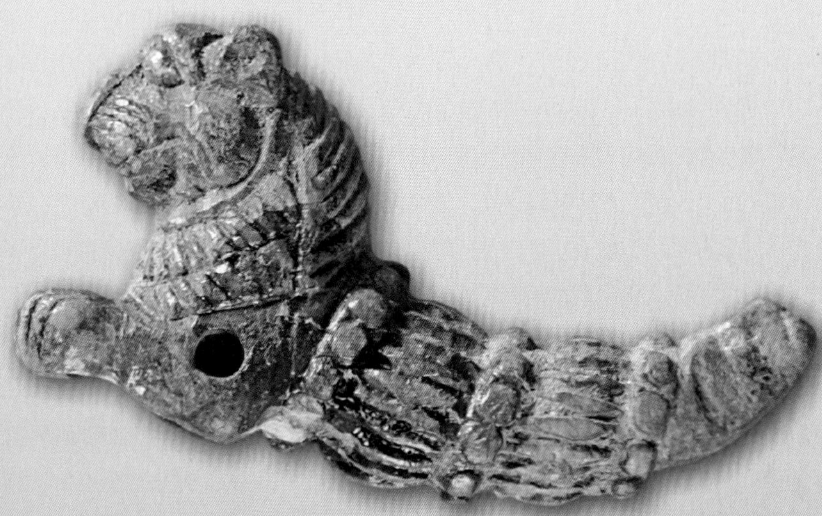

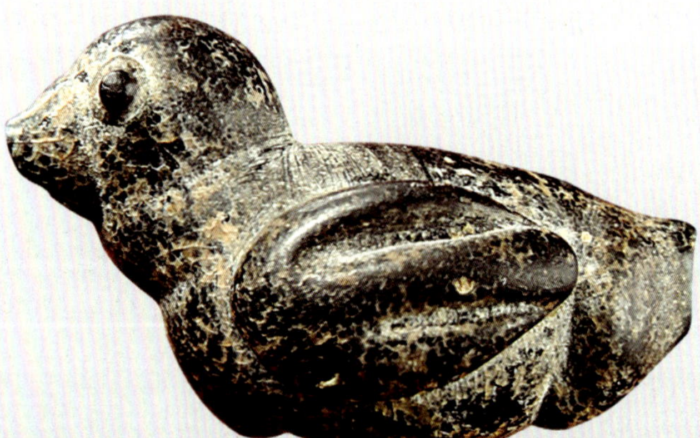

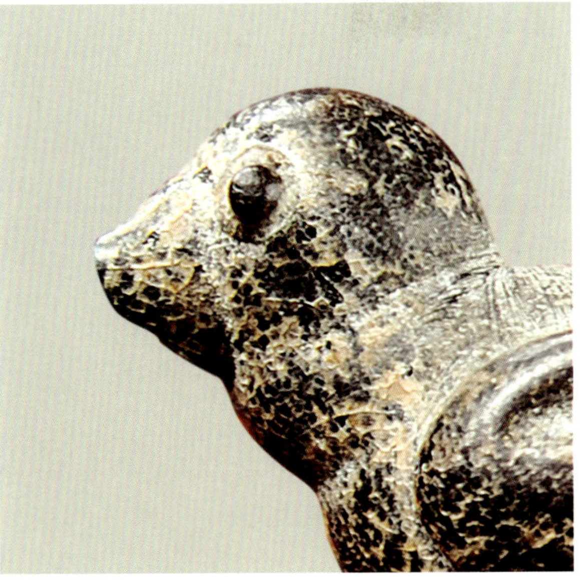

FIGURE OF A BIRD

The terracotta bird-shaped bead in black colour may have been used as a pendant. The beak of the bird is partly broken and wings are in flying posture. The bird may have been auspicious as suggested by the ornamentation on its wings and neck.

Provenance:	Kaushambi, Uttar Pradesh
Material:	Terracotta
Date:	Early Historic
Dimension:	2.8 x 2.5 cm
Acc. No.:	AM-BED-99.86

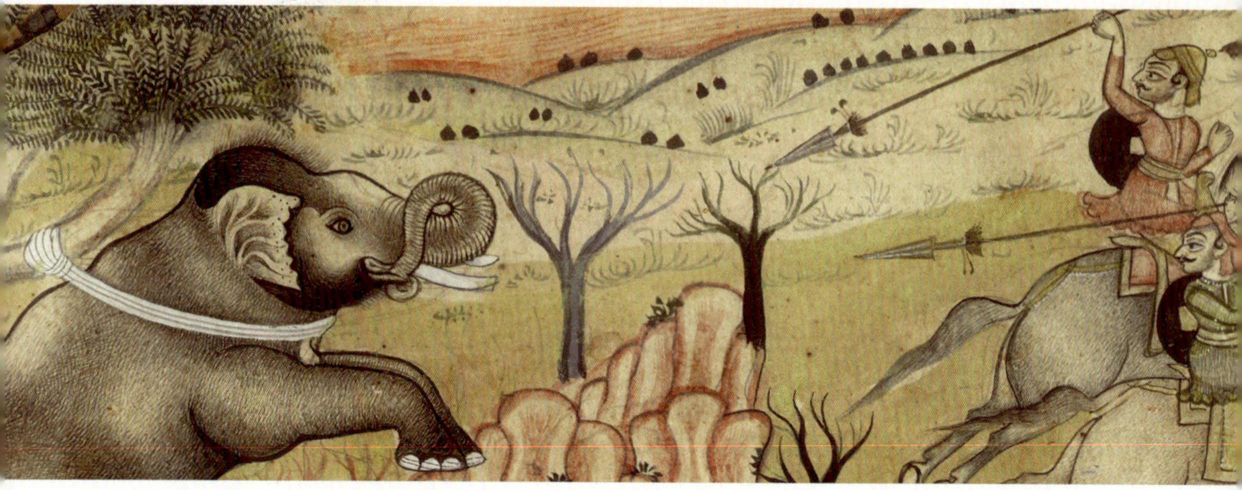

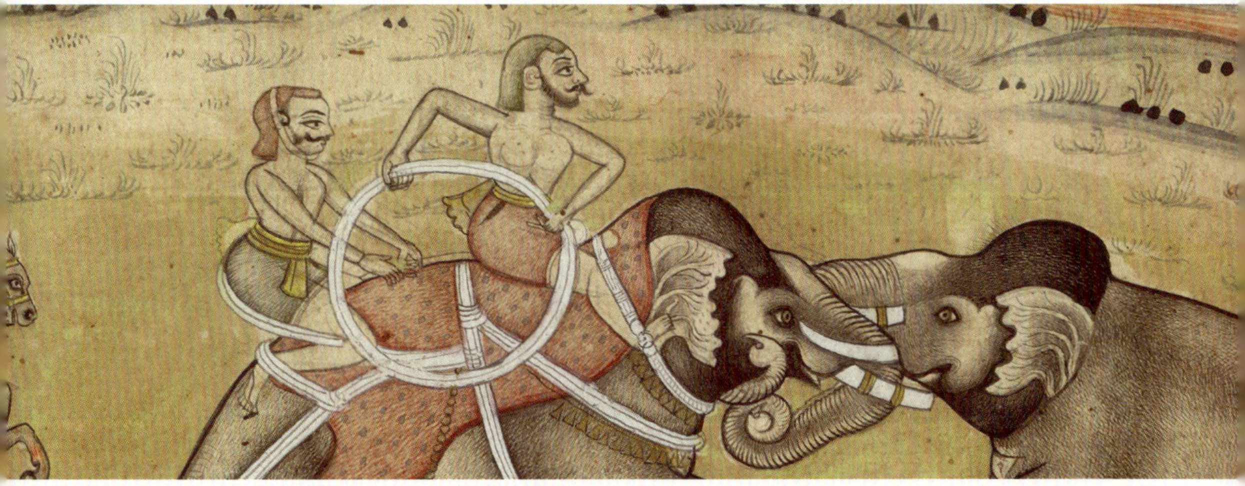

MINIATURE PAINTING
GALLERY

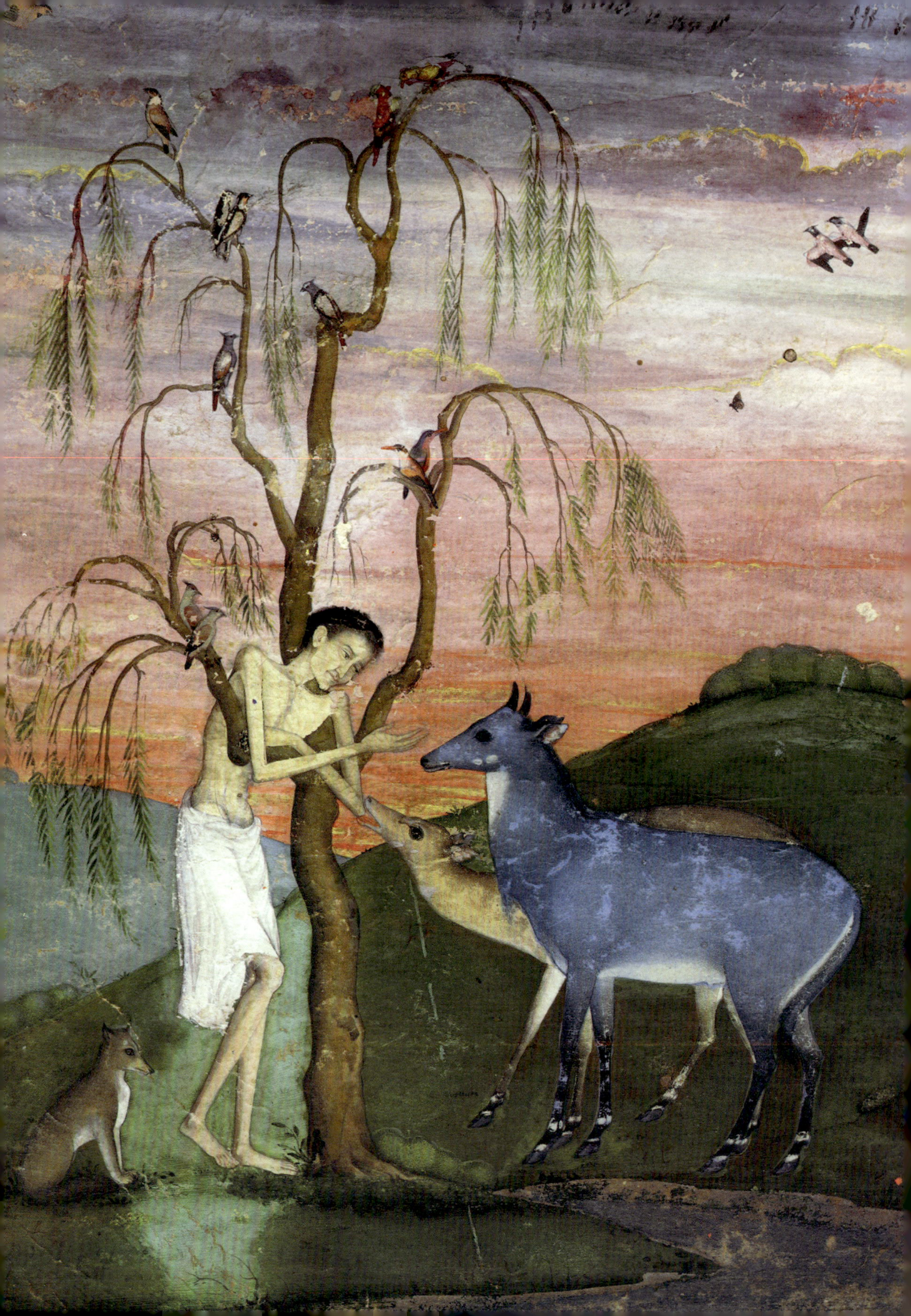

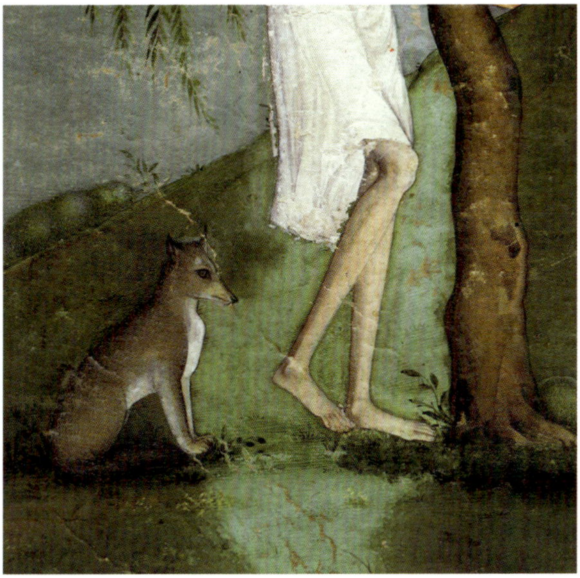

MAJNUN WITH NILGAI

There is a representative collection of Indian miniatures of different schools and kalams in the Allahabad Museum. A fair number of these are Mughal paintings from Delhi and Lucknow, the principal centres of Mughal Art.

This is one such painting. The artist is unknown. It shows an emaciated man (Majnun) with his body leaning against a tree, one of his hands stretched towards a pair of Nilgais in front of him.

Provenance: Malwa, Rajasthan
Material: Paper
Date: 17th century CE
Dimension: 16.51 x 11.43 cm
Acc. No.: AM-MIN-1189

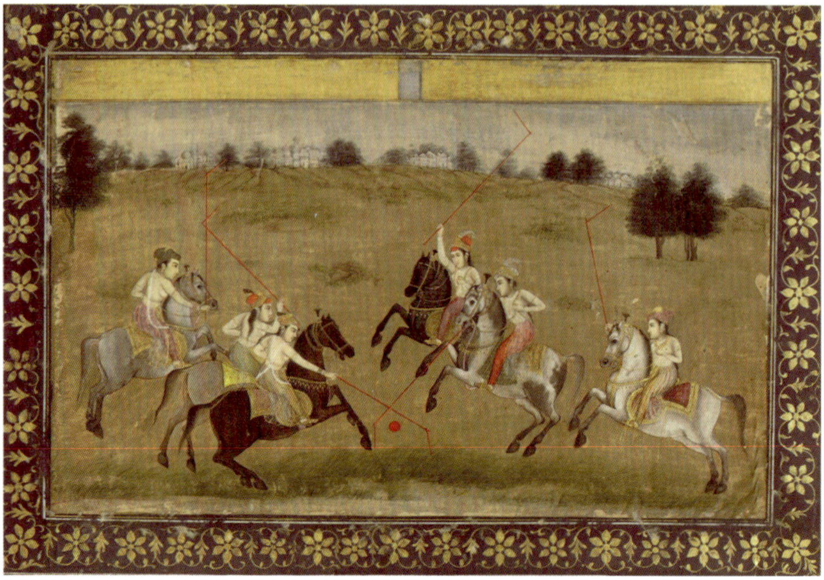

PRINCESS PLAYING POLO

Historically speaking, Mughal women played polo and enjoyed horse riding and hunting as much as their male counterpart as evident from Mughal paintings. This painting shows two groups of three ladies playing polo. Artist unknown.

Provenance: Rajasthan
Material: Paper
Date: c. 18th century CE
Dimension: 22.225 x 13.97 cm
Acc. No.: AM-MIN-1001

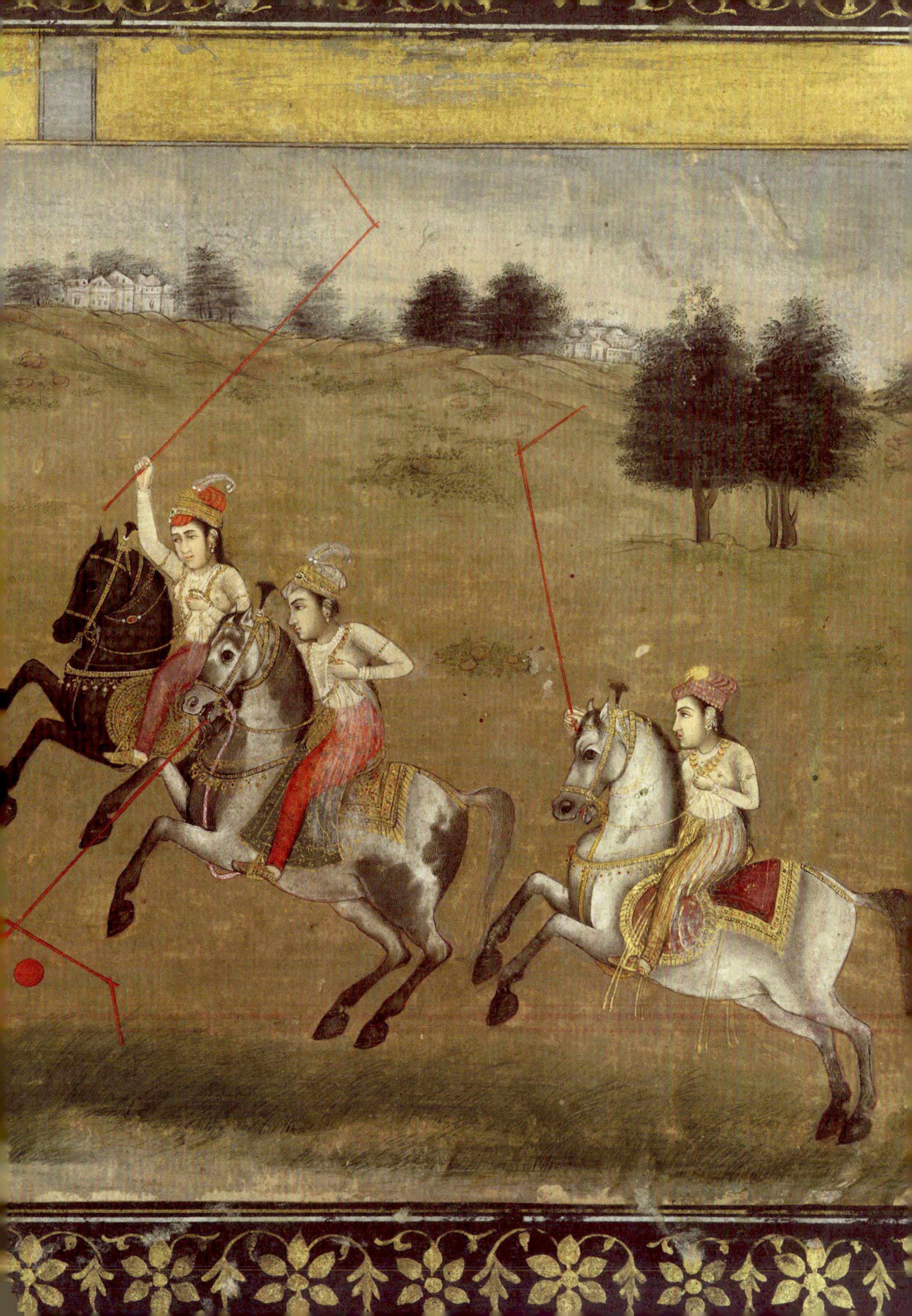

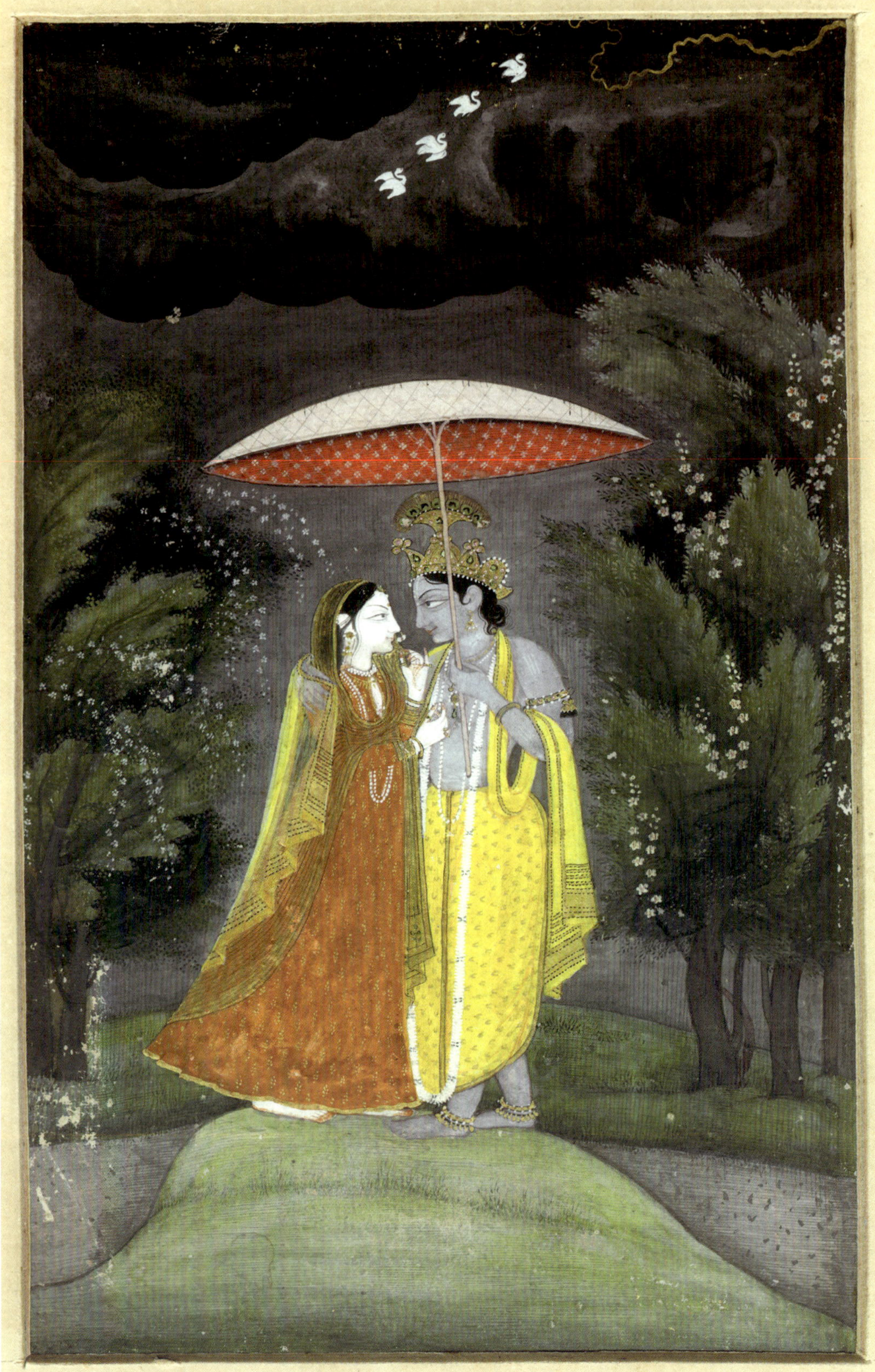

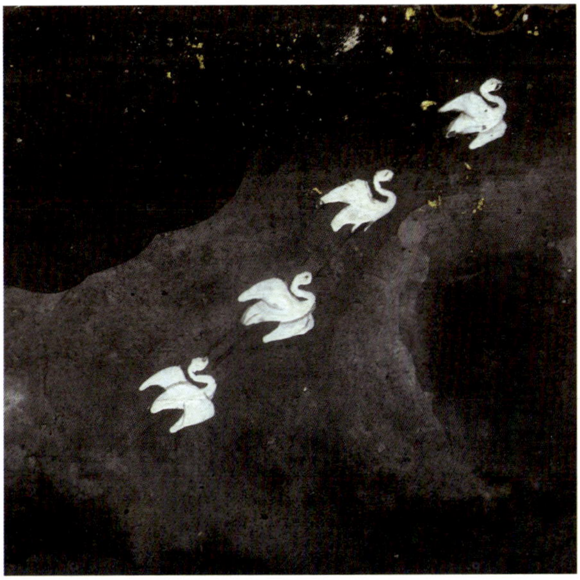

RADHA AND KRISHNA IN THE RAIN

Practically all the schools of Rajasthani Art are represented in the Allahabad Museum collection. The Rajasthani School had its centres at Bundi, Malwa, Mewar, Jaipur, Jodhpur, Nathdwara, and Kishangarh. This painting from Bundi shows Radha and Krishna under an umbrella caught in the rain. A series of herons are shown flying in the sky. Dark clouds and flash lightning indicate rainy day ahead.

Provenance: Bundi, Rajasthan
Material: Paper
Date: 18th century CE
Dimension: 21.59 x 15.88 cm
Acc. No.: AM-MIN-205

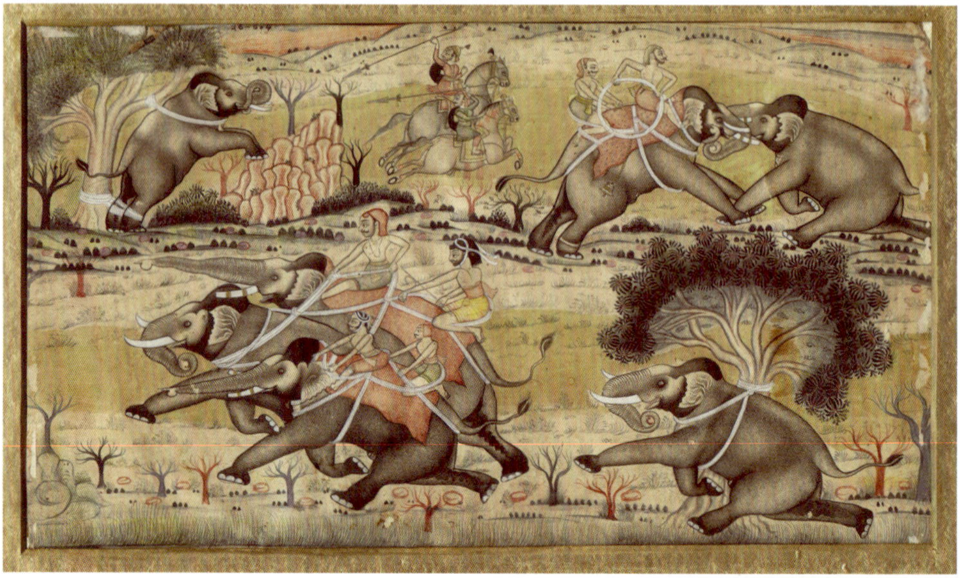

A CAPTURE OF ELEPHANTS

A coloured line drawing, this picture shows the use of elephants at warfare and how wild ones were tamed for that purpose.

In the foreground we see an elephant fastened to a tree with ropes and mahouts of two trained elephants lassoing a wild elephant. In the background we see another elephant tied to a tree struggling to break free, two soldiers on horseback and a tame elephant fighting with a wild elephant as the riders get ready to lasso it with a rope.

Provenance: Bundi, Rajasthan
Material: Paper
Date: c. 18th century CE
Dimension: 37.465 x 22.86 cm
Acc. No.: AM-MIN-1254

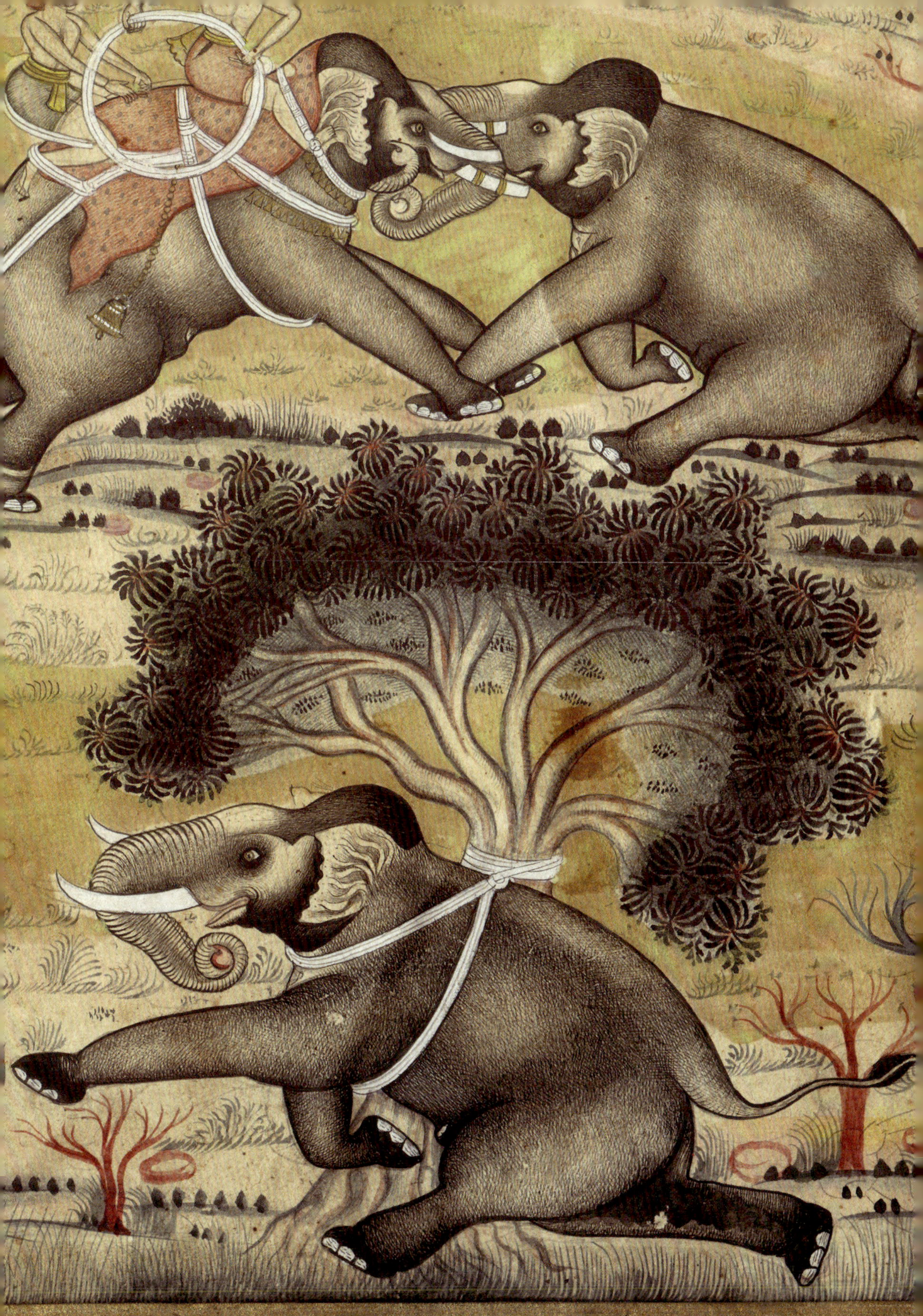

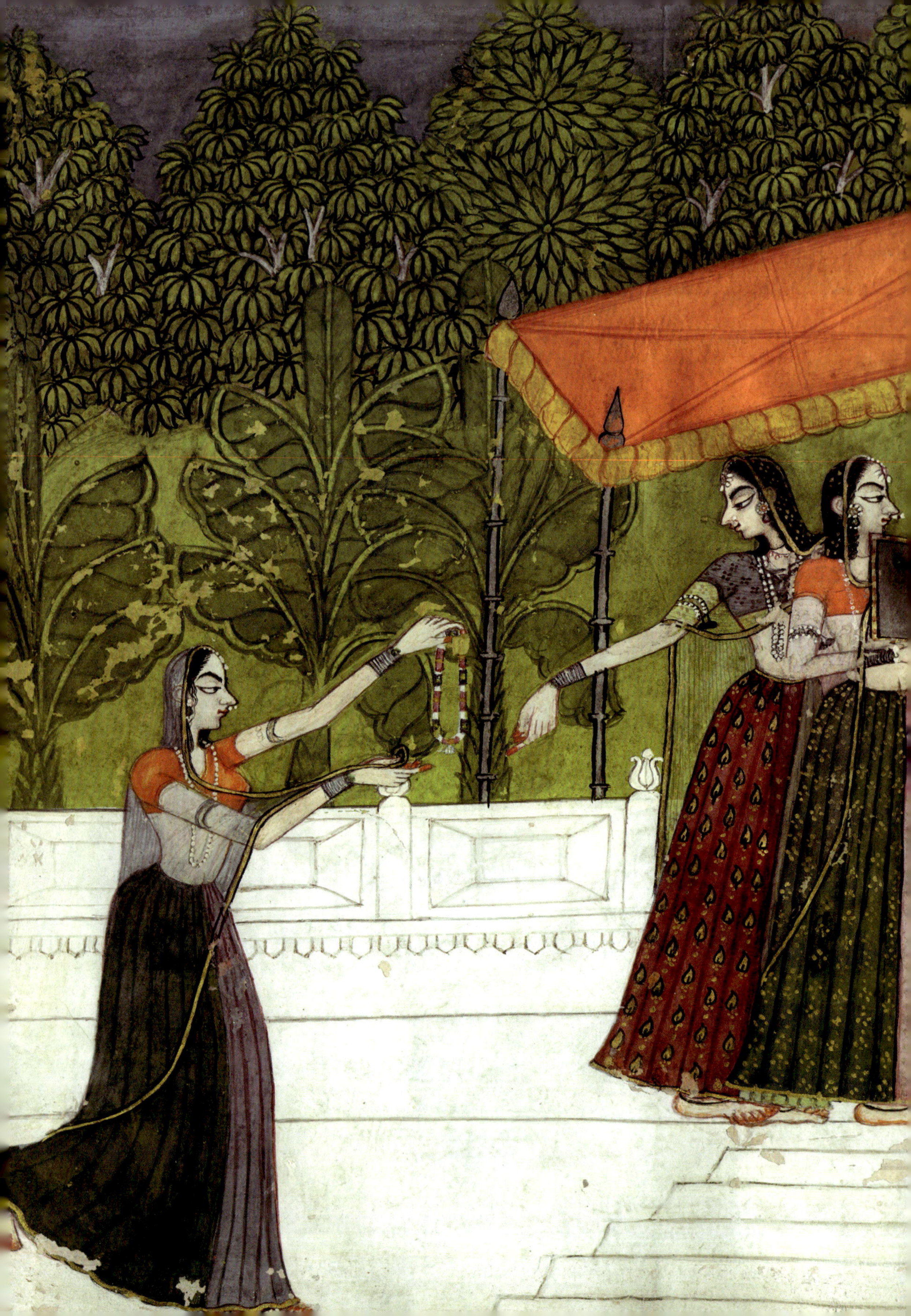

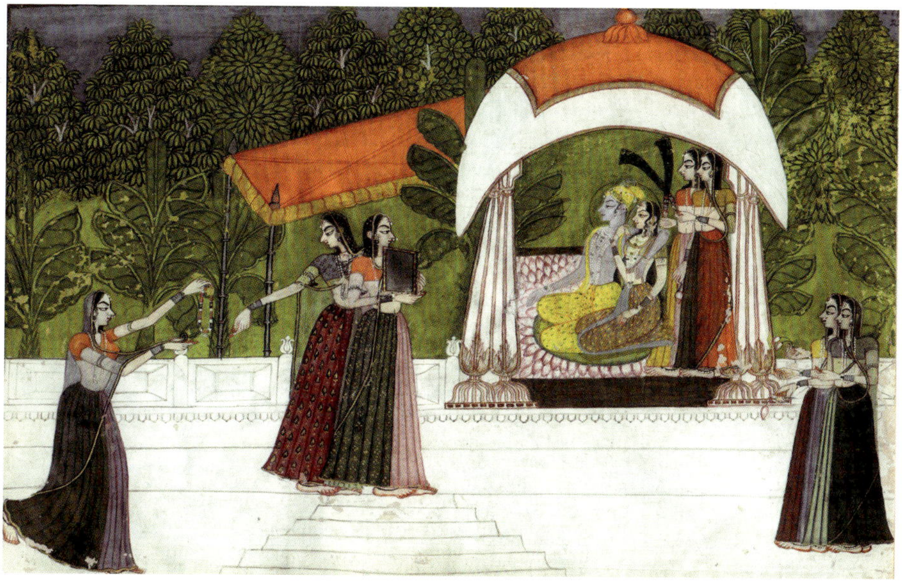

KING AND QUEEN IN A GARDEN PAVILION

In this painting, a king and queen are seen seated under a canopy, set inside the palace garden. Two female attendants stand behind while two are in front. On the extreme left, a lady is holding a garland in her hand and rushing towards the couple.

Provenance: Kishangarh
Material: Paper
Date: c. 18th century CE
Dimension: 33.655 x 22.225 cm
Acc. No.: AM-MIN-593

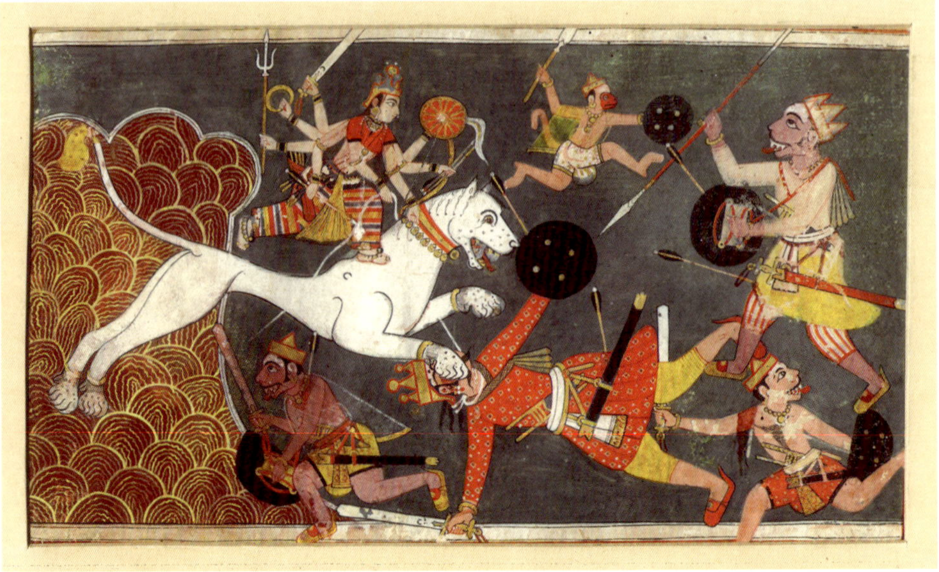

DEVI KILLING THE DEMONS

This image of a Devi with eight arms is seen standing on a white lion, jumping from a hill. One claw of the lion rests on the face of a demon, who has fallen on the ground. It is a battlefield with many demons brandishing their arms to protect themselves.

Provenance: Malwa
Material: Paper
Date: c. 17th century CE
Dimension: 20.955 x 14.605 cm
Acc. No.: AM-MIN-325

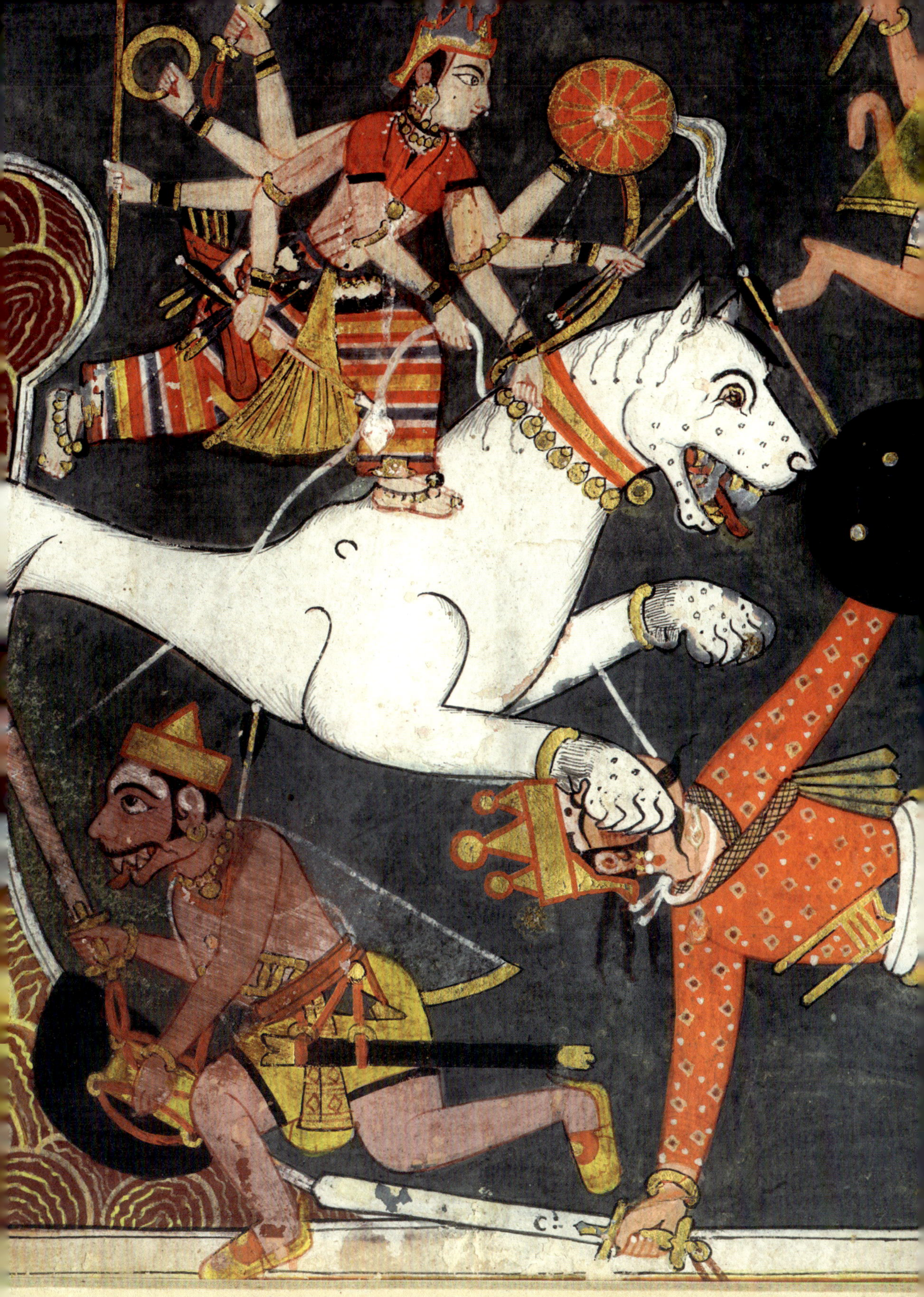

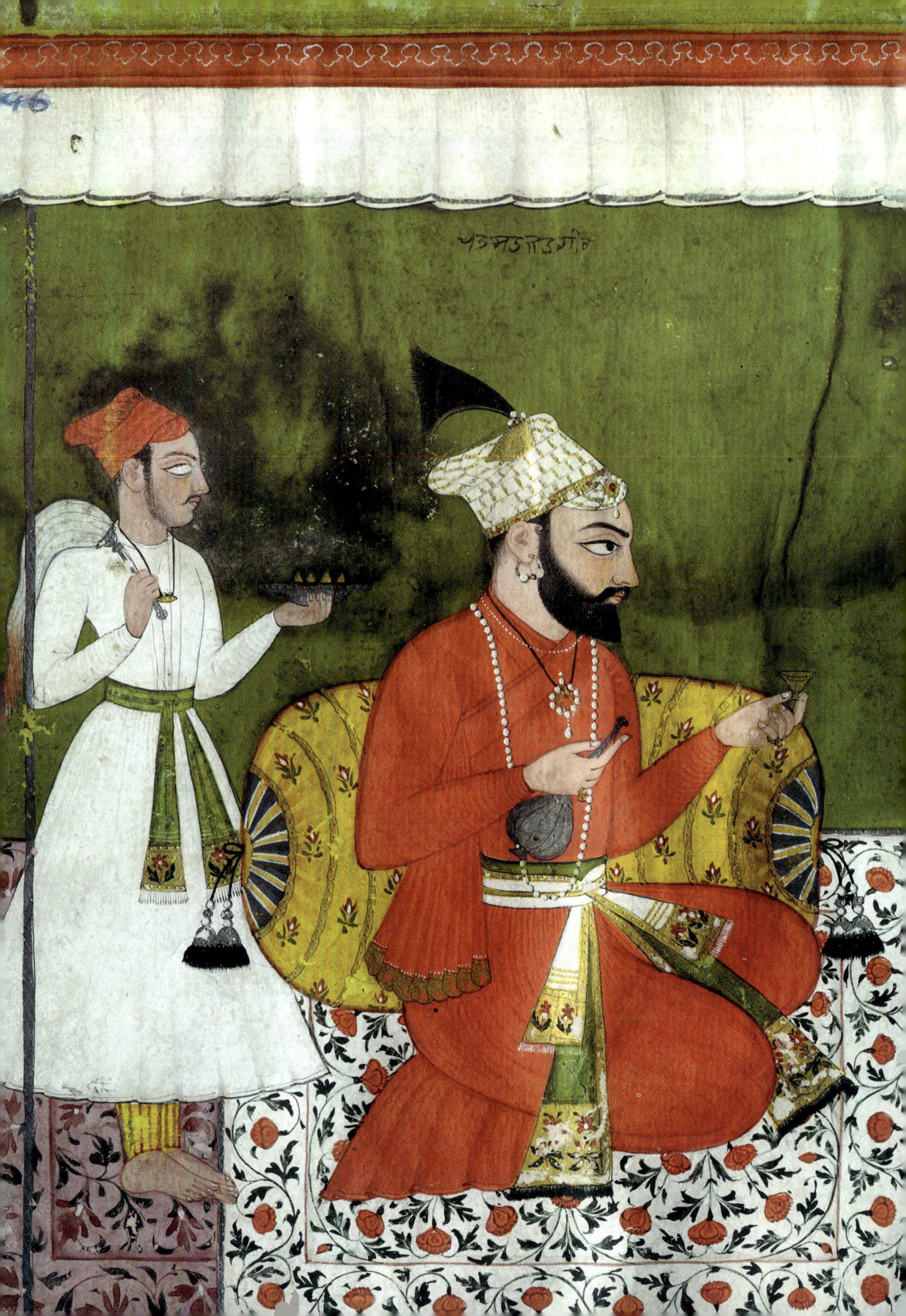

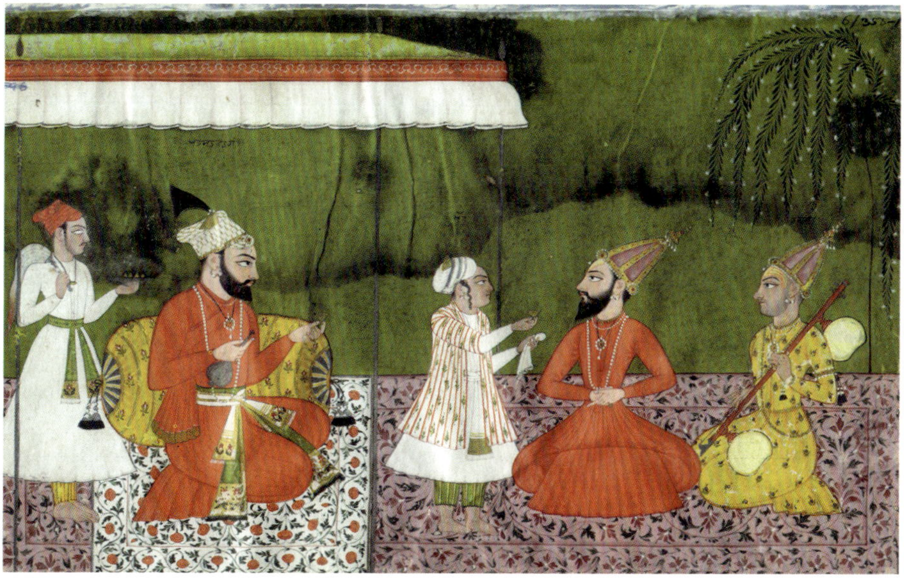

JAHANGIR OFFERING POISON TO THE GOSAIN

A beautiful painting of Jahangir seated under a canopy. He holds a jar in one hand and a cup in the other. Behind him stands an attendant. Facing him are persons wearing conical caps and *jamas*. One of them is playing the *veena*. The other, a bearded person, assumed to be a Hindu ascetic, is being offered a cup by an attendant, assumed to be poison.

Provenance: Basoli
Material: Paper
Date: Early 18th century CE
Dimension: 26.035 x 17.145 cm
Acc. No.: AM-MIN-770

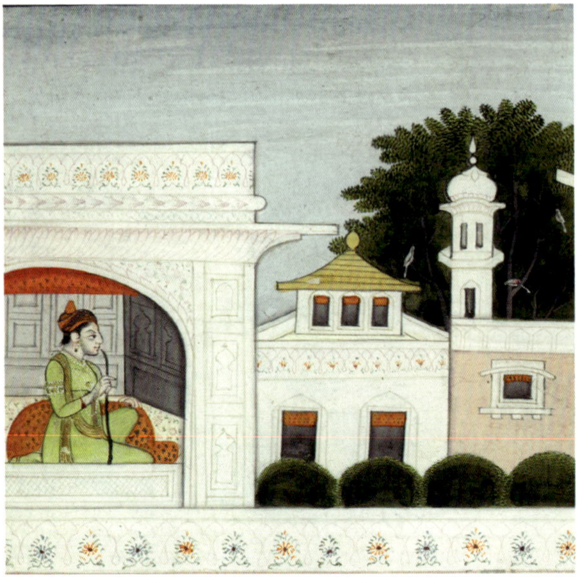

SCENE INSIDE A PALACE

A remorseful queen, with her bent head, is seen seated under a pavilion, inside a palace. She is attended by three female attendants. One of them is seen consoling the grief-stricken lady. Far away a king can be seen on the terrace, under a canopy, seating and smoking a hookah.

Provenance: Kangra, Himachal Pradesh
Material: Paper
Date: Late 18th century CE
Dimension: 25.4 x 17.78 cm
Acc. No.: AM-MIN-336

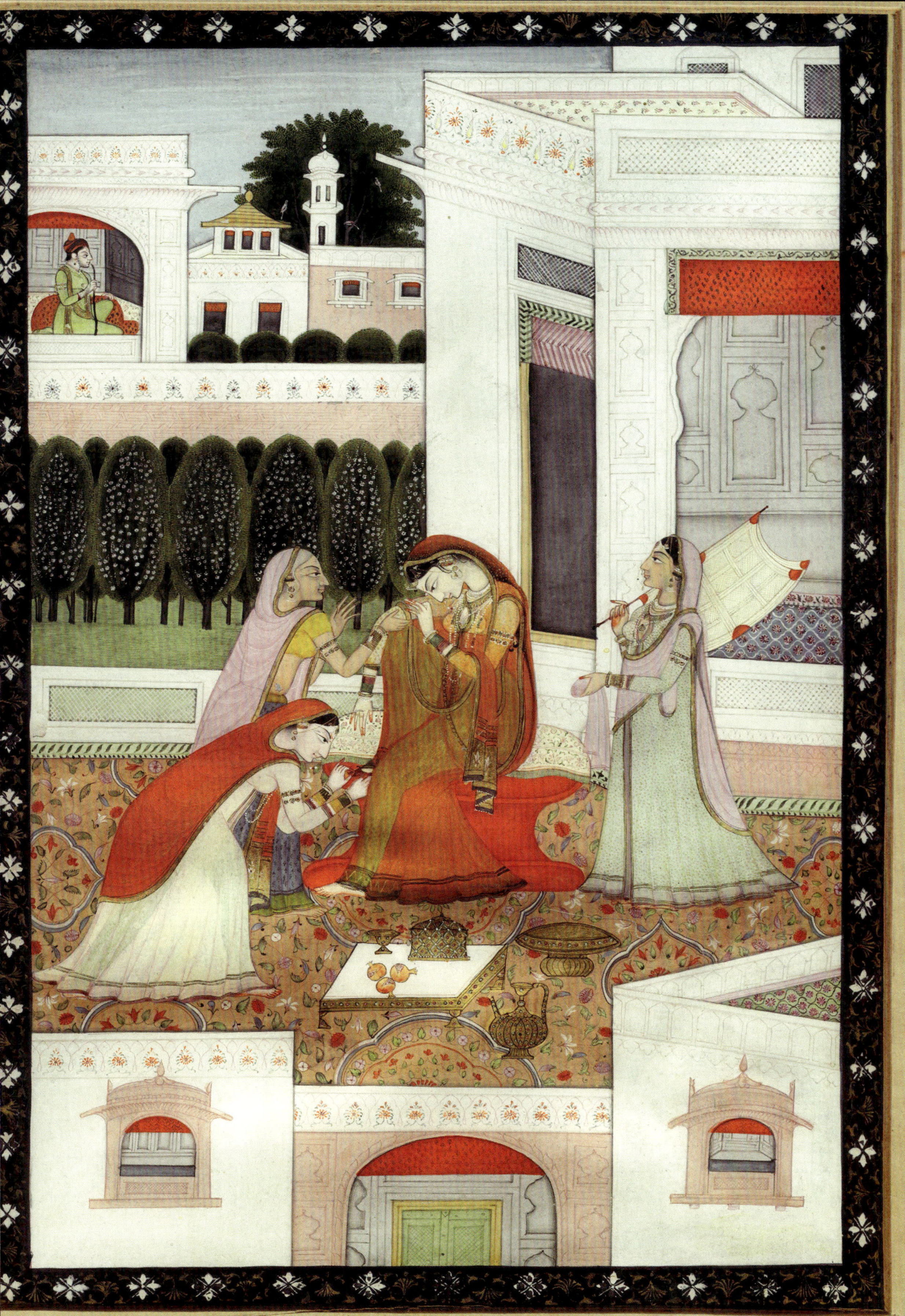

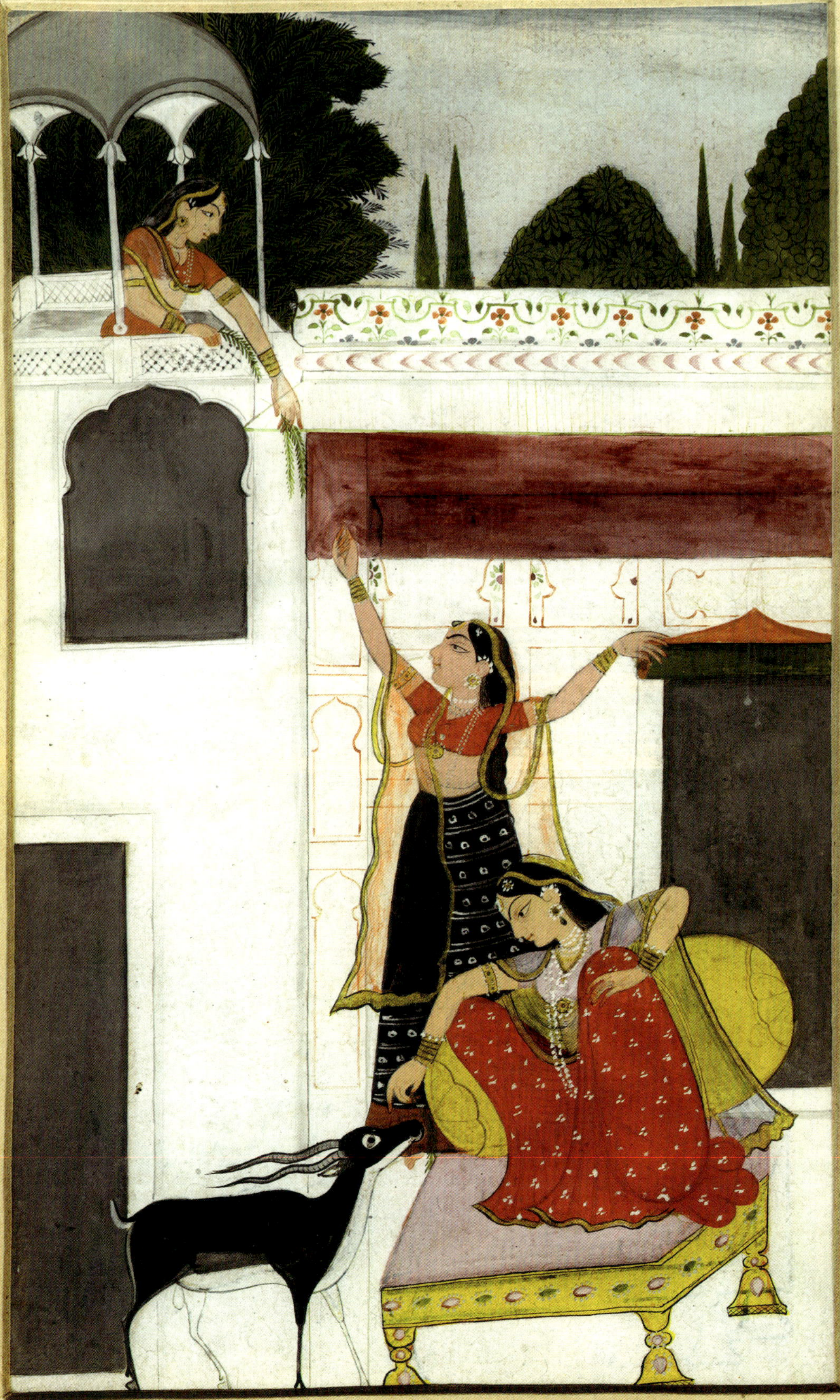

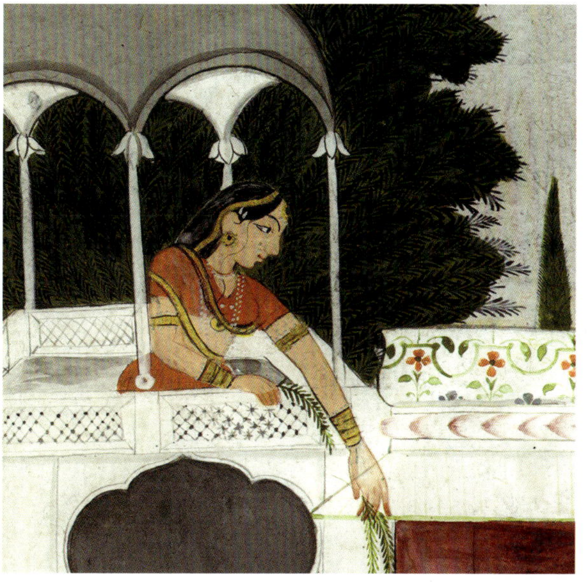

LADIES AND PET DEER

Inside an enclosed pavilion is a lady, seated on a *chauki*, feeding green leaves to a black antelope. Another lady, standing on the same chauki, is being supplied with leaves, from a third one, standing on a turret.

Provenance:	Kangra, Himachal Pradesh
Material:	Paper
Date:	c. 18th century CE
Dimension:	24.765 x 14.605 cm
Acc. No.:	AM-MIN-335

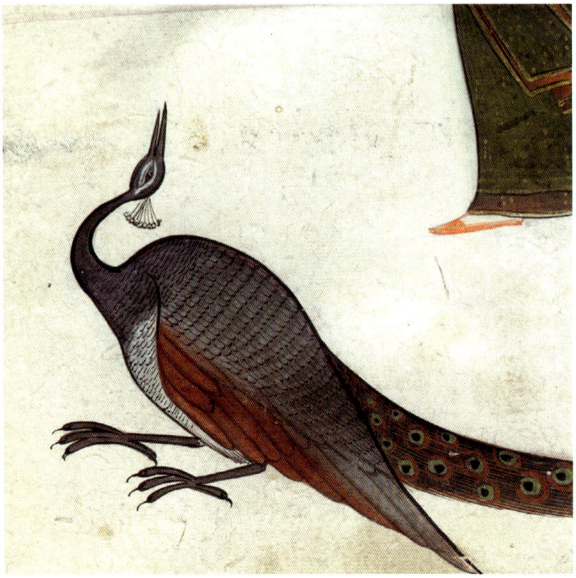

LADY PLAYING WITH A PEACOCK

In this painting a woman is seen holding a necklace before a peacock, which is trying to peck at it. It is a playful scene and probably representative of how women in royal households kept themselves amused when they were by themselves. The painting is presumably from Rajasthan as can be made out from the attire of the lady who wears a lehenga, a choli and an odhani, and the Indian national bird, peacock, which can be found aplenty in those areas.

Provenance: Kangra, Himachal Pradesh
Material: Paper
Date: c. 18th century CE
Dimension: 20.32 x 11.43 cm
Acc. No.: AM-MIN-797

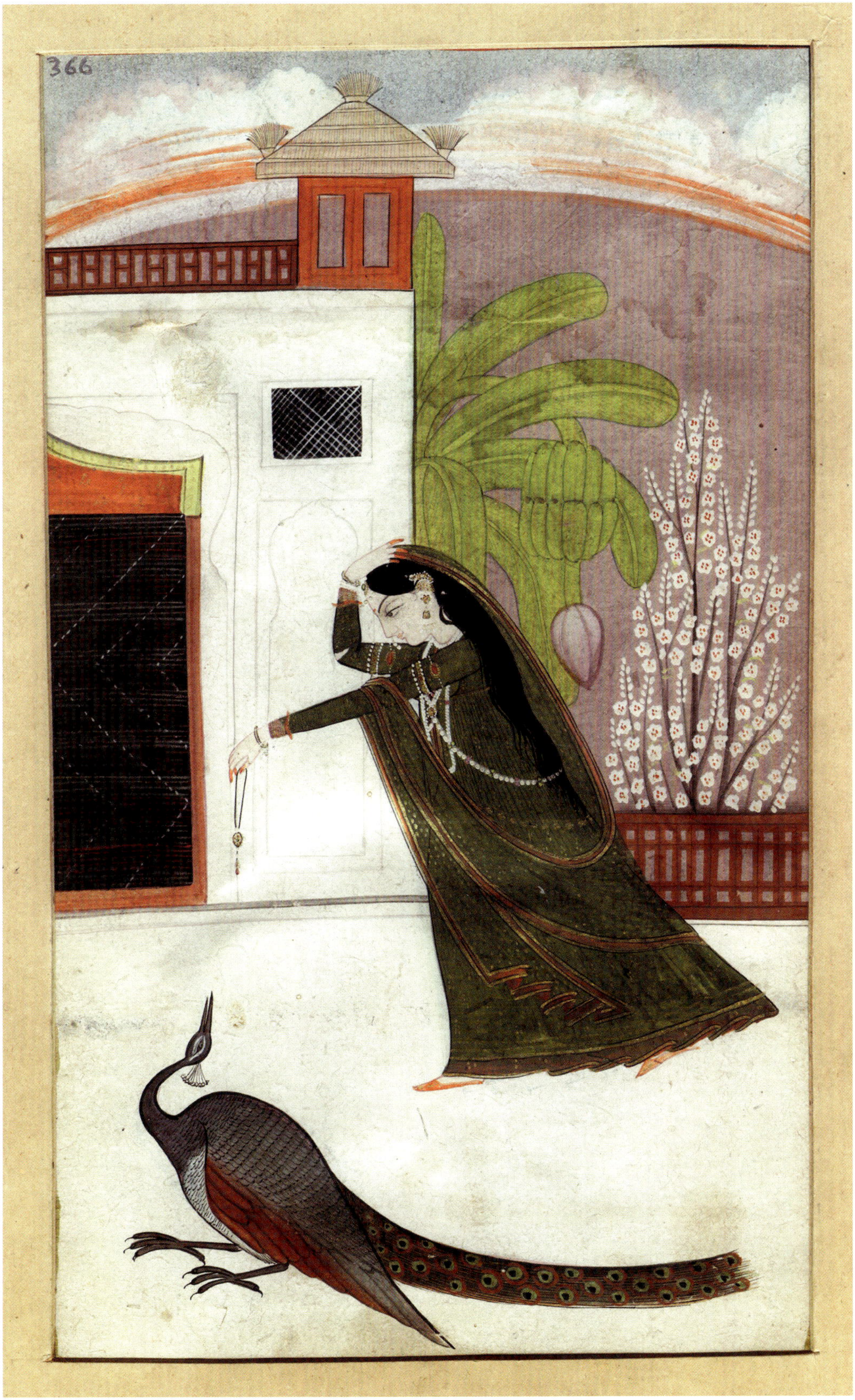
366

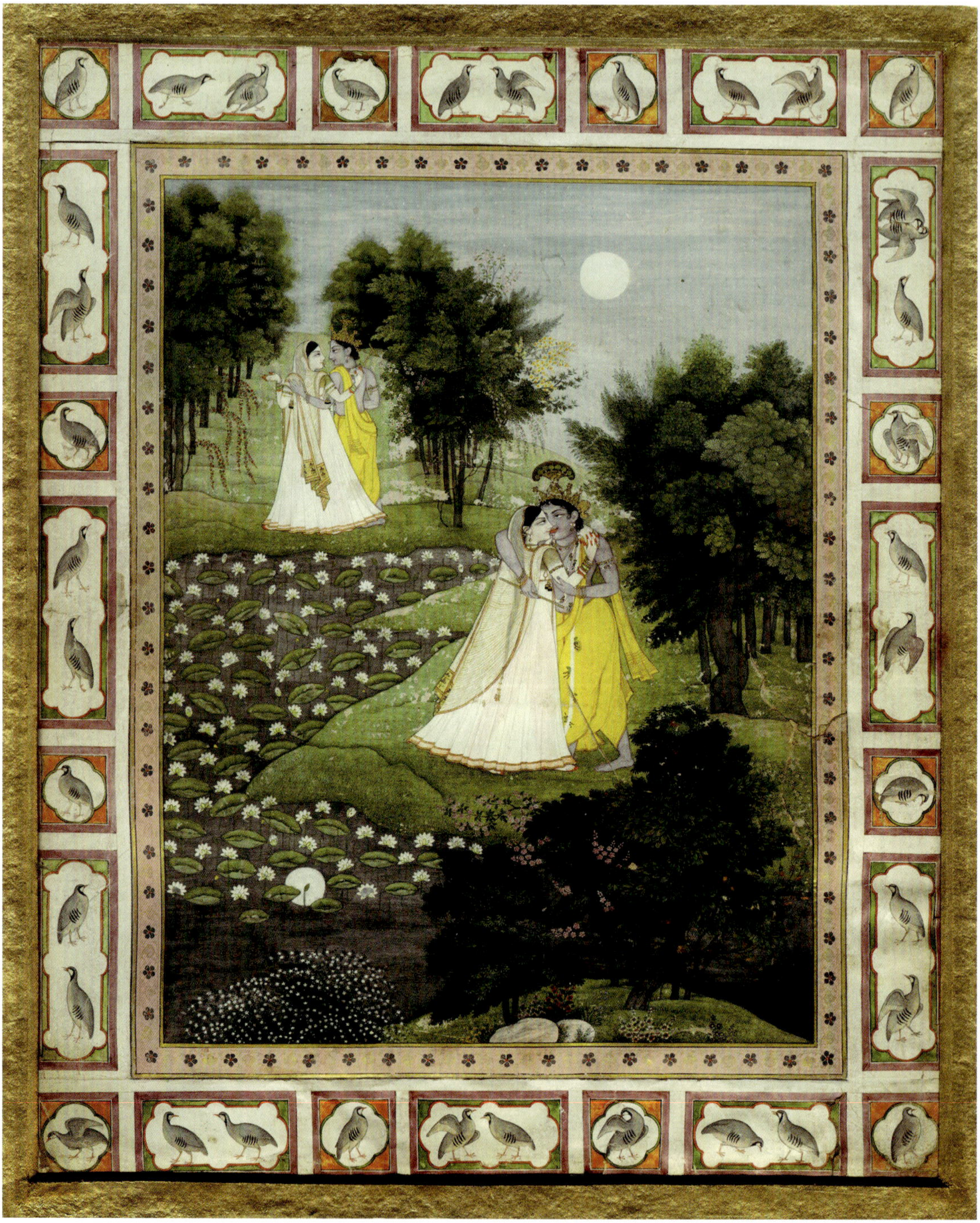

RADHA AND KRISHNA IN MOONLIGHT

The painting shows Radha and Krishna on the bank of a lake in a forest, enjoying moonlight. Both of them are shown together at two different places, embracing each other, in the same picture. The entire border is full of birds. Krishna wears yellow attire while Radha wears a white lehenga and a transparent gold coloured odhani.

Provenance: Kangra, Himachal Pradesh
Material: Paper
Date: c. 18th century CE
Dimension: 24.765 x 19.05 cm
Acc. No.: AM-MIN-632

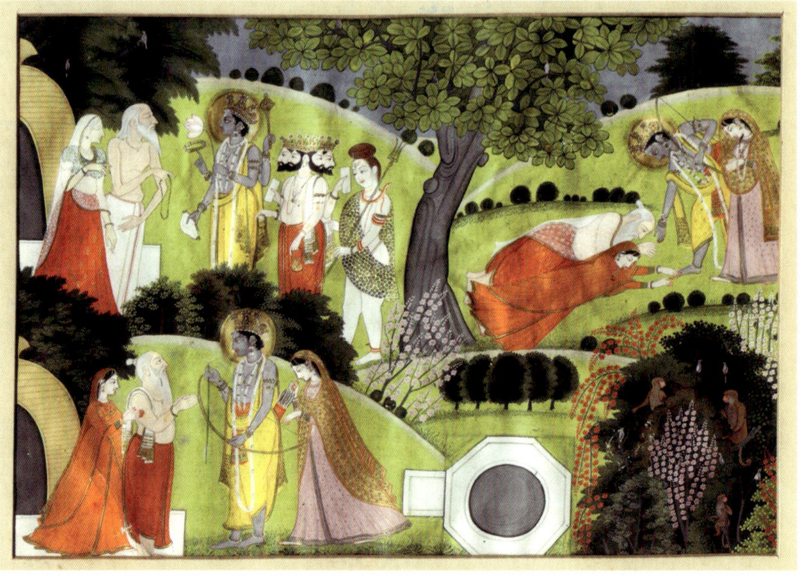

MANU AND SHATARUPA

The painting illustrates the Puranic story when kings Manu and Shatarupa obtained a boon from Vishnu. On the left top corner Manu and Shatarupa are seen standing at the door of their hermitage. Vishnu Brahma, and Siva are standing in front of them and offering boons. On the top right, both are seen lying prostrate on the ground, near the feet of Vishnu, along with Lakshmi. Below on the left corner, Manu and his wife are seen standing before the God with folded hands. On the right side monkeys and birds are playing in a blossomed grove.

Provenance: Kangra, Himachal Pradesh
Material: Paper
Date: c. 18th century CE
Dimension: 13.02 x 23.50 cm
Acc. No.: AM-MIN-35

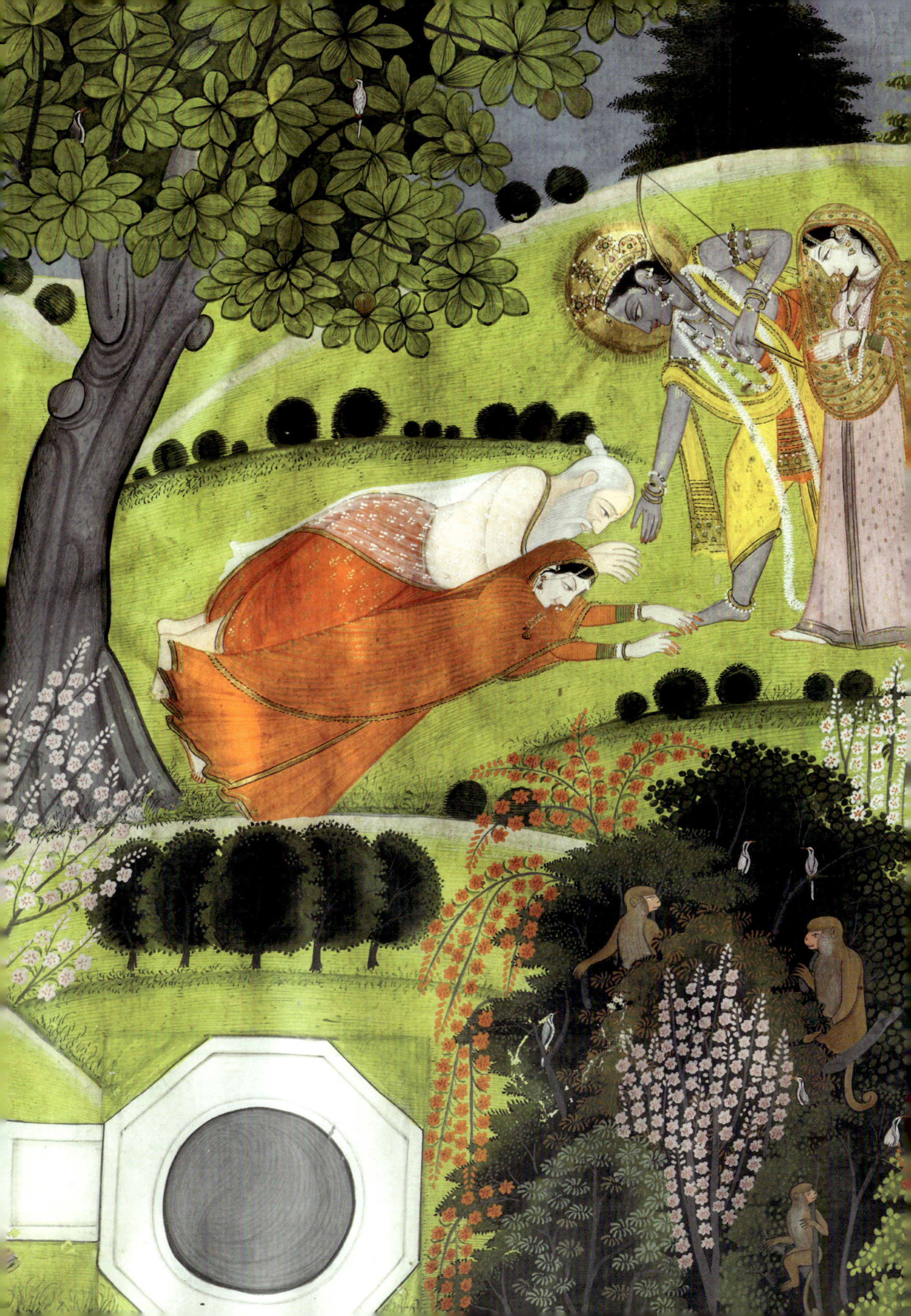

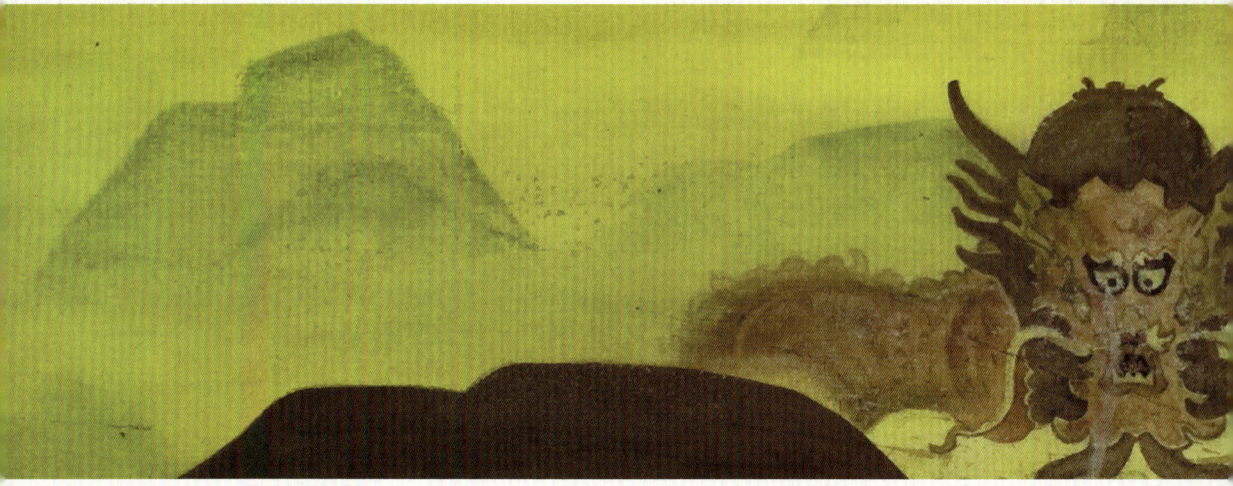

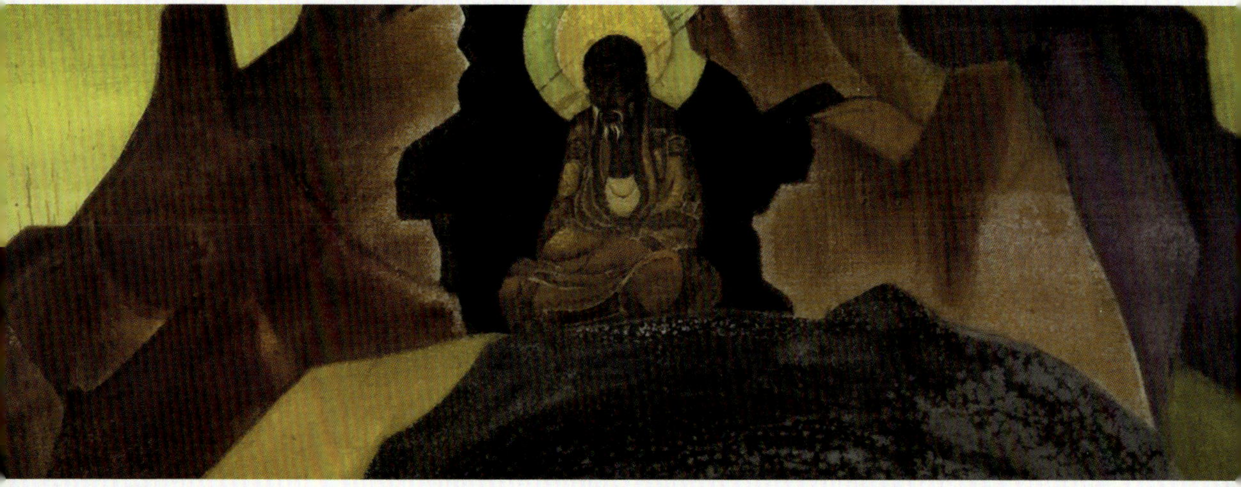

MODERN PAINTING
GALLERY

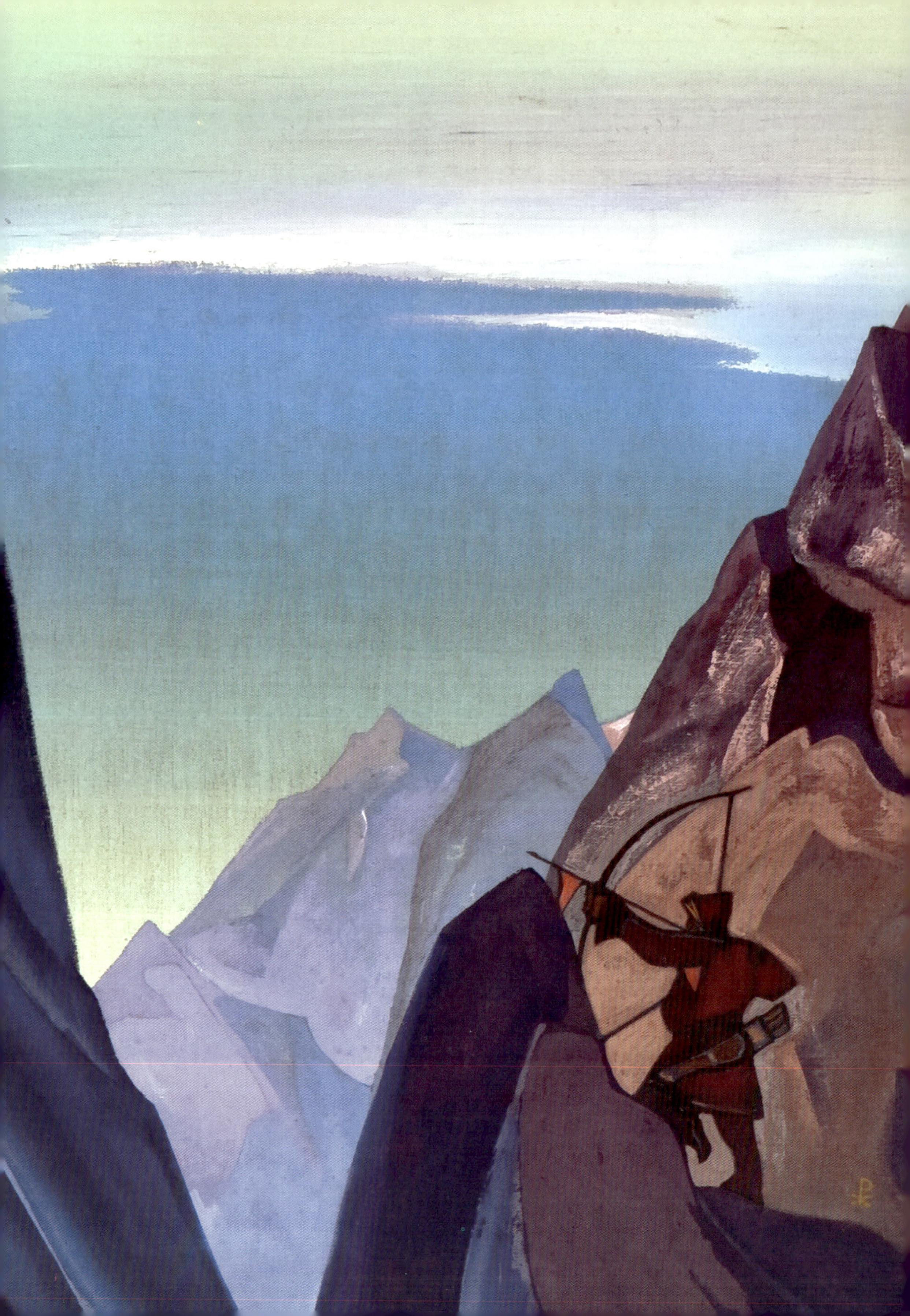

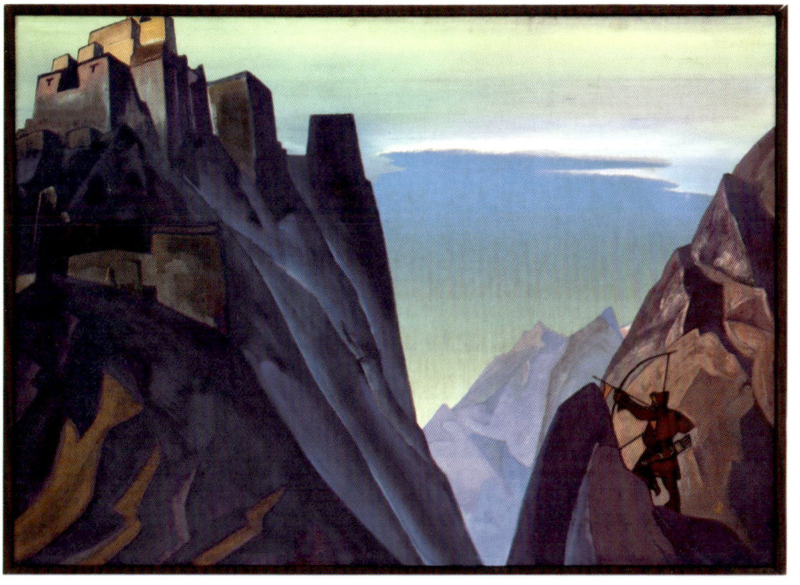

MESSENGER OF SHAMBALA

This picture shows the brilliant colours of a dawn across a deep gorge. From the shadows, a man is preparing to shoot an arrow across the deep valley, towards a monastery on the other side. The title of the painting suggests a Tibetan landscape where the legend of Shambala lives on.

Roerich had painted more than seven thousand canvases out of which nineteen are in the Allahabad Museum, varied in nature and compositions. The paintings of Roerich are the manifestation of his internal experience while 'he was moving from Europe to America to Asia and absorbing the auras of diverse peoples, making pilgrimage to remote places and always and everywhere scattering wisdom, planting seeds of beauty some of which has sprung up flowers, and scattered seeds of their own.' (Barnett D. Conlan in 'Roerich', Riga Museum, 1939).

Provenance: Not known
Material: Canvas
Medium: Tempera
Date: 20th century CE
Dimension: 110 x 83 cm
Acc. No.: AM-MOD-59
Artist: Nicholas Roerich

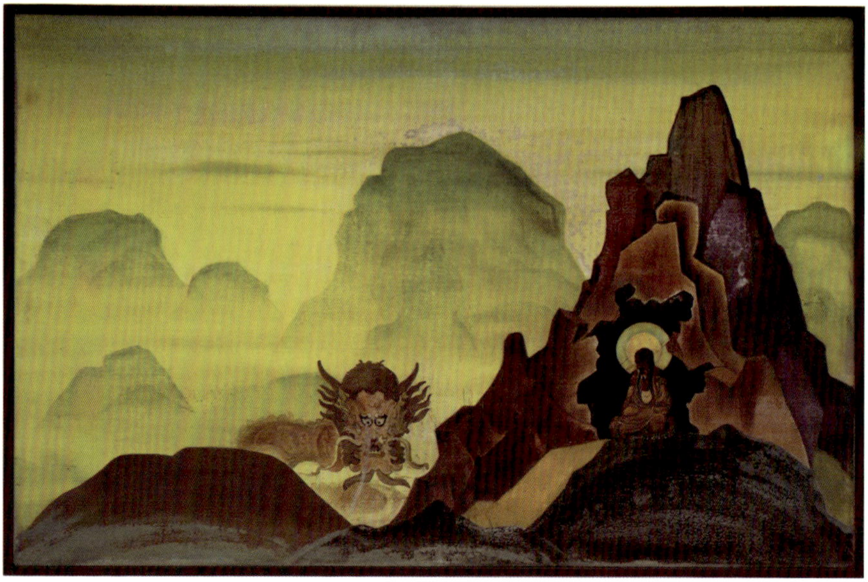

ARHAT

This painting depicts an *arhat* or a Buddhist monk, in advanced stages of spiritual understanding, meditating in a cave while a fearsome creature seems to be approaching him. The entire work is subsumed with an ethereal golden-yellow glow. The soft colours exude serenity against the inevitability of fate. This painting is reminiscent of Roerich's work, executed in Russia, just before the Bolshevik Revolution. Many of them were prophetic in nature, signalling the need to protect and preserve the spiritual and artistic heritage of the world.

The ideas and the ideals of Nicholas Roerich's works reflecting intense humanity and passion for culture and quest for mystic knowledge are vividly expressed in the collection of his paintings in the Allahabad Museum.

Provenance: Not known
Material: Tempera
Medium: Canvas
Date: 20th century CE
Dimension: 136 x 93 cm
Acc. No.: AM-MOD-55
Artist: Nicholas Roerich

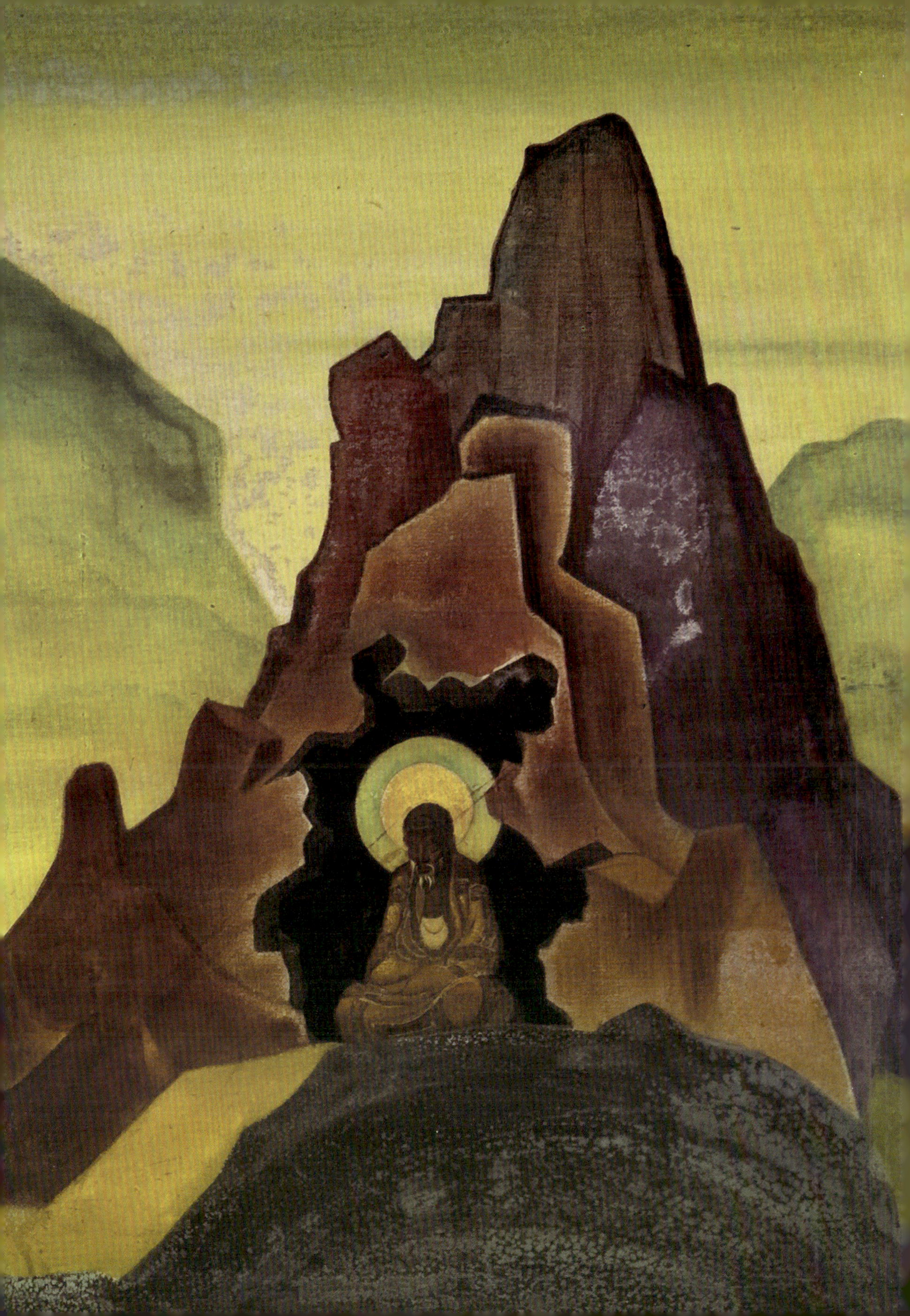

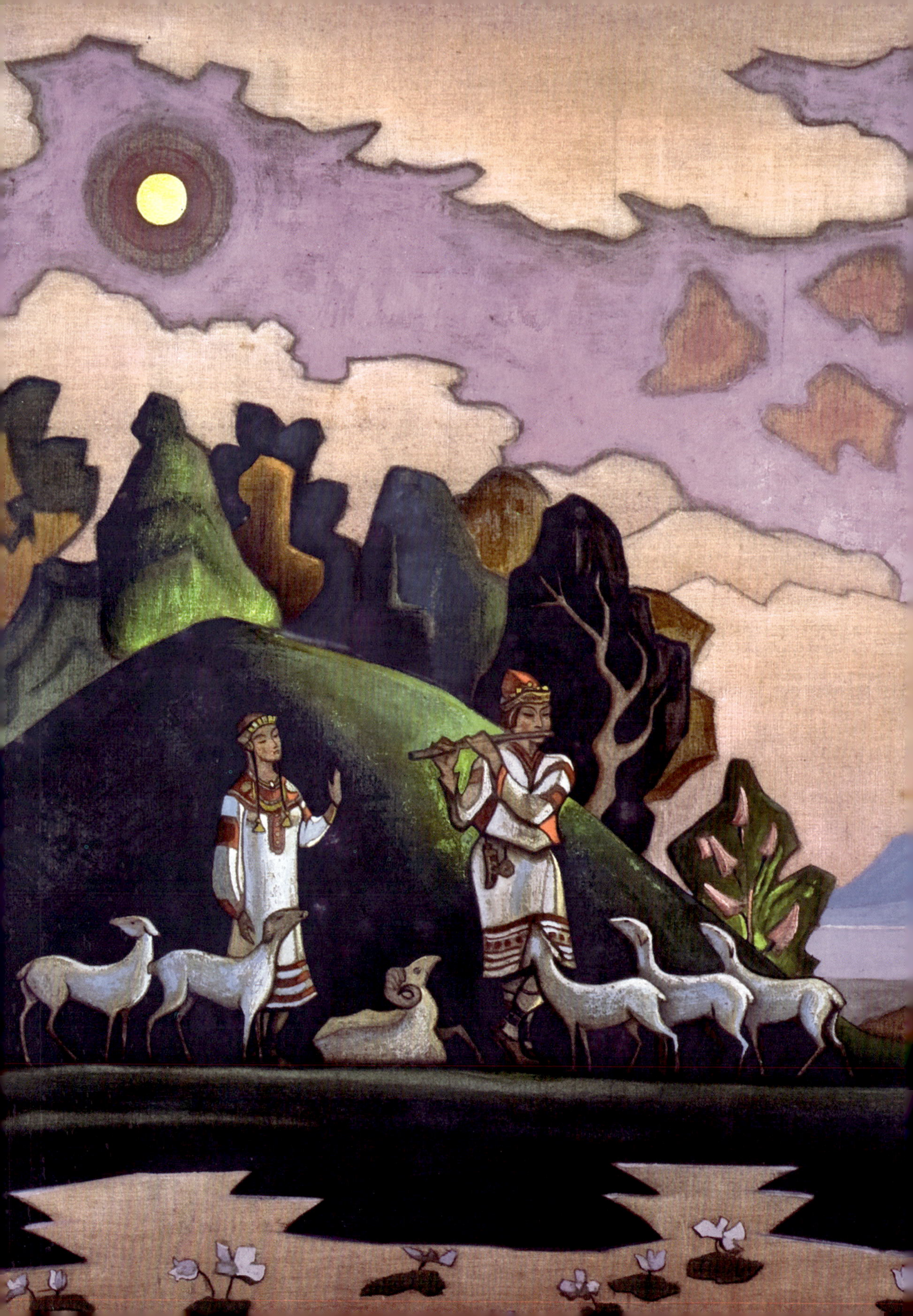

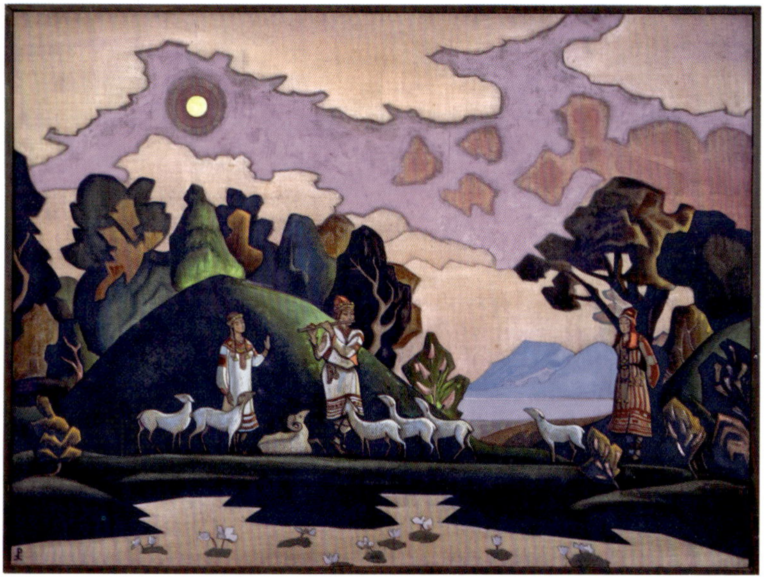

HOLY SHEPHERD

His belief in the universality of religions can be seen in this work where, he blends the figure of Krishna in the persona of the Slavic folk hero, Lel who is holding a flute amidst sheep, in place of cows of Krishna. With him are his two attendants, Kupava and Snegurochaka. The two attendants of Lel can be compared with the *gopis* of the Indian tradition. The painting depicts an idyllic sunset in which sheep graze peacefully.

Roerich's metaphors and vivid symbolisms in his work, which suggests mystical or spiritual experiences are directly inspired by the path followed by Jesus Christ, who too had such deep experiences.

Provenance:	Not known
Material:	Canvas
Medium:	Tempera
Date:	20th century CE
Dimension:	130 x 100 cm
Acc. No.:	AM-MOD-63
Artist:	Nicholas Roerich

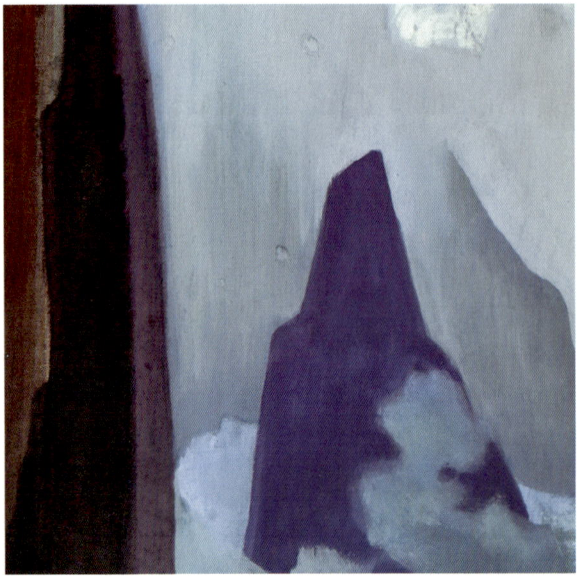

ECSTASY

The painting shows an ascetic seated on the pinnacle of a high peak, performing penances. Above him is the blue sky with clouds. With its brilliant colours of a monsoon sky, the picture shows the rishi eternally striving for communion with the great heights. It is a work suffused with a raw spirituality, capturing the moment of enlightenment.

Provenance:	Not known
Material:	Canvas
Medium:	Tempera
Date:	c. 20th century CE
Dimension:	136 x 93 cm
Acc. No.:	AM-MOD-48
Artist:	Nicholas Roerich

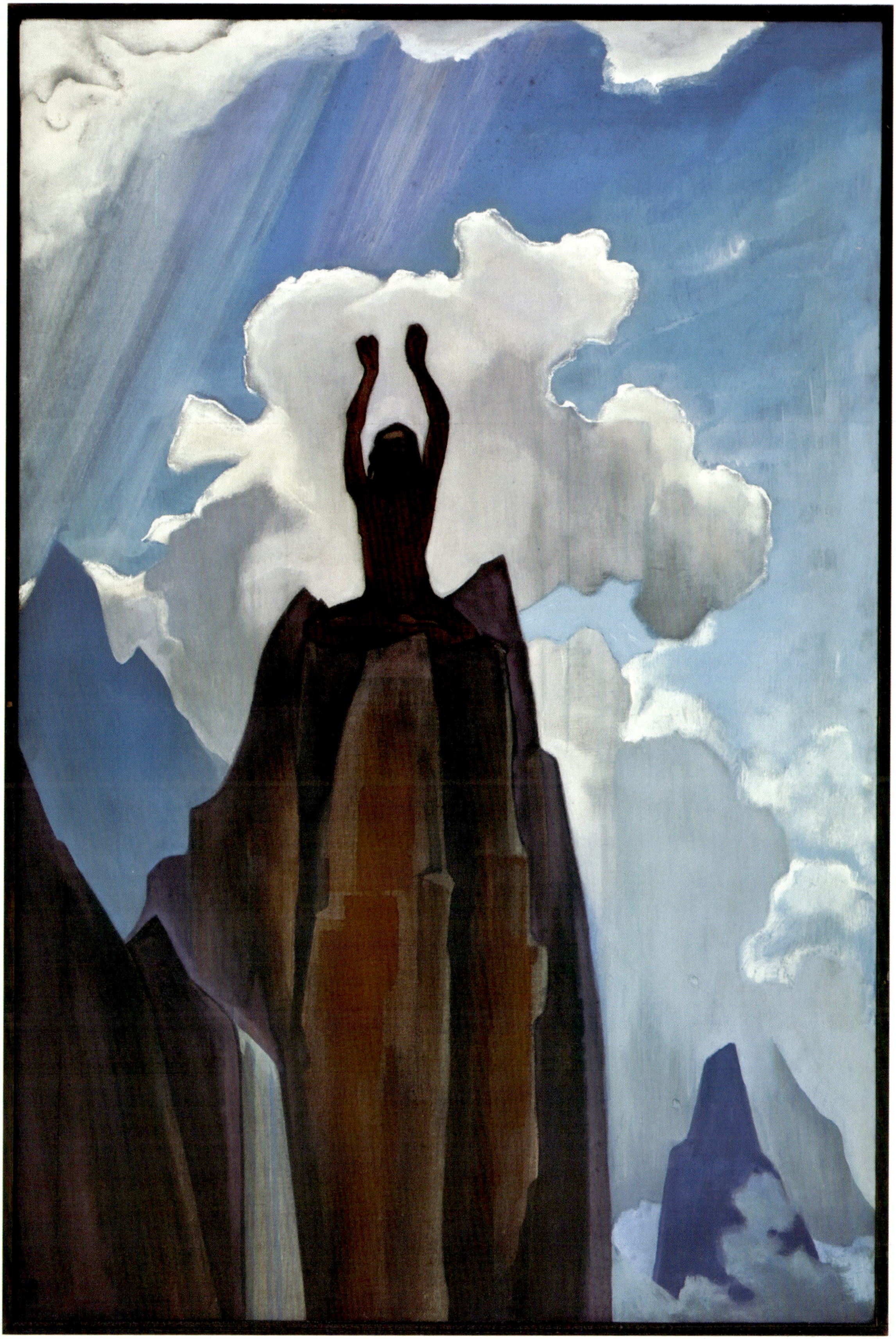

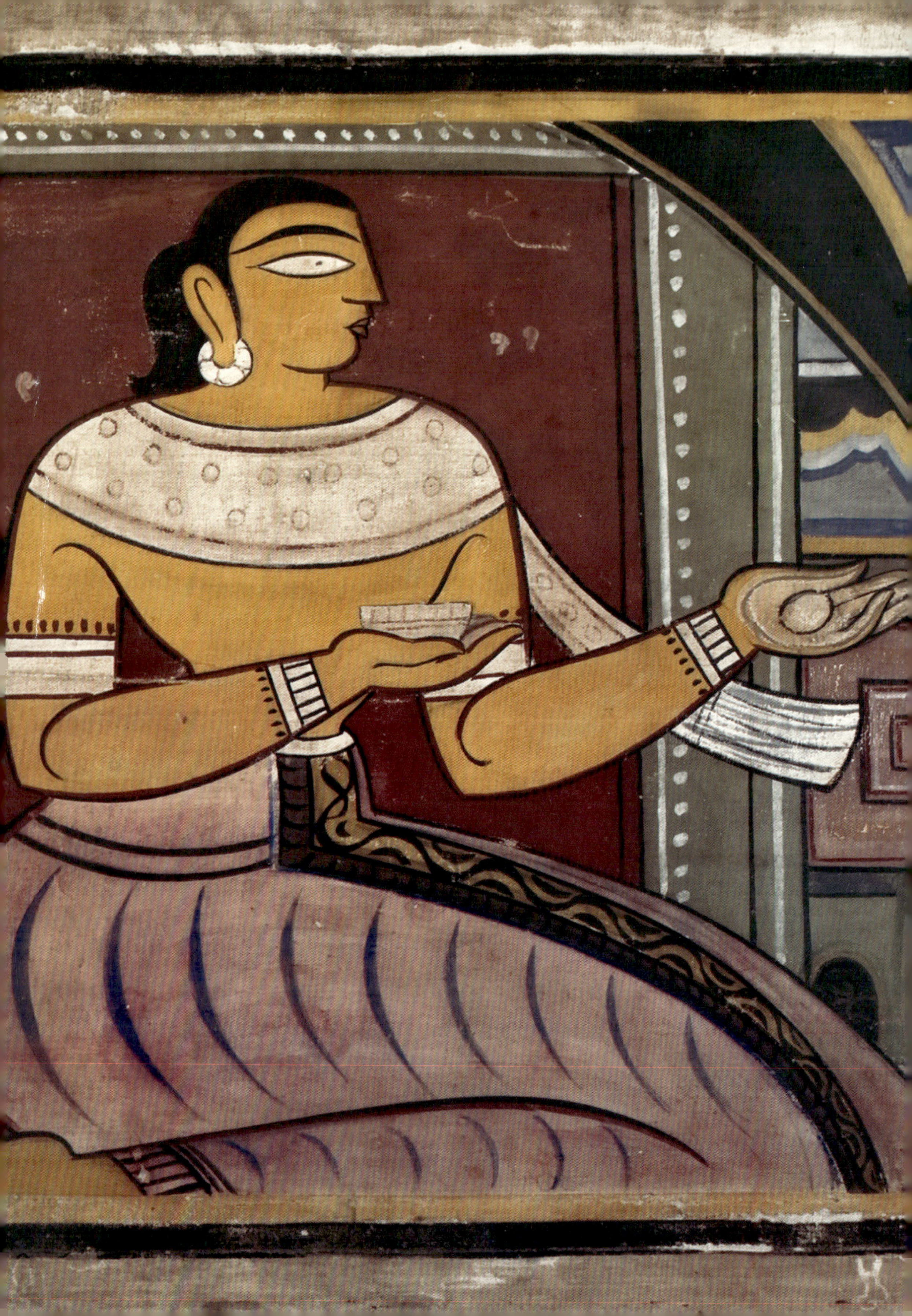

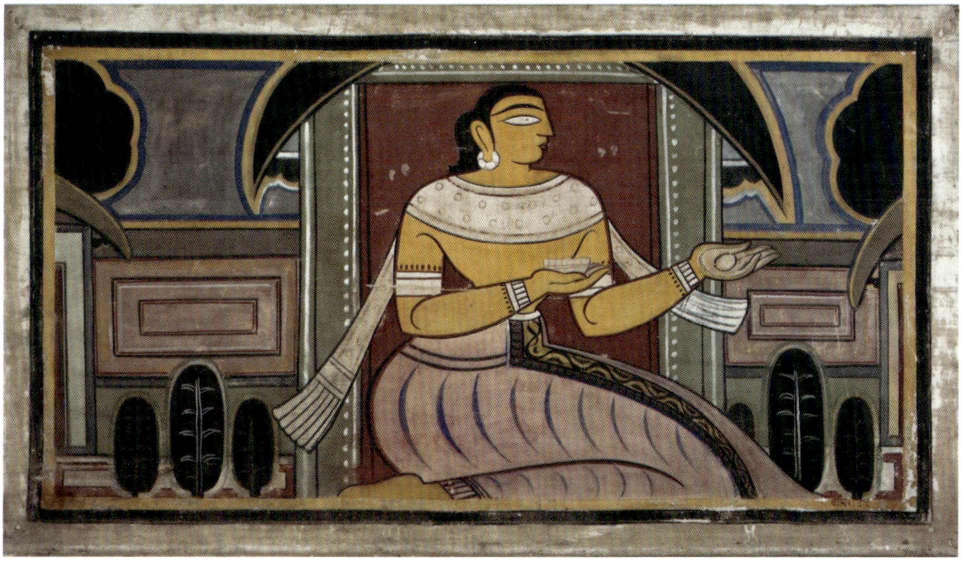

LADY SEATED IN FRONT OF A HOUSE

A lady sitting, holding a cup, probably at the front porch of her house. This is a typical Jamini Roy, inspired by the Kalighat Pata paintings. This painting is representative of a mature phase of his artistic repertoire. Jamini Roy had been honoured with the Padma Bhushan in 1955. One of the most famous pupils of Abanindranath Tagore, his artistic originality and contribution to the emergence of Modern Art in India remains unquestionable.

Provenance: Not known
Material: Cloth
Medium: Tempera
Date: 20th century CE
Dimension: 142 x 76.5 cm
Acc. No.: AM-MOD-311
Artist: Jamini Roy

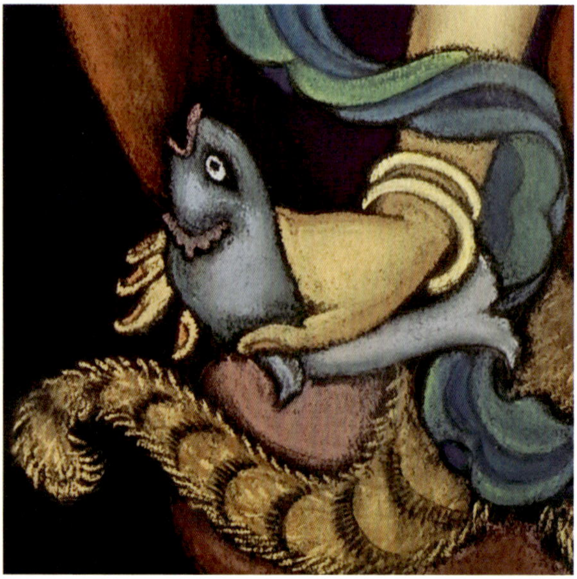

VAJRASATTVA

The painting depicts the seated figure of Vajrasattva of Buddhist religion. It is a deity with a pot and fish in his hand, an aureole encompassing his body. He represents the scary aspects. The painting resembles Buddhist thangakas of Vajrayana.

Anagarika Govinda (1908–1985), the German bhikkshu whose paintings are a part of the Modern Painting collection of the Allahabad Museum, was born Ernst Lothar Hoffman in Waldhiem, Germany. He was a precocious child who took to philosophical thinking at an early age. He became attracted to Buddhism at the age of eighteen. In 1928, Hoffman moved to Sri Lanka and acquired the name of Anagarika Govinda. He founded the International Buddhist Union in 1929 and therefore joined the teaching profession at Shantiniketan in 1932.

Provenance: India
Material: Paper
Medium: Pastel
Date: c. 20th century CE
Dimension: 64 x 54 cm
Acc. No.: AM-MOD-29
Artist: Anagarika Govinda

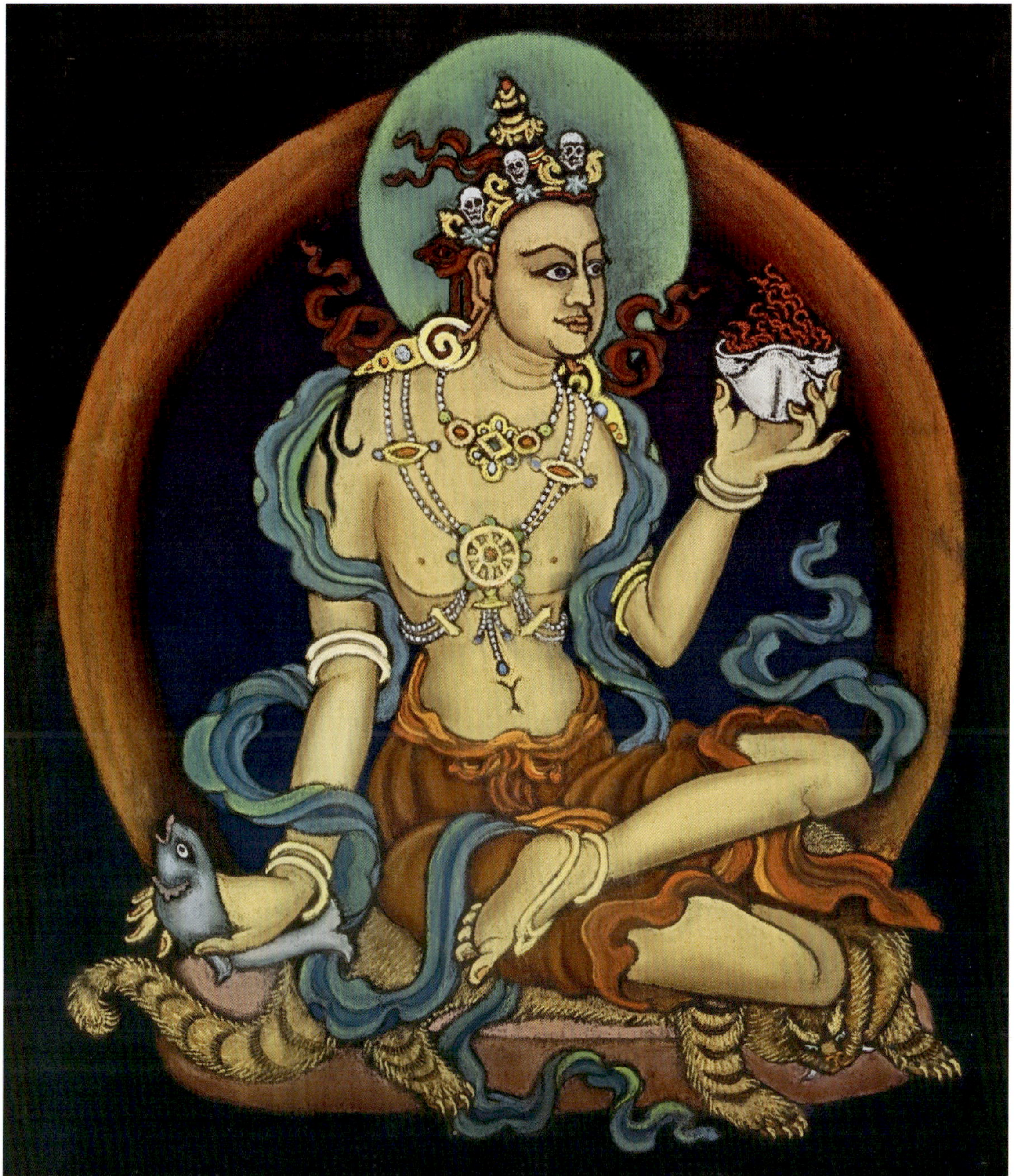

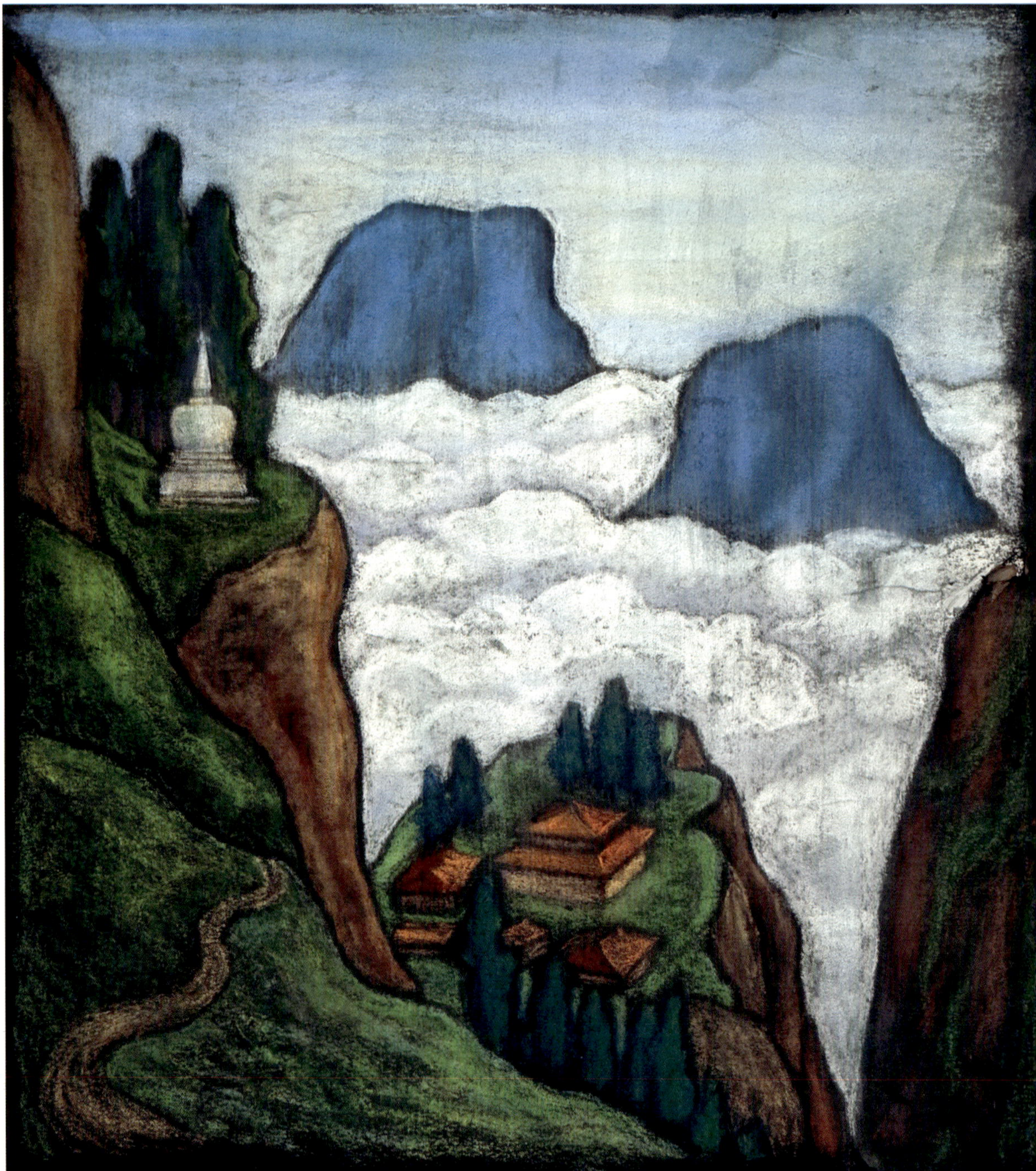

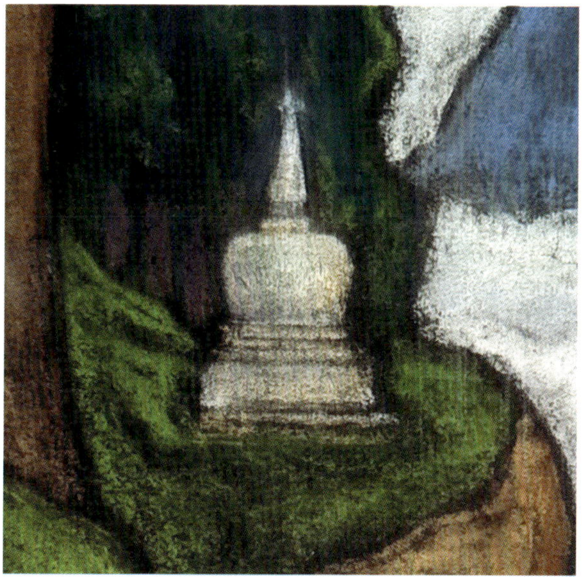

ABOVE THE CLOUDS

A painting that depicts a landscape with green, blue, and white colours, evoking high spirituality. It is a beautiful watercolour 'wash' by Anagarika Govinda, with a poem in Bengali.

The Allahabad Museum has his paintings permanently displayed in the Anagarika Hall. In his speech, Anagarika had said, 'my paintings have been wandering about in three continents. They have lived with me the life of a homeless pilgrim. From the blue shores of the Mediterranean through the burning deserts of Africa, the green paradise of Ceylon, and the eternal snows of the Himalayas, they have found their way to this sacred land of Aryavarta.' The paintings of the Anagarika Govinda, executed in pastel colours are reflective of his myriad experiences.

Provenance: India
Material: Paper
Medium: Pastel
Date: c. 20th century CE
Dimension: 40 x 34.5 cm
Acc. No.: AM-MOD-46
Artist: Anagraika Govinda

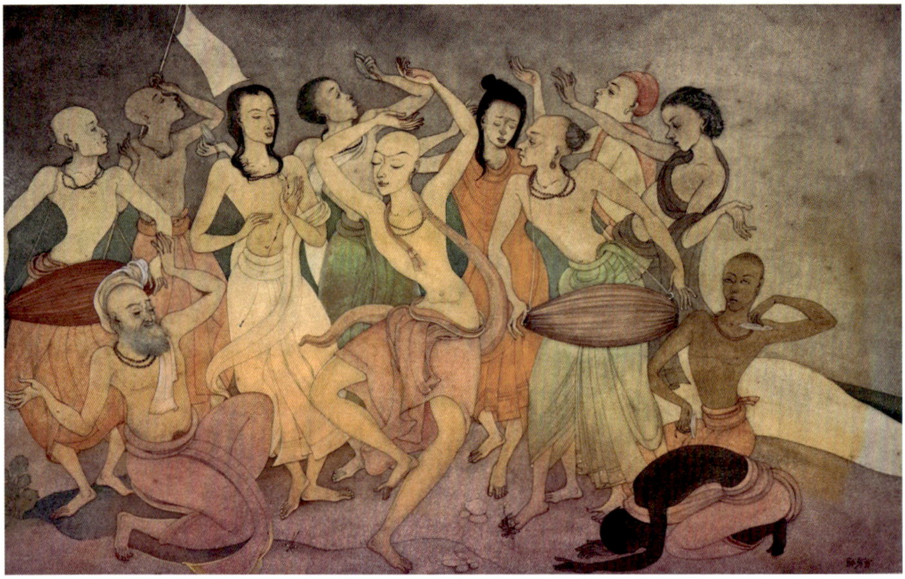

KIRTAN

The Allahabad Museum has a rich representation of the Bengal School of paintings in its collection. This painting is by artist Kshitindranath Majumdar. Most of his paintings are reflective of the Bhakti theme and shows the deep spiritual nature of the artist, who had been inspired by the mystic Bhakti reformer, Chaityanya Mahaprabhu. This painting depicts devotees, singing and dancing, with one of them playing a *mridangam*.

Other paintings in the museum collection from this school of art belong to Abanindranath Tagore, Gyanendranath Tagore, Nandalal Bose, Asit Kumar Haldar, Kshitindranath Majumdar, Ranada Ukil, Bireshwar Sen, Ram Gopal Vijayvargiya, and Sudhir Ranjan Khastgir.

Provenance:	India
Material:	Paper
Medium:	Watercolour
Date:	c. 20th century CE
Dimension:	45 x 29 cm
Acc. No.:	AM-MOD-16
Artist:	Kshitindranath Majumdar

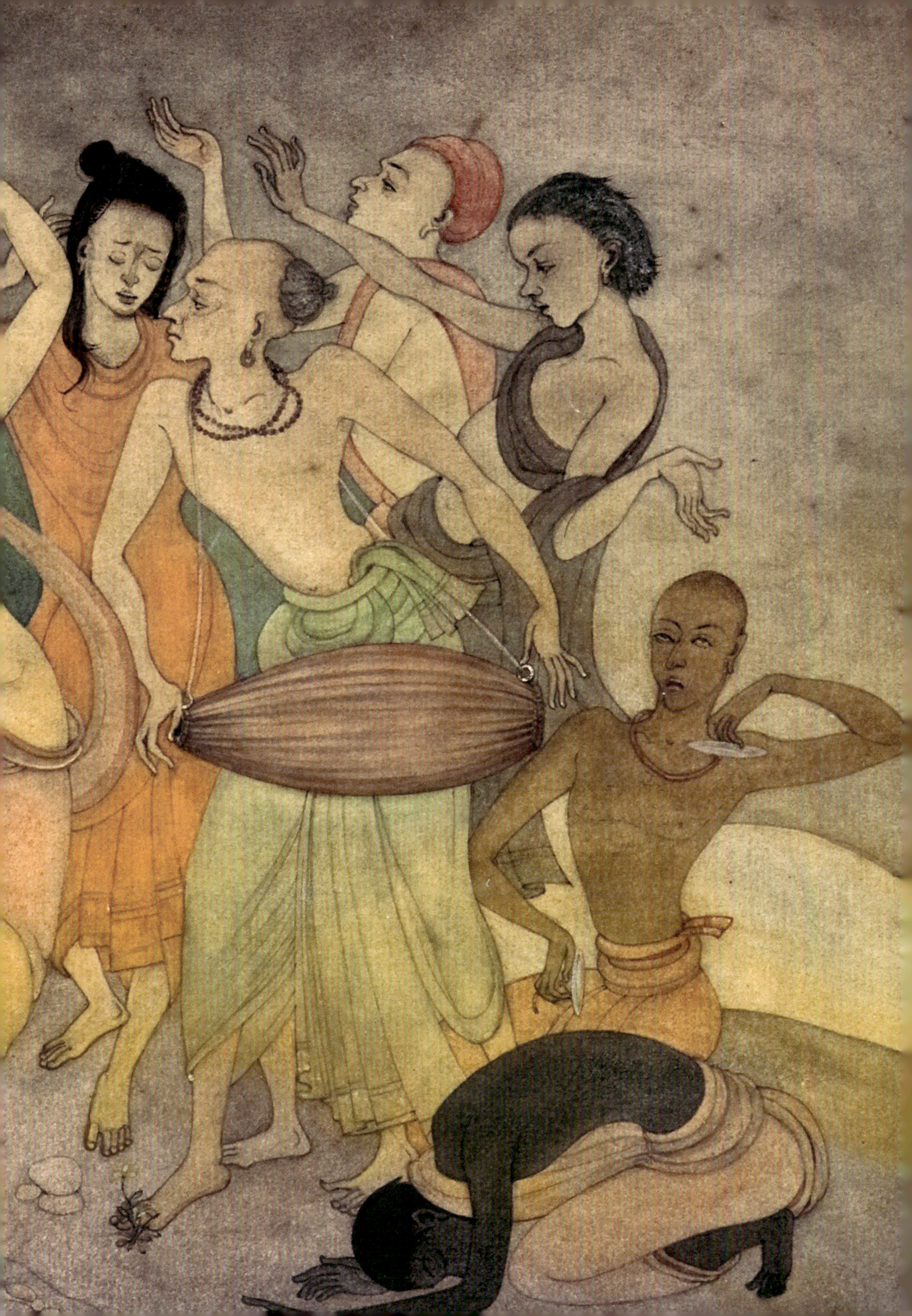

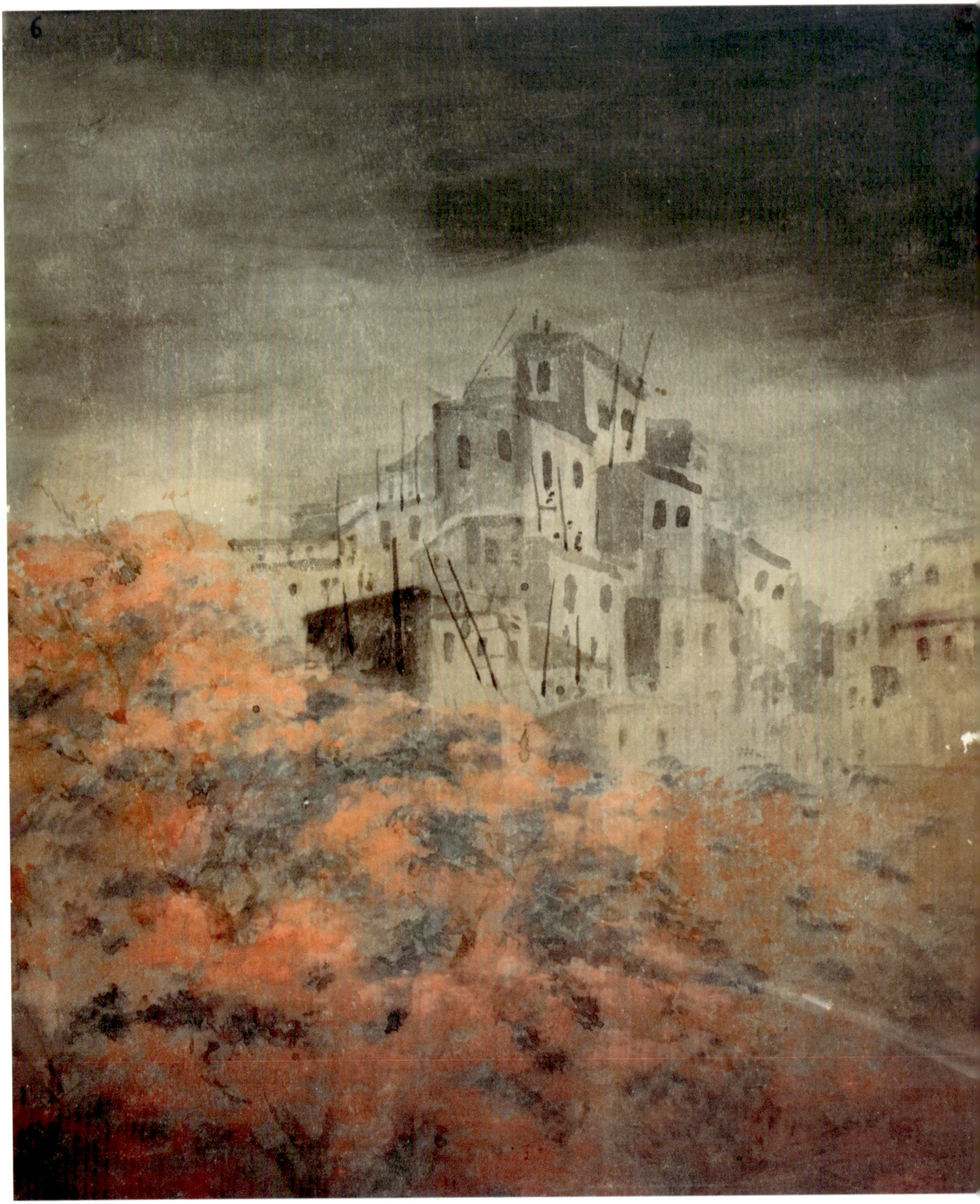
6

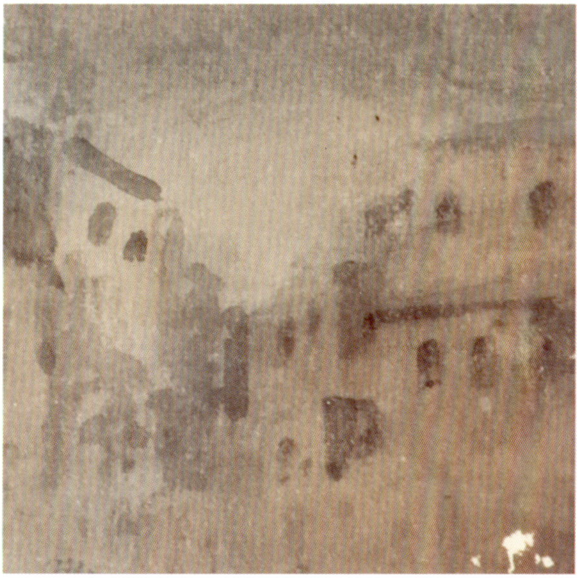

GULMOHAR

This watercolour painting depicts gulmohar trees in full bloom. This painting by Gaganendranath Tagore is a classic example of Bengal School of Art. Gaganendranath Tagore perfected the 'cartoon' style of sketching, often ignoring fine strokes.

Provenance: India
Material: Paper
Medium: Watercolour
Date: c. 20th century CE
Dimension: 31 x 25 cm
Acc. No.: AM-MOD-407
Artist: Gaganendranath Tagore

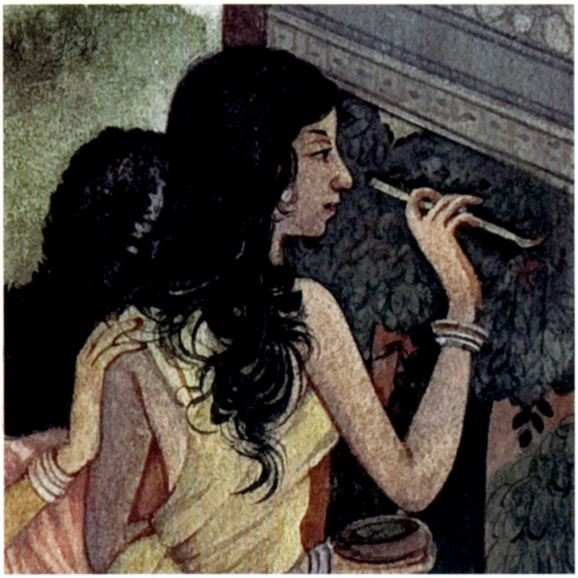

SISTERS

This painting by Nandalal Bose depicts two young ladies. One of them is drawing something on the wall. The painting is inspired by Mughal miniature style and is lyrical in its theme. The work has soft pastel colours, which evokes a romantic mood.

Provenance:	India
Material:	Paper
Medium:	Watercolour
Date:	c. 20th century CE
Dimension:	32 x 22.5 cm
Acc. No.:	AM-MOD-421
Artist:	Nandalal Bose

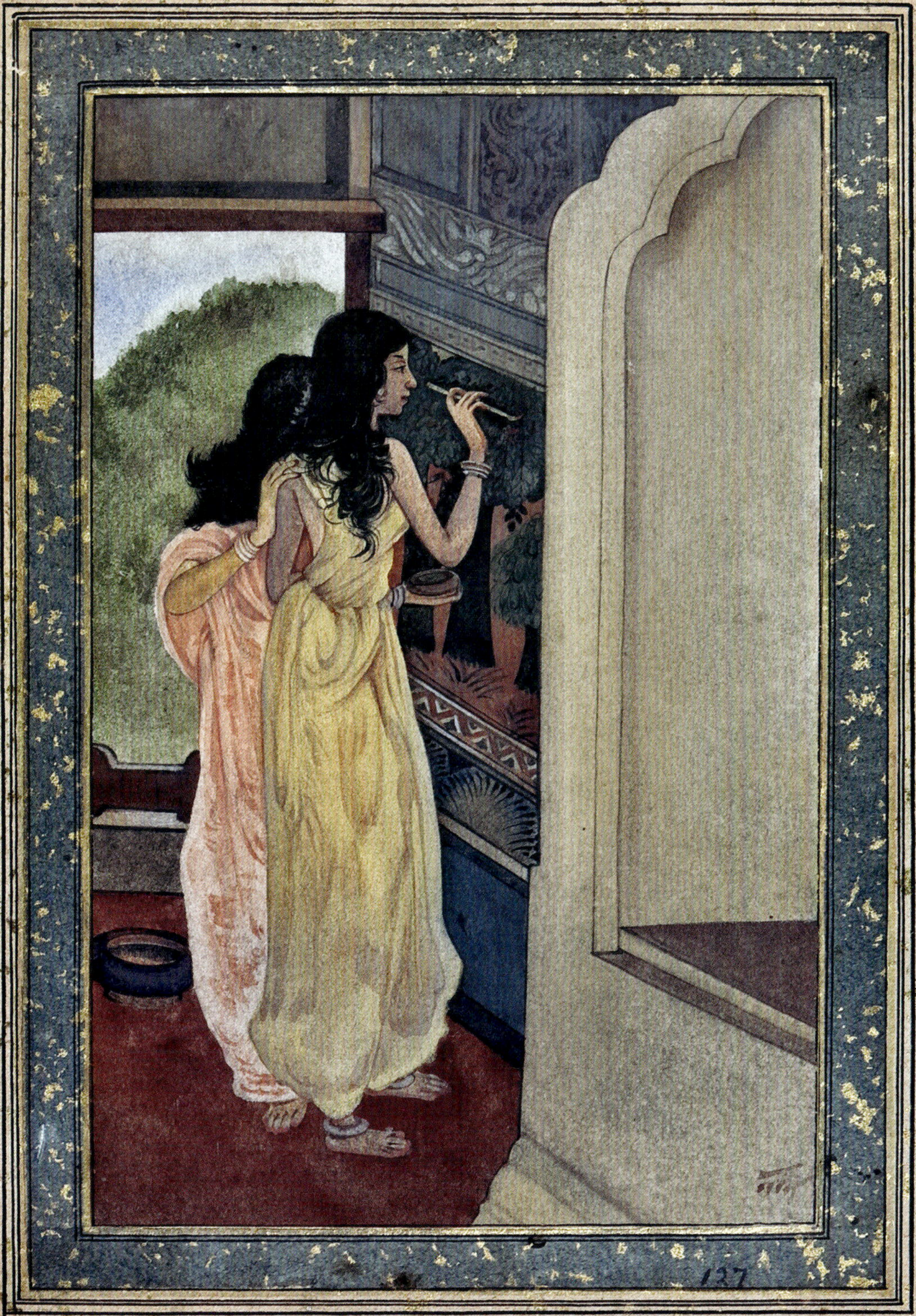

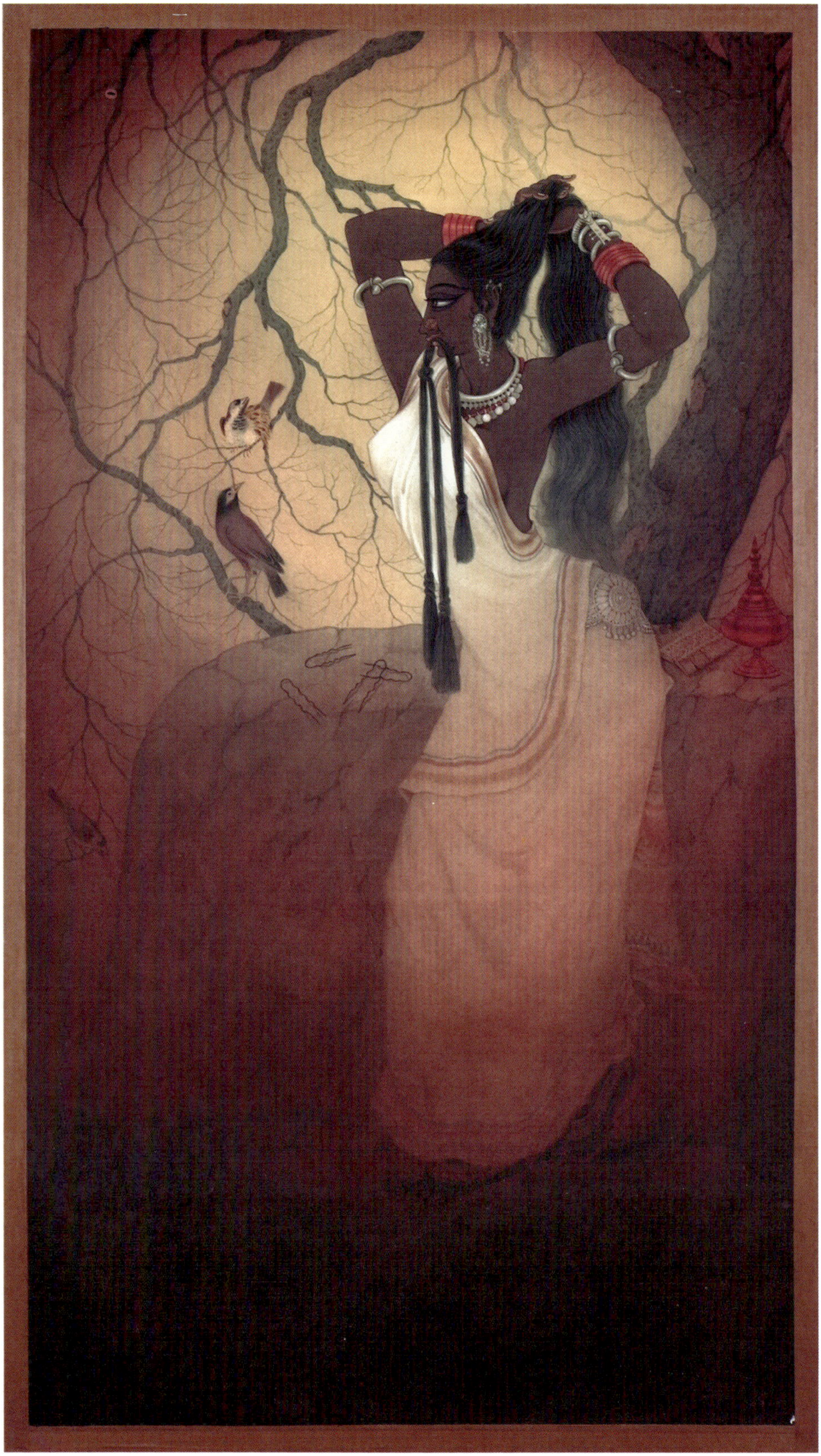

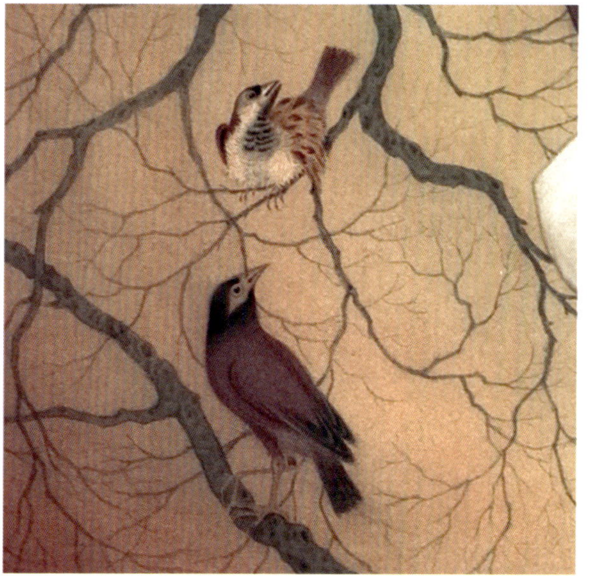

SANVARI

This is one of the largest wash paintings by B.N. Arya, depicting a Santhal tribal woman sitting under a tree, tying her long hair into a knot. She wears popular tribal jewellery, which enhances her beauty. She is holding a black hair *paranda* (hair tassel) in her mouth. A few bun pins are spread in front of her. Two birds are staring at her. There is a red vermilion or sindoor case kept on an elevated platform behind her. A spectacular combination of light and shade has been used by the artist in this painting.

Provenance: India
Material: Paper
Date: c. 20th century CE
Dimension: 141 x 80 cm
Acc. No.: AM-MOD-7
Artist: B.N. Arya

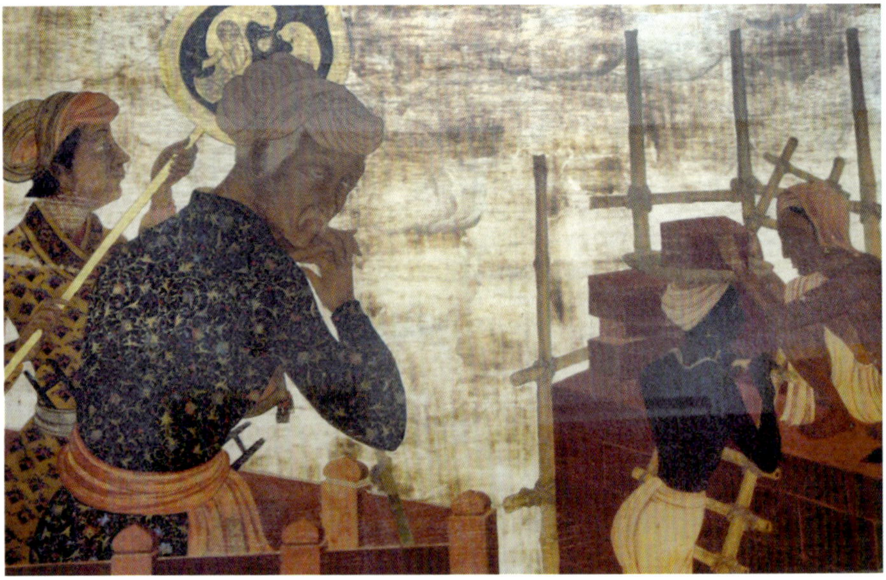

AKBAR WATCHING CONSTRUCTION OF FORT

This painting depicts Mughal Emperor Akbar watching the construction of the Allahabad Fort. A scaffolding can be seen in the background. The emperor is wearing an *achkan* with beautiful zari embroidery work. An attendant stands with a sunscreen (*chhatra*). Two labourers are shown lifting stone blocks.

Provenance:	India
Material:	Wood
Medium:	Tempera
Date:	c. 20th century CE
Dimension:	115 x 166 cm (with the frame)
Acc. No.:	AM-MOD-80
Artist:	Asit Kumar Haldar

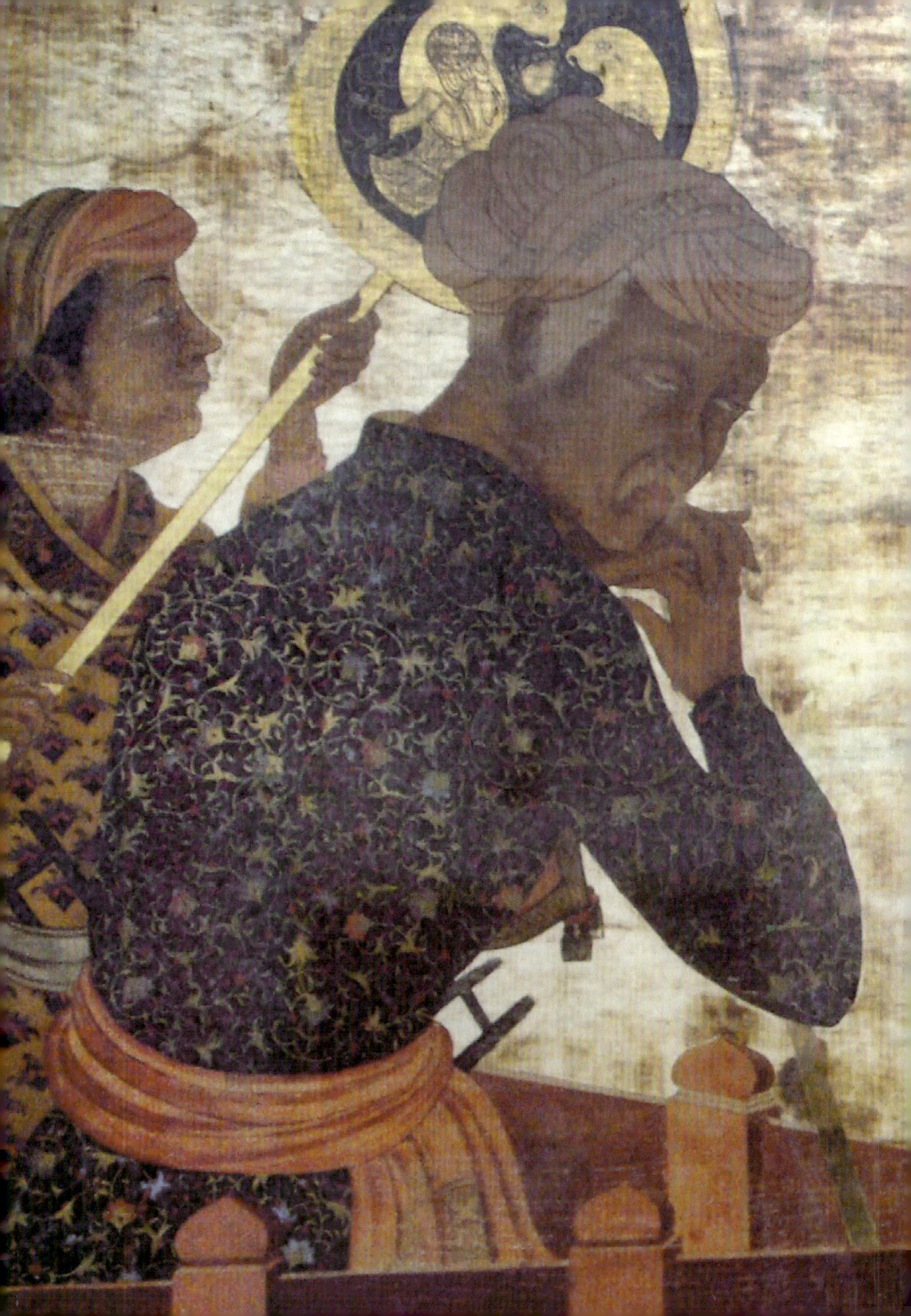

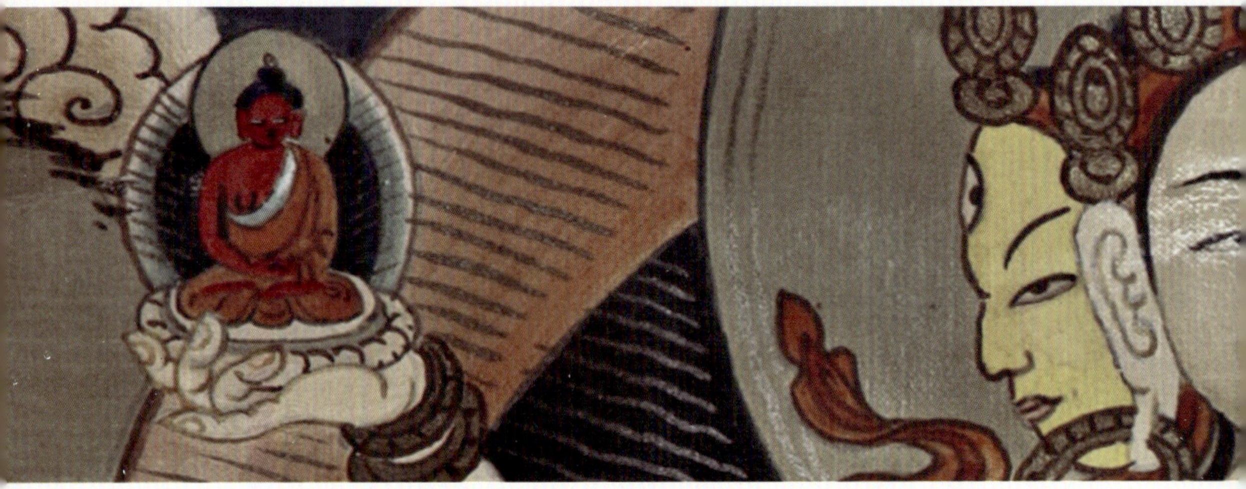

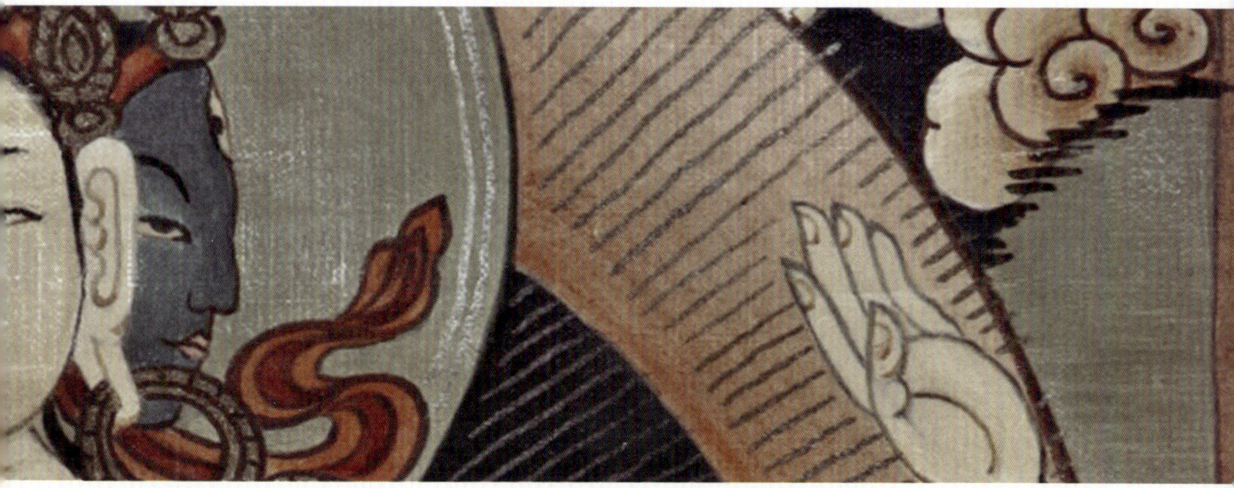

THANGKAS
GALLERY

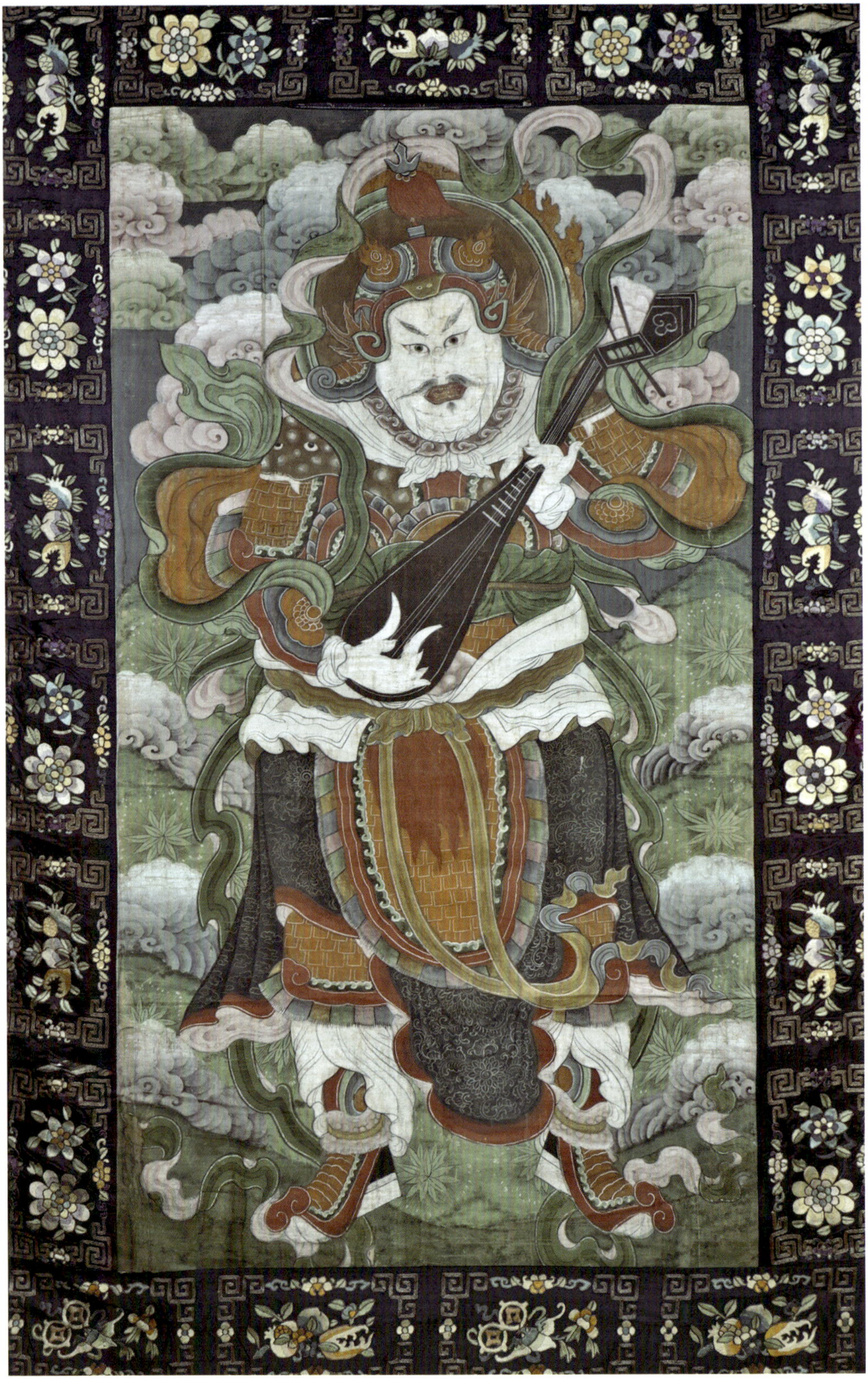

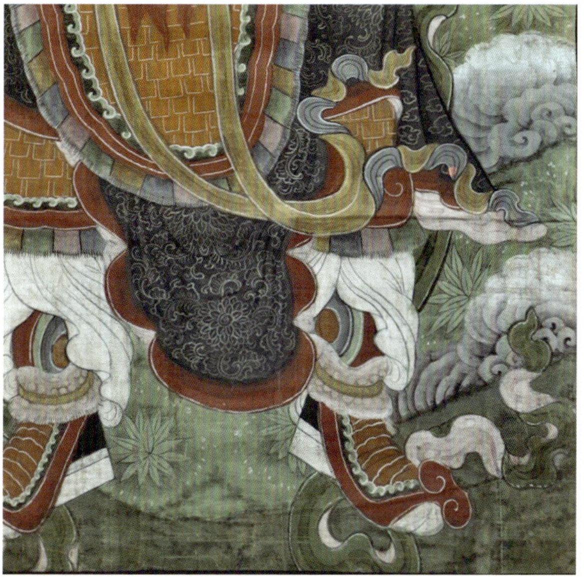

DHRITARASHTRA (LOKAPALA)

Here is a Buddhist thangka, featuring the Guardian King of the east, Dhritarashtra, who is shown with his lute, dominating the picture space. He is in a colourful attire with a crown on his head, playing his musical instrument.

Provenance: Peking, China
Material: Silk
Date: c. 18th century
Dimension: 82 x 151 cm
Acc. No.: AM-MIN-THNK-1809

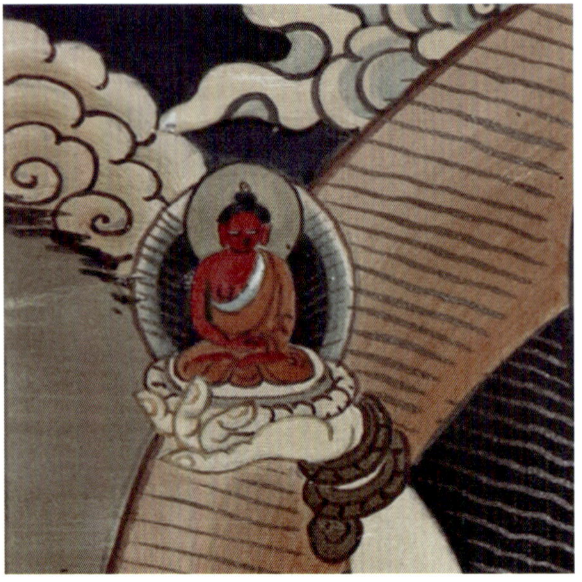

USHNISHAVIJAYA

This painting mounted on red silk brocade portrays Ushnishavijaya, the Queen-mother of enlightenment—emphasised by her enlightened elevation. She has three faces and eight arms. Her main symbol is the crossed thunderbolt, which she holds in front of her breast. Her special recognition symbol is the Buddha image raised by her right upper hand.

Provenance: Peking, China
Material: Silk
Date: c. 18th century CE
Size: 55 x 55 cm
Acc. No.: AM-MIN-THNK-1913

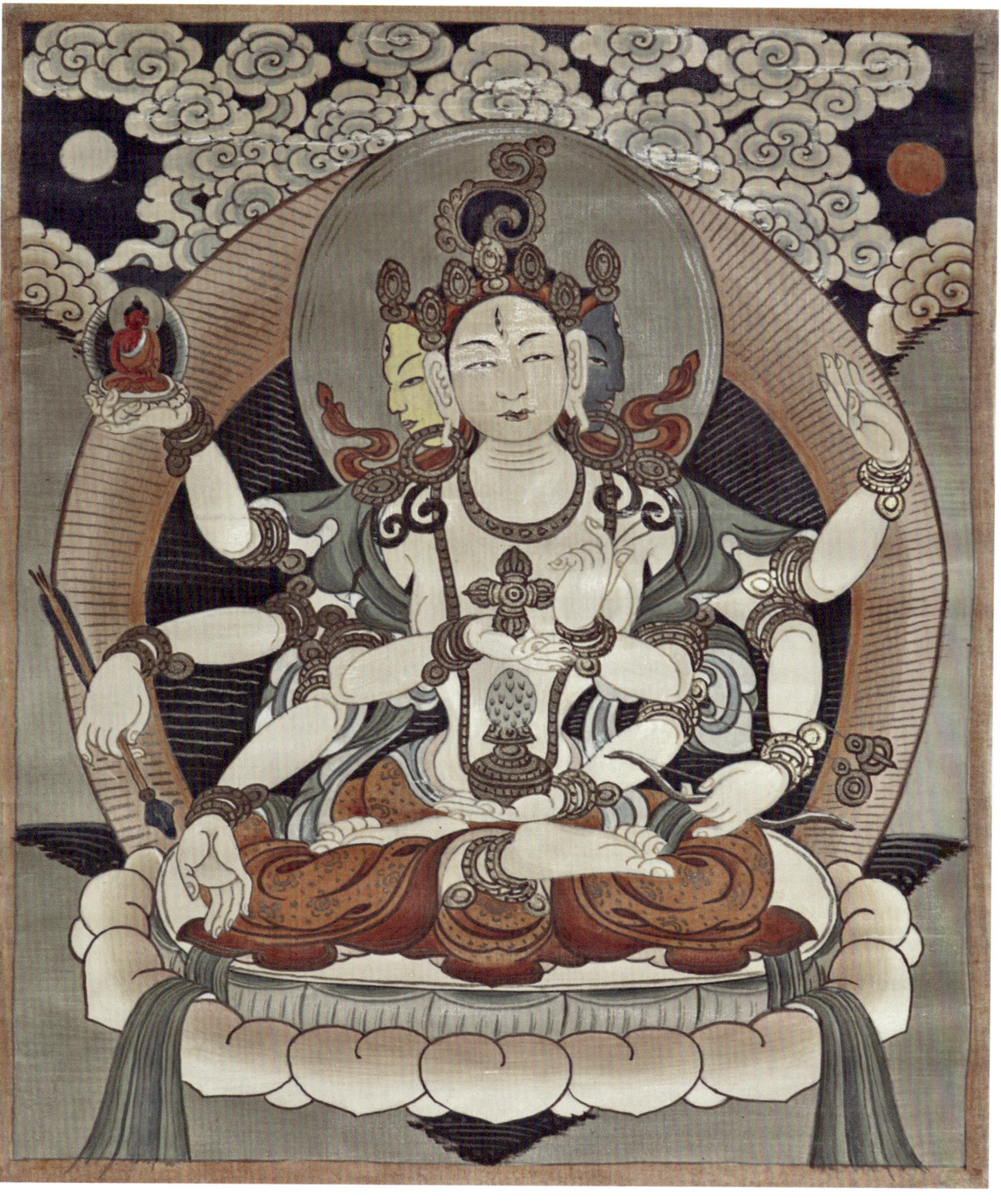

NATIONAL CULTURE FUND
TOWARDS CREATIVE PARTNERSHIPS

The National Culture Fund's (NCF) primary mandate is to nurture Public Private Partnerships (PPP) to mobilise resources for the restoration, conservation, protection and development of India's rich, natural, tangible and intangible heritage. NCF believes that cultural diversity and heritage conservation are vital pillars of inclusive national development.

Established by the Ministry of Culture in 1996, NCF is a Trust under the Charitable Endowments Act of 1890. It is governed by a Council with the Hon'ble Minister for Culture as its chairperson and managed by an Executive Committee chaired by the Secretary, Ministry of Culture, Government of India.

NCF welcomes contributions from private companies, PSUs and organizations under their CSR policies or PPP mode, to develop, safeguard and preserve Indian art and culture. NCF provides 100 per cent tax exemption (under section 80G (2) of the Income Tax Act) and prominent visibility to its donors for their contributions.

NCF is proud to collaborate with this project.

ACKNOWLEDGEMENTS

Allahabad Museum

Mr Rajesh Purohit, Director

Dr S.C. Kala

Dr R.R. Tripathi

Dr S.P. Gupta

Dr S.D Trivedi

Dr Pramod Chandra

Shri Krishna Deva

Dr S.R. Shukla

Dr Sunil Gupta

Dr Onkar A.Wankhede

Dr Prabhakar Pandey

Dr Ajay Kumar Mishra

Dr Rajesh Kumar Mishra

Dr Waman A. Wankhede

Dr Sanju Mishra

Photography

Sanjai Kumar, Pradeep Shrivastava, American Institute of Indian Studies, National Mission for Monuments and Antiquities